Emerging Issues in Education

Emerging Issues in Education

Policy Implications for the
Schools

Edited by
James E. Bruno

Lexington Books
D.C. Heath and Company
Lexington, Massachusetts
Toronto   London

Main entry under title:

Emerging Issues in Education

   Based on a series of 14 seminars sponsored by the Rand Corp., 1969-1971.
      1. Education—United States—1965-   Addresses, essays, lectures.
   2. Educational sociology—United States—Addresses, essays, lectures.
   3. Educational research—United States—Addresses, essays, lectures. I.
   Bruno, James E., ed. II. Rand Corporation. III. Title.
   LA210.E62   370.9'73   72-4893
   ISBN 0-669-84152-8

LA
210
.E62

Published simultaneously in Canada.

Printed in the United States of America.

International Standard Book Number: 0-669-84152-8

Library of Congress Catalog Card Number: 72-4893

Contents

70244

List of Figures

List of Tables

Foreword

In July 1969, the Carnegie Corporation awarded Rand a grant, matched by an equal contribution of Rand funds, to study three sets of issues facing California—public education, environmental policy, and intergovernmental relations. During the following two years, Rand staff and consultants produced a series of studies on these topics. Work in these and other public policy fields of importance to the State has continued since 1971, under the sponsorship of the state of California and several California school districts.

This volume, edited by Professor James Bruno, is one product of the Carnegie-Rand collaboration. Since October 1969, we have conducted a regular seminar series for Southern California school administrators and educational researchers. The seminar series is designed to provide this audience with a current summary of the major emerging policy issues facing education during the 1970s. The success of the series, which reflects the high quality of the guest speakers, has prompted Rand to issue this volume, based on the first fourteen seminars in the series, for a wider audience of educators and other citizens interested in educational policy issues. If the reception of this volume warrants it, additional volumes based on the seminars may be issued, as part of a more general series of Rand Educational Policy Studies.

John Pincus

Director, Rand Education
and Human Resources
Program

Preface

The assumption that inequalities in schools resulted in or were the major cause of inequalities in adult life was one underlying theme which permeated much of the school controversies in the decade of the 1960s. As a result of this overriding concern for schools as a social force in American life, a large body of research was directed toward studying various segments of inputs, outputs, and instructional processes, of public elementary and secondary education. This book attempts to consolidate in one volume what seem to be the relevant emerging issues in each of these important areas of inquiry and to extract their implications for educational policy.

The material for this volume was provided by The Rand Corporation which sponsored a series of thirteen monthly seminars on emerging issues in education. At these seminars nationally prominent speakers were invited to address school district officials and educational researchers on important policy questions facing elementary and secondary education. The objective of these presentations was to examine and summarize the policy implications of research findings in important areas of educational inquiry.

The book is divided into four sections. The first section serves as a general introduction to the emerging issues in education. Parts II and III concern themselves with issues related to school district inputs and instructional processes. The final section explores issues and directions for promoting educational change.

The introductory section on the context of educational change contains two chapters, one provides an overview and perspective to educational issues by examining the complex, evolving roles of the four participants in education—students, teachers, administrators and society. The second chapter in this section gives a futuristic orientation to the organization of the schools and discusses how educational practices might change with different alternative futures of society.

The next two sections on school district inputs and instructional processes are the portions of the volume which should be of particular interest to school district policy makers. Part II discusses various inputs to the education sector—student, legal, community, teacher and financial. The chapters in this section attempt to define boundaries for change and important influences which govern the shape and organization of education in America.

Part III examines issues related to the instructional process itself and focuses on topics such as early childhood education, instructional technology, curriculum policy making, teacher characteristics and their relationship to pupil performance. The purpose of these chapters is to examine the broad policy issues related to improving instruction.

The concluding section in this volume contains three chapters and deals with issues and directions for promoting educational change. The first chapter discusses accountability or educational quality control and its influence on educational practices. The second chapter examines the emerging issue of guaranteeing student outcomes or performance contracting. The final chapter explores future directions for educational research and examines the intersection of the psychometric and econometric research methodologies for studying the education phenomena.

The purpose of these chapters is to give to the reader an up-to-date appraisal of recent developments in educational research and practice which although not directly related to school inputs or instructional processes will have an important effect upon educational policy in the 70s.

Included at the end of each chapter is a list of references for those interested in more comprehensive treatments of specific educational issues. The reader, of course, should be aware of the necessary limitations imposed by a one-volume treatise on such a broad subject as the emerging issues in education and is therefore encouraged to make extensive use of the bibliography.

With these references, the book can be used as a reader for courses in areas of school administration, psychology, and evaluation in graduate schools of education. The book can also serve as a basic text for an introductory survey course on policy issues in education. For the professional educator, the researcher, the student, or the concerned layman interested in a broad and concise overview of school district policy and its future directions, this book satisfies an important need; namely to survey the emerging issues in education and to extract their significance for educational policy. Since most of the text is narrative in form and typically summarizes current thought and empirical research, a minimum amount of statistics and rigorous mathematical analysis is used.

Naturally, some of the policy related implications and findings reported in this book may cause controversy among some educators. All, however, will gain a better overall impression of where educational practice seems directed, what research has told us about the schools, and finally, what seem to be the principal issues facing public education in the seventies.

The preparation of this text required the insights and knowledge of a host of nationally prominent educational researchers. I would, therefore, like to thank each of the contributors to this volume. In addition, I would like to commend The Rand Corporation and the Carnegie Corporation for sponsoring the educational seminar series and for providing the resources and mechanism which eventually led to this text. Finally, I want to express my gratitude to Los Angeles County school officials who certainly provided the "real world" insight to our seminars and indirectly influenced the themes and implications for policy found throughout the text.

James E. Bruno

Coordinator,
Seminar Series

Sept. 20, 1972

**Part I:
Introduction to the Emerging
Issues in Education**

1 Emerging Issues in Education: An Overview and Perspective

James E. Bruno

Introduction

During the 1960s America's established institutions such as the school, family and church were faced with únprecedented challenges. In only one decade attitudes towards sex, patriotism and drugs changed drastically. With a "youth culture" conveying values which were totally counter to those held by their parents, it was natural that the schools, being the principal formal mechanism for culture transmission and imparting of societal values, would be caught and embodied in the middle of the controversy surrounding these changes. The educational establishment was given the almost impossible task of absorbing, interpreting, interjecting, and tempering these changes into a structured school program which would provide meaningful educational experiences for all students. Needless to say, the schools failed in this endeavor.

As the news media became interested in public education and as educational practices became topics of political concern, more Americans became aware of the serious problems in education than at any other time in the nation's history. Issues such as voucher plans, accountability, performance contracting, received and are still receiving great attention in the news. Educators are faced with a growing demand for change in the present educational system: a system characterized by its high costs, low productivity, and inability to be fully responsive to identified national and student needs. The net result of this public concern has been thorough reexamination of educational practices and the development of innovations to make the learning process more efficient and more effective. As public support for its educational system wanes, school administrators will seek insights and present alternative procedures which might result in improved educational efficiency and effectiveness. Findings contained in research literature on the education phenomena have been the primary source of such insights.

This chapter attempts to explain why educators have been unable to utilize many of the findings in the educational research literature, by relating change in the schools to the evolution in role and influence of the four principal participants in the education "game." Analogous to players in a poker game with bluffs, strategies, systems, etc., the principal players in the education "game" are becoming collectively better organized for exerting influence, more sophisticated

3

and vociferous in demonstrating this power, and equipped with better information to make demands upon the system. The *teacher* imparting instruction, the *student* receiving instruction, the *administrator* providing the structure for instruction to take place, and finally *society* which oversees the whole game and sets goals, rewards, or incentives, either overtly or covertly for the other three players and influences what is taught, are the principals in the education "game." While society has the "high cards" in the game, since they set the incentives for the other three to participate, the students are the most important players because they can refuse to play. A visit to any local high school in an urban area is usually enough to convience even the greatest skeptic that the students are beginning to exert their influence by merely refusing to participate.[a] This transformation in student power, attitudes, and influence has tended to upset the "balance of power" in education and might have enormous consequences upon educational policy in the future.

Before discussing the changing roles of these participants, however, it is important to examine what research has told us about educational effectiveness in the schools and what organizational, resource inputs, and teaching methods produce effective learning.

Educational Research and Educational Practice

One frequent and seemingly justified criticism of educational research is that real-world problems of the school administrator are not fully investigated. Typically, it is under "limitations to the study" or "areas of future research" that one finds the real-world analog to the school district planning or policy situation described in the research. Thus the educational administrator faced with resource allocation problems, the federal judge faced with equal opportunity decisions, the parent faced with the type of education to expect from the schools, the school board faced with methods of improving educational effectiveness, and teachers involved with seeking better teaching strategies, had to rely on information usually generated by poorly designed, theoretical research studies to assist them in making policy-related decisions. While some decisions made by school officials were faulty, most likely all decisions, good and bad, were made in the absence of consistent and conclusive research evidence.

In essence, educational researchers at the university, who performed most of the research in education, had political and professional interest which, up until very recently, were somewhat incongruent with those of school district policy-

---

[a]Evidence of the "newfound" influence and power of students can be found in an extraordinary book titled "Up Against the Law." In essence, this "cookbook" on legal rights for those under 21 informs students how to deal with parents, teachers, and school officials while staying within their legal rights. Strouse, Jean, *Up Against the Law: The Legal Rights of People Under 21*, New American Library, Macmillan Company, 1970.

makers. There was little reason for educational researchers to subordinate their theoretical, empirical research interests to "real-world" or policy-related problems of school administrators simply because colleagues labeled this type of research as "pedestrian." In fact, the concept of regional educational laboratories and research centers was developed to satisfy the need for bridging the gap between research and practice. Incentives and financial rewards for the researcher, especially at a university, are placed primarily in theoretical studies and studies which advanced the body of knowledge. This type of "theory-related" research is in sharp contrast to research commissioned by industrial concerns where contractual guarantees are frequently employed to subordinate research exclusively to practical policy-related concerns.[b]

In addition, universities never really developed a tradition in either multi-disciplinary or problem-centered research. Even within departments of a university such as education, sociology, or economics, it was difficult to involve its various disciplines in applied research; although in recent years this phenomenon is changing. It is interesting to note that the systems approach and interdisciplinary approaches to problems came principally from the private and military sectors of the economy rather than from colleges and universities. A national institute or "think-tank" corporation with emphasis on interdisciplinary research is intended to deal with the problem of channeling skills and expertise from various disciplines towards the solution of a problem. The recently passed legislation to create a National Institute of Education was a response to the need for interdisciplinary educational research.[c]

Unfortunately, researchers during the last decade also became obsessed with quantitative analysis and Peter Drucker's expression, "Let's not make the quantitative important but the important quantitative," became the exception in research instead of the rule. This quantitative trend is continuing as traditionally qualitative and policy-oriented areas of inquiry such as sociology, psychology, education, and political science are becoming more quantitative. By necessity, the problems addressed in such research are based upon more stringent assumptions, hence entail more limitations, and are less generalizable.

The decade of the seventies should see more government-sponsored research directed at school district policy as national institutes and nonprofit research organizations begin to consume larger shares of the education research dollar. Legislators are also beginning to take an interest in the scope and direction of

---

[b]Of course there were some exceptions to the theory-related research in education, the most notable being the curriculum reform research such as SMSG, CHEM, etc., which did have an impact upon the schools.

[c]In proposing NIE, the full house committee on education issued a report underlying the fact that past research efforts were less than startling. O.E. research, it said, "has been plagued by a negative image; poor management resulting in research of poor quality and little substance; failure to focus on genuine problems in education; and insensitivity to any interests except those of the established educational leadership." James Brann, "NIE: New Life for Research," *Saturday Review*, September 16, 1972 (p. 43).

educational research. In an address at the 1971 annual AERA (American Educational Research Association) in New York City, Senator Walter F. Mondale (D-Minn.) commenting upon the future directions for educational research proposed that educational researchers direct more attention to practical solutions and politically available goals. At this same conference, Rep. John Brademas (D-Ind.), who is Chairman of the House Subcommittee on Education, emphasized the need for educational research to focus upon "real-world" problems in education.[1]

Finally, as economists begin to study the education phenomenon, there is a concerted effort to incorporate some type of benefit-cost analysis in educational research studies. Many previous research studies showed that Treatment A showed no distrinct difference in student outcomes than Treatment B. Findings of "no difference" in outcomes with various methods have implications for cost-effectiveness analysis, and if there is no difference in the effectiveness of various teaching alternatives, then cost should become the major discriminating factor in the selection of an approach.

With billions of dollars already invested in educational research, many fine theoretical studies have been completed, but these findings for the most part are not consistent and cannot be generalized across schools. The Rand Corporation recently completed a study for the President's Commission on School Finance, which had as its objective to survey the research literature and summarize or assess what we have learned about education and schooling using five research paradigms:[2]

1. Input/output approach
2. Process approach
3. Organizational approach
4. Intervention
5. Experiential

Each study used in the experiment was placed in one of the above paradigms and critiqued for its internal validity or methodology and interstudy consistency. Studies surviving these evaluation criteria were summarized and combined with the results of the other approaches. Policy implications of the research were then extracted. Table 1-1 contains a summary of the findings in each of the research areas.

These were the major conclusions of the Rand study:

1. Research has not identified a variant of the existing educational system that is consistently related to student educational outcomes.
2. The larger the school system, the less likely it is to display innovation, responsiveness, and adaption, and the more likely it is to depend upon exogenous shocks to the system.

3. Research tentatively suggests that improvement in student outcomes, cognitive and noncognitive, may require sweeping changes in the organization, structure, and conduct of educational experience.

The Rand report did not imply that no school policy variables make a difference or that nothing works, but emphasized that research has found nothing that consistently and unambiguously makes a difference in student outcomes.

The major policy implications of the Rand study were:

1. Increasing expenditures on traditional educational practices are not likely to improve educational outcomes substantially.
2. There seem to be opportunities for significant reductions, and in some cases reductions in educational expenditures without deterioration in educational outcomes.

In the absence of any clear-cut, educational practices that work, the "why change" attitude seems to prevail and variables in the political and social organization begin to exert a greater influence upon decision making in school districts.

The Rand Corporation's recommendation that pouring more money into current educational practices will not affect student outcomes seems valid. Of course, the same statement can probably be made for present educational research practices. While there is no question that the billions invested in educational research have had minor impacts upon the schools, especially in curriculum, the lack of consistent findings has not resulted in significant changes in educational practices. One possible reason for lack of consistency in research findings might be that the schools have to define goals and set criteria for evaluating effectiveness in a society with constantly evolving goals and objectives. In addition, as a social organization, the schools no matter how sophisticated the analysis, can refuse to accept the researcher's conclusions. It is important, therefore, that educational policy analysts consider the aspirations and interests of the four players in the "education game." Tracing the evolution of these roles and the status maintenance procedures involved in legitimizing them in the organization might offer researchers insight into where the schools seem to be headed. More important, however, this type of analysis can improve the researcher's understanding of the boundaries to policy research in education or how much the schools can be changed without upsetting the "game," i.e. to achieve practical solutions and set politically available goals.

Participants in Education

Teacher

Research has examined how teaching styles relate to such important areas as student attitudes and pupil performance. A number of important questions

Table 1-1
What We Have Learned About the Schools Using Different Research Approaches

Research Paradigm	Principal Concern	Researchers	Results
Input/output approach	How resource inputs are related to school district outputs (production function)	Economists	Production function seldom explains student outcomes very well Background factors consistently dominate Little evidence that school resources influence student outcomes when background variables are controlled
Process approach	Improve the way education takes place—examine the processes and methods by which resources are applied	Ed. psychologists Curriculum specialists sociologists	Many findings, but usually no benefit cost analysis, and until recently no aptitude treatment interaction
Organizational approach	Case study—educational practice a reflection of history social demand and organizational change. How these factors impinge on the various decision-makers and affect their behavior	Political scientists Organization theorists	Innovations in large school systems are based upon exogenous shocks Difficult to assess validity or reliability of studies since most are nonquantitative

Evaluation	Examinations of the effects of large-scale interventions in the school systems and how they affect student outcomes	Evaluation research methodologists Statisticians	Virtually without exception, all large national Comp Ed programs have shown no beneficial results Large fadeout of results Level of funding not sufficient for success
Experiential	Student centered; how the system affects students; the Reform literature	Sociologists Philosophy of Ed. Former teachers Radicals	Many observations; no empirical data School focus on unimportant objectives Student learning can't take place in authoritarian environment Substance of educational practice is irrelevant Children should not be required to attend school

concerning teachers, however, remain unanswered. In the last decade teachers perceptions of their own functions in the educational process changed considerably. As teachers began to form collective bargaining groups, perceptions of their role in education also changed. Teachers are becoming more militant, and this new found militancy should have dramatic effects upon future school district policies. An examination of the recent evolution of the teacher's function in the schools might shed light on possible reasons for this militancy.

The enormous growth of elementary and secondary education enrollment in America during the 1950s, as "war babies" entered then moved through the educational system, had a strong impact upon the teaching profession. In addition, the economic climate in the country was generally favorable toward education since competition for tax dollars from welfare and other social service items in state and municipal budgets was minimal. The growth of school enrollment, due either to migration—urban to suburban, rural to urban—or to "war babies" and a favorable financial posture permitted an ideal setting for educational enterprises to function and contributed to stability and contentment in the teaching profession. During this period the industrial sector of the economy also expanded and absorbed large numbers of college graduates, some trained under the G.I. Bill, to fill middle and lower managerial positions. The industrial demand for college-educated manpower during the fifties and early sixties for middle management positions was significant to education. These industries tended to attract and absorb high-aspiring, upwardly mobile men by offering them high starting salaries, leaving mainly low-aspiring, security-minded men for education. The removal of these high aspirers thus left only women and smaller numbers of men to constitute the education work force.

Once in teaching the relatively few upwardly mobile men and women could serve their internship of a few years in a classroom and then move into higher-salaried administrative posts. Women who decided to stay in teaching usually remained at salaries much higher than any comparable salary for women in industry. Those women who wanted administrative posts filled the host of middle supervisory positions in the schools: girls' vice president, director of counseling, curriculum coordinator, etc. Most women teachers during this period, however, stayed in teaching a few years, then left the profession to raise a family, and possibly returned to teaching at a later date.

One would find very little support for teacher strikes or other activities associated with teacher militancy from teachers of the fifties and early sixties, due primarily to high turnover rates and the built-in mechanisms for upward mobility for those who desired higher salaries through positions in school administration (teaching being the stepping-stone to school administration). As long as the bulk of the teacher work force was women, and it would remain that way until job options for men in industry decreased, and a mechanism was provided for creating administrative jobs for upwardly mobile men and women, the situation in education could be described as one of cooperation between teachers and administrators. Both groups enjoyed the "professional" and "teamwork" atmosphere because their ideals and material goals were very similar. The expansion of school districts permitted this harmonious relationship to maintain itself through the 1950s and early 1960s and resulted in a relationship between teachers and administrators characterized as one of mutual professional interests and generally close identification with school district policies.

In the middle and late sixties, however, the climate for education began to change, as more men entered the teaching profession due both to the tremendous output of male graduates from American colleges and universities and decreasing job options and security in the industrial sector. In addition, the exodus to the suburbs, with few exceptions declined along with the birth rate, and the "war babies" entered college. Enrollments leveled off drastically and the number of new schools built each year diminished. Finally, the financial honeymoon education enjoyed with the taxpayer ended as competition from other social service items in state budgets increased; notably welfare, transportation, and health. Bond issue and tax override election defeats began to appear in increasing numbers[d] and upward mobility for teachers was, therefore, constrained by the lack of additional administrative posts. This scarcity of financial resources for education also resulted in increases in class size and deterioration in working conditions for the teacher. The few administrative posts that did become available were reserved for minority ethnic groups who justifiably claimed underrepresentation in administrative appointments. Finally, control over student behavior deteriorated badly as problem students generally stayed in school instead of dropping out and the counter-culture influence began to exert itself. All of the above trends contributed to the development of the militant teacher movement, fostered the rapid growth of teacher unions and resulted in today's estrangement between teachers and school administrators.

The evidence of the growing polarization between teachers and administrators can best be understood by noting the evolution of the National Education Association official policies over the last two decades. In the 1950s the NEA was a "professional" association with a large number of school administrators as members. A teacher strike was unthinkable during this early period, since both teachers and administrators, having similar goals, worked in a spirit of professional harmony and cooperation to advance the cause of education and their mutual interests.

In 1966, a poll of the NEA membership revealed that over 53 percent of the teachers felt a strike was justified.[3] In 1971, it was 73 percent. The 20 percent increase in militant attitudes toward strikes reflects a period in which the actual number of teacher strikes increased fifteenfold, from 12 in 1965 to 180 in 1970.

---

[d]In the first quarter of 1971, voters rejected more than half of the 248 proposed issues, denying 307 million dollars to education. ("News Front," *Education USA*, May 17, 1971, p. 206).

About 15,000 teachers in 1965 and 118,000 in 1970 were directly involved in work stoppages in American public schools. One impact of changes in the teacher work force, namely the recent influx of men, was also demonstrated by the NEA survey. The study showed that male teachers were more militant in their views concerning teacher strikes than women. Among male teachers 87 percent supported teacher strikes, while only 66 percent of the women approved. The survey also revealed that most of the former regional differences in opinion concerning teacher strikes disappeared. Teacher strikes are presently considered viable options for teachers throughout the country from conservative rural areas to liberal urban areas. In 1970, the largest teacher organization in the country (NEA) had adopted a forceful plank emphasizing that "teachers may have no choice" but to strike as "the only means of attracting public attention to, and correcting unfavorable school conditions."

To summarize, in the past, schools accomplished their difficult tasks by relying on the dedicated and poorly compensated efforts of thousands of teachers who assumed responsibilities above and beyond their job specifications. During the 1970s, as the "idealistically oriented teacher" becomes the "materialistically oriented teacher," and desires extra compensation for each additional task performed, financial gains resulted from making teachers more efficient might be over-shadowed by rising costs in necessary support functions. The decade of the 1970s will most likely see increased conflict between teachers and administrators as the last vestiges of joint concern and goals are eliminated and both try to insure their jobs and status in the organization with the teacher as a worker-student accountability and the administrator as a manager-fiscal responsibility.

The role and influence of the teacher in the instructional process will probably change as economic efficiency considerations in the instructional process begin to assume greater importance and society demands more accountability. The large influx of paraprofessionals, declining budgets and enrollments and the "breaking" of teacher strikes with substitute teachers might tend to neutralize the militancy of some teacher unions at the local level. But state organized or even nationally organized teacher strikes could give enormous bargaining power to teachers and will affect what educational practices actually reach the schools at the classroom level.

Students

Teachers have changed in their attitudes toward the schools, but students who are most important players in the education game have undergone the most marked changes in values and attitudes. The quiet, obedient, generally passive students of past years have evolved into disrupting, activist students.

The following quote by Mario Savio, spoken during the free speech movement at the University of California in 1964, paraphrases the sentiments of all students at all levels of education:

The university is best characterized as a corporate board of directors. The faculty as workers, the students as raw materials, and the entire process of higher education is dehumanizing, illiberal, irrelevant, and immoral. Worst of all, it is boring.

The last phrase, "Worst of all, it is boring," is a typical comment of many high school students. The great adventure of education which Alfred North White-head speaks of in his *Aims of Education*[4] has not materialized for some students in the structured learning environment with all its syllabi, courses of study, grades, examinations, and emphasis on rote learning which characterize American education. The ethic of deferred gratification, with the expectation of eventual entry into high-status jobs, which motivated Americans to stay in school and tolerate its shortcomings during the last three decades has now begun to weaken. The schools are now faced with the problem of having to develop alternative mechanisms for exerting control over students.

To illustrate how school control over students has deteriorated, a study conducted by the National Association of Secondary School Principals (NASSP) in 1967 revealed that 59 percent of the 1000 schools studied had experienced some form of organized activism or protest against school policies. In a survey conducted by the House Subcommittee on General Education of the nation's 29,000 high schools (public, private, and parochial), over 18 percent faced *serious* student protest in 1968-1969 (riots, boycotts, strikes, etc.).[5]

Such apparent lack of control, an unparalleled occurrence in American education, points to the basic flaw in the mechanism which controlled students in the past—e.g., the relating of being good in class with, a grade received, a recommendation for college and ultimate entry into a high-status job. The materialistic goals of money, position, and power for a significant number of students seem to have been displaced by more intrinsic goals such as self-aware-ness, social service, and community involvement. Students today are asking themselves such "dangerous" questions as: Who am I? Who do I want to serve? And do I want the life style of my parents?

An educational system based largely upon materialistic incentives of an older generation cannot provide a meaningful educational program for these types of students.

In an illuminating book, *The Making of a Counter Culture*,[6] Theodore Roszak attempts to trace the blame for today's troublesome younger generation to psychological problems in early childhood:

If we ask who is the blame for such troublesome children, there can only be one answer: it is the parents who have equipped them with an anemic superego. The current younger generation is the beneficiary of the particularly permissive child rearing habits that have been a feature of postwar American society. Dr. Spock's latitudinarianism (go easy on toilet training, avoid discipline) is much more a reflection than a cause of the new conception of proper parent-child relations that prevails in our middle class.

Speaking of the schools, Roszak continues his analysis:

They (the young) passed through the school system which dismal as they all are in so many respects, have nevertheless prided themselves since World War II on the introduction of progressive classes having to do with creativity and self-expression. These were also the years that saw the proliferation of all the Mickey Mouse courses which take the self-indulgence of adolescent "life problems" so seriously. Such scholastic pap mixes easily with the commercial world's effort to elaborate a total culture of adolescence based on nothing but fun and games. The result has been to make of adolescence not the beginning of adulthood, but a status in its own right: a Limbo that is nothing so much as the prolongation of an already permissive infancy.

The prolongation of infancy or the term some writers use, "extended adolescence," might provide a clue into the recent student unrest and dissatisfaction with the educational establishment.

The adult phase of life, which in some parts of the world begins at 12, in other countries with marriage, or with a first full-time job, or with the first child, does not develop in America until the late twenties or early thirties, because of the schooling needed for credentialization. Degree, credential, and certificate requirements proliferate, creating a "paper caste" system. For these "pieces of paper," students have to stay in school and defer their life and adulthood. When the student finally leaves the educational system he often realizes to his dismay that the job does not require all of the education he received. It was reported in *Time*[7] that 80 percent of all jobs available in the United States are within the capabilities of those with high school diplomas. It was also stated in *Time* that the Commission on Human Resources and Advanced Education reported that 25 percent of all college graduates will be working at jobs where a college education is not needed.[8] The massive increase in educational requirements, seemingly unrelated to job requirements, must have a discouraging effect upon high school students possessing the "instant gratification," "live now" attitude. At least these students would prefer some incentive for possessing the deferred gratification ethic of their parents; such as a high status job at the termination of their formal education.

The radical shift in student attitudes, perceptions, and expectations concerning the schools does not seem to be a temporary phenomenon; in fact, these attitudes might even become more radical or at least more widespread in the future.

Roszak nicely summarizes his view concerning the depth of the youth revolt:

Such developments make clear that the generation revolt is still in the process of broadening down through the adolescent years, picking up numbers as time goes on.

The conflict will not vanish when those who are now 20 reach 30; it may only reach its peak when those who are now 11 and 12 reach their late 20's (1984). We may then discover that what a mere handful of beatniks pioneered in Allen Ginsberg's youth will have become the life style of millions of college-age youths.

The apparent outcome of this trend towards overschooling results in the attitude that the schools are used as mere "parking lots" where students defer their lives with no apparent real reward in terms of a meaningful job. Many students and some researchers, such as Reimers (*School is Dead*), believe that schools as presently constituted have outlived their usefulness in a technologically based society. The notion of actually abolishing the formal schools is now being considered by followers of Ivan Illich, a Roman Catholic priest, who is currently head of the Free University in Cuernevaca, Mexico. He says, for example:[9]

Allowing schools to monopolize learning gives arbitrary power to "academic priests" who mediate between the faithful and the gods of privilege and power.

While abolishing the schools seems very remote, there are researchers who are concerned how schools affect students and their future lives. These researchers of the "experiential" movement, such as Illich, Herndon, Kozol, Kohl, Silberman, and Reimers, have proposed sweeping educational reforms.

Most of the educational reform literature points to the fact that the educational system does not serve the purpose for which it was originally intended, that schools focus on unimportant objectives and teach irrelevant material, and, worst of all, that learning takes place in an authoritarian, boring environment. Educational reformers desire schools which are student-centered and can accommodate the different learning styles of students. There are some public schools which incorporate some of these educational reforms and are attempting to make students more "adult-like" in their attitudes and responsibilities toward school.[10] The Parkway School in Philadelphia uses the city as a classroom; at the Munay Road Annex of Newton High School, Newton, Massachusetts, students contract for and accept responsibility for their own education; and the John Adams High School in Portland, Oregon, approaches education as a menu of courses or interests for students from which students choose their course of study. These three experimental programs might provide hints concerning the future directions for educational reform in the seventies, but widespread adoption of these schemes seems remote due to the institutional rigidity of the educational system.[e] Some changes and reforms will have to come

[e]In an article appearing in *Saturday Review* September 16, 1972 (p. 42) Christopher Jencks on the basis of his research on schooling and inequality concluded that possibly the only

about, however, if for no other reason than to keep students (the most important players) in the education game.

One concern over widespread educational reform is that it might result in even more confusion, when these students become adults, and are unable to cope with "real-world" situations which require discipline, self-control, and regimentation. Thus, a great contradiction manifests itself for educators, namely, how does one individualize and humanize instruction to prepare students for a world that for most is largely based upon group norms and is dehumanized? How does one impart serious values to a generation knowing only abundance and a prolonged adolescence and, to use Roszak's expression, "fun and games"? How can parents, teachers, and administrators, most of whom experienced scarcity, had a short adolescence (World War II), and deferred gratification, relate to these students with their extended adolescence, do-it-now attitude, who have only experienced abundance? These are a few of the more difficult questions which educators must resolve to keep students involved in education and to give meaning and purpose for educational institutions. It seems that the purpose of schools and schooling in a technology-based society is destined to be one of the key educational issues of the seventies. The enormous federally sponsored spending programs of the 60s, which attempted to provide everyone entering the job market with comparable skills by massive remedial educational programs, has been of dubious value. Even the traditional American belief that doing well in school can help the poorest and most culturally disadvantaged child achieve economic success has to a great extent been disproved. In fact Jencks, in his book *Inequality: A Reassessment of the Effect of Family and Schooling in America*, asserts, on the basis of Project Talent and USOE data, that schools do nothing to close the gap between rich and poor; moreover the quality of education that public elementary and secondary students receive has little effect upon their future income. If these findings are verified and if students perceive their full meaning, the difficulty of keeping students involved in the education game will increase considerably. In addition other social institutions will probably assume a greater role in education as the perceived need for formal structured schooling dissipates.[f]

As far as students are concerned in the next decade, the greatest challenge to educators will be to devise nonmaterialistic incentives or intrinsic rewards which will elicit voluntary student involvement in educational activities.

---

basis for evaluating a school should be whether students and teachers find it a satisfying place. He reasoned that since schools do little for economic success, schools which value ideas because they enrich the lives of children are far superior to schools which value reading scores because of their supposed importance in later life.

[f]Edward Zigler, a Yale psychologist and former director of the U.S. Office of Child Development commenting on this trend has said "school people keep saying we should do more, whereas the real wave of the future is for schools to do less and let other social institutions do more." *Saturday Review*, Sept. 16, 1972, p. 41.

Administrators

The third participant in the education game is the school administrator whose primary responsibilities include keeping the system functioning, resolving conflicts, maximizing efficiency and setting objectives for meeting continually changing societal goals. With these diverse responsibilities and rapidly deteriorating influence, the average tenure of school superintendents and administrators is only a few years. The school administrator was treated harshly by some researchers and many of education's problems were blamed on poor planning and poor management. There is little question that the school administrator was generally unprepared in the areas of analysis, but so were his counterparts in private business and industry during the early fifties and his counterparts in other areas of the public sector are, even today, generally unprepared in the areas of analysis.

The school administrator has to make decisions in one of the most political institutions in America where everyone from a parent with little education to professors at universities has an opinion on how the schools should be run. Most school administrators in the past decade performed under conditions of perpetual conflict as they assumed roles of systems analysts, public relations men, professional educators, etc., in order to succeed in leading the organization.

If any one group or principal player in the education game represents the educational establishment, it is the school administrator. Of the four players he is in the most delicate or insecure position because unlike the teacher he has no tenure, and unlike the student, no law requiring him to be in school. To appreciate the basic policy of most administrators on some of the important contemporary issues in education, consider the following official resolutions of the AASA (American Association of School Administrators) at their 1971 convention.[11]

Vouchers. The tentative AASA statement on vouchers views the proposed system of renumeration of parents for their children's education "with grave alarm"; the Resolutions Committee cites such possible abuses as infusion of racial, ideological, or other noneducational concerns into the selection and administration of schools. Only a "massive bureaucracy" to oversee such a program could prevent these problems, claims the AASA.

Performance Contracting. Administrators should "foster experimentation" but demand that such projects be "under the strict supervision of persons thoroughly competent in relevant aspects of the field of education."

Teachers' Strikes. AASA would "abhor in principle and condemn in practice" all work stoppages while teachers are under contract as they disrupt the education of children and bitterly divide communities.

Student Rights. While rejecting violence by students, a resolution would have administrators seek "better channels for communicating" with students and provide youths with a "meaningful role in policymaking."

Some of the above resolutions are contrary to views held by most teachers, and as both players compete for public attention, it should be interesting to see the resolution of this "battle" between teachers and administrators. The term "battle" seems appropriate, especially considering the statements of the new President of the AASA, Paul Salmon, when he says:[12]

The American Association of School Administrators (AASA) is going to *seize* the role of educational leadership, exercise it wisely and relinquish it to no one. Since the National Education Association (NEA) has become "obsessed with collective bargaining and bread and butter issues for its members," it has "vacated a position that it had held for a long time from which it spearheaded the development of policy for the education profession."

Of course there is a hierarchy of administrative posts in a school district. The person caught directly in the middle of this battle between superintendents and teachers is the school principal who might be considered to represent middle management in school organizations. The insecure status of the principal was best described at the 1970 annual convention of the National Association of Secondary School Principals (NASSAP) in Washington, at which Martin Kalsh, President of the Detroit Organization of School Administrators and Supervisors, said:[13]

in this day of teacher power, community power, and student power, principals must use collective bargaining to get the power they need to survive. Any other approach is naive because education is a rough business today. You cannot depend on the good will and trust of the board and superintendent anymore. "When his back is to the wall, even the strongest superintendet will *sell you out.*"

The above quotes generally describe the current conflicts in the former "harmonious" educational establishment—the frustrated principal who has a dual identification as teacher and administrator, the teacher who has to be held accountable for pupil performance, and the administrator who is now fiscally accountable for his decisions.

One of the major problems of the school administrator, which make educational programs seem ineffectual, is that the principal goals for elementary and secondary education are constantly changing. Dr. Harold Spears, in a paper delivered at the 1971 Convention of the AASA, listed the following issues, priorities or concerns of educators during the past decade:[14]

1956   the great engineering shortage
1957   the Sputnik blame
1958   schoolhouse safety, the Chicago fire
1959   the Conant report

1960	the application of the National Defense Education Act
1961	the search for excellence—for the gifted
1962	attention to the child's racial background
1963	the search for the dropout, MDTA, and the Vocational Ed Act
1964	compensatory education—a new term for a forgotten concept
1965	the Economic Opportunity Act—Headstart and the Job Corps
1966	the Elementary-Secondary Education Act
1967	quality education, the search for a quality school
1968	the teacher rebellion
1969	the student rebellion
1970	accountability
1971	reading

As teachers organized to insure their jobs and status in the school district organization, administrators tried to develop skills to distinguish themselves from teachers and become the "managerial class" of education. One status form for administrators is to have skills in analysis. During the late sixties there was great interest generated in improving educational effectiveness through analysis as superintendents and administrators sought solutions to problems in educational management and planning from those skilled in economics, business administration, and systems analysis.

Unfortunately, no matter how sophisticated his analysis, the school administrator is locked in a position which compromises his whole decisionmaking base and deprives him of the flexibility which decisionmakers in other sectors of the economy take for granted. Funds for giving his program flexibility are scarce and the replacement of people in the organization who do not perform to the organization's standards is difficult. As previously mentioned, the growth of public education in terms of enrollment was phenomenal during the late fifties and early sixties. Almost anyone with a college degree was hired to teach and, as they completed requirements for credentials, became permanent or tenured employees after three or four years almost in spite of their competence. Now in the 1970s, with declining enrollments and budget, the school administrator has to make decisions where in some districts over 90 percent of the teachers are over 40 with tenure; most having been hired during the rapid growth era of education. Due to the fixed-step salary schedule, as these teachers get older they get more salary, so costs are continually rising while performance might actually decrease. Infusion of new teaching talent in these districts has been curtailed drastically and many districts will only hire teacher aides as older teachers retire in order to create surplus money for innovations and provide more flexibility in their educational program. The tenure problem is of such overriding concern and importance that some legislators are beginning to discuss its elimination. This concern of both teachers and the public over teacher tenure is exemplified in a short note reported in *Education USA:*[15]

Pressure to ease or eliminate teacher tenure laws is reported developing from public and political sources across the nation. In California, Governor Reagan is leading the attack. He said tenure laws tend to protect the "incompetent." The California State Board of Education has given the issue "top priority." One Board member said the goal is to cut down the umbrella which protects mediocrity. The California Teachers Association is counterattacking. It charges that "current irresponsible and ill-informed attacks on the state's teacher tenure laws are putting California schools in danger of becoming unprotected targets for radical political and social interests and the spoils system."

Caught directly between students who want more freedom and less regimentation, and society wanting to exert greater control over the schools, the school administrator's position and influence in the organization is being seriously undermined. His principal ally, the teacher, is contributing to this erosion of power as teacher-student, teacher-school board coalitions exert their power and influence. To maintain his status in the school district organization, the school administrator will probably have to continue acquiring skills of the managerial class, so that his role is legitimized before the school board. The teacher-administrator professional education team philosophy, characteristic of education in the past, seems to have vanished. Locked into a tenure personnel system, declining enrollments, budget restrictions, and on the firing line for his decisions with no job security, the school administrator will face difficult times during the next decade.

While there is little question that school administrators, because of their lack of analytical sophistication, might have caused some waste of public funds, the really important waste in education was not financial but waste of human resources. Dropouts, turned-off students, unmotivated teachers and students, are not problems of resource allocation but problems of a more fundamental and philosophical nature. The recent emphasis on tests, examinations and training teachers to boost these test scores accomplishes its objective of raising scores— but what does this mean? Is it even relevant to later social adjustment of the student? The "traditional" goals of the schools and the 1946 USOE stated goals for the schools, mainly social adjustment, self-discipline, acceptance of authority, deferred gratification, seem more related to later adult success and economic rewards than boosting scores on a reading test.[g]

Without clear delineation of goals, educators might devise very efficient reading, math, vocational education, etc., programs with little or no overall effectiveness since they do not know how these programs satisfy society's overall

---

[g]For a complete analysis of the relationship between schooling and later economic success, see *Inequality: A Reassessment of the Effect of Family and Schooling in America* by Christopher Jencks, Marshall Smith, Henry Acland, Mary Jo Bane, David Cohen, Herbert Gintis, Barbara Heyns and Stephan Michelson (Basic Books October 1972). The Coleman data, Project Talent and several other large data bases were reanalyzed under a Carnegie Grant with the conclusion that schools have few longterm effects on the later "success" of those who attend them.

goals or utility; or, more important, how they relate to the future lives of the students. The ambiguity of goals makes the school administrator's job particularly difficult.

Society

The influence of society on educational practices is most difficult to discern although there has been a drastic polarization of societal attitudes during the last decade.

The following excerpt, taken from a recent book by Philip E. Slater, *The Pursuit of Loneliness*, best sums the recent trends in the attitudes of society:[16]

There are an almost infinite number of ways to differentiate between the old and new cultures. The old culture, when forced to choose, tends to give preference to property rights over personal rights, technological requirements over human needs, competition over cooperation, violence over sexuality, concentration over distribution, the producer over the consumer, means over ends, secrecy over openness, social reforms over personal expression, striving over gratification, Oedipal love over communal love, and so on. The new counterculture tends to reverse all of these priorities.

The polarization of society into proponents of the old culture and counterculture philosophies will most likely result in great confusion in school district policy during the decade of the seventies. Legal, social, and economic indicators seem to indicate that counter-culture philosophies are gaining in strength, although political power is still mainly concentrated in the old culture. Thus the last player in the education game, the player who influences the course of education by setting goals and incentives, seems divided between pre-World War II scarcity-oriented society and post-World War II abundance-oriented society.

One, of course, could argue that the above is merely another cycle of abundance/scarcity in civilization. Slater, however, feels that the new counterculture has permanently affected the value and incentive system which influences people:

It should be stressed that affluence and economic security are not in themselves responsible for the new culture. The rich, like the poor, have always been with us to some degree, but the new culture has not. What is significant in the new culture is not a celebration of economic affluence but a rejection of its foundation. The new culture is concerned with rejecting the artificial scarcities upon which material abundance is based. It argues that instead of throwing away one's body so that one can accumulate material artifacts, one should throw away the artifacts and enjoy one's body.

Concerning attitudes toward work or study and happiness, Slater points out:

It is a central characteristic of the old culture that means habitually become ends, and ends means. Instead of people working in order to obtain goods in order to be happy, for example, we find that people should be made happy in order to work better in order to obtain more goods, and so on.

One finds some rational and systematic appraisal of society's changing values in codified form if one studies the law.

Since about 1950 the law has been used by some judges and lawyers to effect far-reaching changes in the educational system—and hence in society itself.[h] This development is clearly seen in recent federal and state court decisions which have been concerned with policy-making and school management.

"Today, education is perhaps the most important function of state and local governments"—*Brown v. Board of Education of Topeka* (1954); as a consequence, the federal courts, in attempting to infuse educational policies and practices with constitutional *minima*, have exercised an unprecedented influence upon the direction of education. Decisions concerned with "equality of educational opportunity" under the Fourteenth Amendment constitute a great proportion of the cases, but also at issue have been the personal rights and liberties of students and teachers guaranteed by the First Amendment, especially rights to "freedom of expression." Hence, both the First and Fourteenth Amendments have had a profound influence on educational policy and decision-making. This influence of the courts should be even more pronounced in the next decade as state courts increase their participation in policy-making for the schools in areas such as due process of law, school discipline, teacher rights, and the activities of school boards.

United States Supreme Court cases affecting education have involved four sections of the Constitution: Obligation of Contracts (Article 1, Section 10) and the First, Fifth, and Fourteenth Amendments. In the 135 years between 1819 and 1954, Spurlock identified some 45 decisions in the United States Supreme Court affecting education.[17] In the 15 years between 1954 and January 1970, there were some 45 decisions of the Court dealing with racial discrimination in the schools.[18] Each new Supreme Court case appears to open the door to more litigation affecting the schools. Whereas the Supreme Court in *Brown v. Board of Education of Topeka* (1954) was careful to say that pupil segregation, "pursuant to state law permitting or requiring such segregation," violates the equal protection clause of the Fourteenth Amendment, by 1970 later courts were saying that, insofar as the harm to the child is concerned, there is no difference between *de jure* and *de facto* segregation. The *Brown* decision has resulted in many subsequent court cases involving the administration and management of

[h]Recall the role that law and lawyers played in the abolition of slavery and in the rise and the fall of the judicial formula of "separate but equal" in public education. Cf. Horowitz and Karst, *Law, Lawyers, and Social Change*. Indianapolis: The Bobbs-Merrill Company, Inc., 1969, Chapters 1 and 2.

the schools, e.g., teacher and pupil assignments. The Supreme Court having applied the Fourteenth Amendment to education resulted in invalidation of the Washington, D.C. "tracking system (*Hobson v. Hansen*, 1967), and the assignment of teachers to minority schools, sometimes on a "three week or more . . . exchange basis" (*Northcross v. Board of Education of Memphis City Schools*, 1970).

The final major area of influence of the courts has been in school finance. State schemes for financing public education which discriminate against the poor on the basis of wealth have been measured by the courts against the standards of the equal protection clause of the Fourteenth Amendment. In the recently decided case of *Serrano v. Priest* (1971) the Supreme Court of California held that such financing schemes based on local school district wealth were unconstitutional. The implications of this decision could have far-reaching consequences for the organization of educational systems.

The period of educational history through which we are passing, as one educational legal researcher has noted, may be characterized as "education under the supervision of the courts."[19] In fact, there is some evidence that in some school districts in the South the courts are the "actual administrators" who are running the schools.

In conclusion, the emerging legal thinking seems to be that educational policies and practices, which were formerly evaluated on the basis of "reasonableness" alone, must now withstand the stricter test of court scrutiny. Education is now considered an activity which affects a person's whole life and livelihood which depend, in a large measure, upon his obtaining an "equal educational opportunity" in the public schools.

Another societal phenomenon seems destined to exert its influence upon education—the declining birth rate, with obvious implications, and changes in the structure of the family unit. In many areas of the country, principally urban areas, the family structure has changed drastically from the period of the fifties as the now common single-parent home requires that schools, *if nothing else*, keep students for a set number of hours per day so that the parent may work.[i] The design of future educational systems will have to consider the aspect of a "work-oriented" parental structure. Thus, while parents will still be asked to provide the resources and oversee the objectives and priorities of education, values and attitudes toward education for the students themselves, formerly derived from their parents, presently derived from peer group relationships as demonstrated in the research literature such as the Coleman Report,[20] will become more peer group dominated in the future.

Finally, society places many demands on the educational establishment, some

[i]In the annual survey of marital and family characteristics, conducted by the Bureau of Labor Statistics, it showed that nearly 26 million children under 18 had mothers working or looking for work in March 1970. (Six million of these children were under 6 years old.) In 1960, 15.7 million children under 18 had working mothers.

of which are dysfunctional to the principal aims of education, and some of which are outright contradictory. Many of the reform writers address themselves to these contradictions, especially Reimers who has outlined the functions of the schools, as society views it, in order of importance:[21]

(1) Control
(2) Socialization
(3) Role Formation
(4) Instruction

Educational reformers, of course, would like to parcel out each of these functions among other social institutions, and point to the fact that control and instruction sometimes work against each other in the present institutional setting of education. Preliminary evidence of up to 80 percent of teaching time being spent in class discipline in ghetto schools certainly underscores Reimers' concern over the intended and unintended functions of the schools.

In summary, school officials have a complex task of having to defend themselves against those who desire change toward less structured or a liberal education less tied to changing so-called national priorities, and those who desire a more formal, efficient, and accountable structure for education. The difficulty of coping with societal demands is made more acute for administrators faced with enormous shifts in student and teacher attitudes. The successful innovations of the future must therefore not only satisfy the criterion of educational benefit, but must now placate the demands of teachers, students, and society. The task ahead is extremely difficult, and cost-effectiveness analysis and PPBS of present programs are not answers to problems which are basically philosophical and subject to political compromise.

School policymakers in the seventies will have to possess not only analytical skills, but insight to read the long and short range needs of society and be able to distinguish politically inspired educational innovation from innovations which truly prepare an individual for a productive adjusted life in an increasingly complex world.

To conclude this overview and perspective of the emerging issues in education, it would be appropriate to convey some personal thoughts.

In a now famous quote Margaret Mead remarked: "My grandmother wanted me to get an education so she kept me out of school." Her view is now shared by millions of Americans. The public school system has to cater to at least four types of student demands: The lower-class—who perceive the need for education in terms of social and economic mobility, the middle-class—who are interested in education for status maintenance in the community, the humanists—primarily interested in education for individual growth, finally the escapists—who use education as a parking lot.

Although the present school system does a little of everything, it cannot satisfy any of these differing demands very well. In addition, the traditional ethic of the school—achievement, self-control, social independence, deferred gratification—has been displaced with a new student ethic of self-actualization, self-expression, interdependence, and instant gratification.

If education is to be at all responsive to the only certain things we know concerning the future, namely, rapidly accelerating change in uncertain directions, then the implications for the schools will be to emphasize individual flexibility and emotional stability under varied conditions. The emphasis of the schools will have to change from acquiring a skill to developing the ability to gain a skill. Memorization of knowledge will have to give way to developing skills related to access of knowledge. The rigidity and reliance in the structure of the present system will have to be transformed to one of adaptability and flexibility. Materialistic incentives characteristic of schools of the older generation will have to yield to intrinsic incentives for learning. Finally the concept of continuing education will have to replace the concept of fixed amounts of education.

Schools will also have to change instructional methods. Music, records, radio, TV, and magazines do a far better job in the presentation of knowledge, imparting values and in attracting the attention of the youth than the schools.

Socially relevant movies, white papers, news programs, and talk shows have had an enormous impact on changes in knowledge and values.

Conflicts in values pose the most serious problem for education. The conflicts between educators, students, and society is what makes meaningful policy-related research in education so difficult. Everyone in the education "game" has a voice and usually *all* important educational decisions are compromises. The notion that educational decisionmakers often presume that people who resist a change in an approach to education do not understand the implications of that change is not necessarily true. It is precisely because parents, students, and others fully perceive the implications of an innovation that they may resist it. This is the case particularly when the innovation may affect established values of the student or impart new ones in a way which conflicts with the values established in his home or community or with those of his background or culture. Sex education, for example, has generated enormous controversy in many communities because the schools are attempting to instruct in an area which has been private to the family. The instruction given by the teacher may directly challenge the values set by the family.

The decade of the 1970s will offer the greatest challenge to educators. School districts will have to function with an "idealistic" youth culture and a "materialistic" teacher, which is the exact opposite of previous generations where youth had the "materialistic" values and teachers had the "idealistic" values. In addition, schools will have to contend with the increasingly powerful mass media for capturing the imagination of the youth. The task ahead for all those concerned with the operations of the schools—researchers, teachers, parents, administrators—is enormous. Dedicated teachers, interested parents, risk-taking administrators, and a tolerant society are the only hope for improving an educational system which, compared to most other countries is excellent both qualitatively and quantititavely, yet is being criticized and discredited with unparalleled intensity. Quite possibly, the schools can be reformed as suggested by Silberman, or might have to be abolished completely or drastically altered, as suggested by Illich; all the trends seem to suggest that the decade of the seventies will be critical for American education.

Notes

1. "Practical Results: The New Edict for Research," *Education USA*, February 15, 1971, p. 127.

2. Averch, Harvey A., et al, "How Effective is Schooling: A Critical Review and Synthesis of Research Findings," R-956, PCSF/RC, March 1972.

3. "NEA Opinion Poll," *Education USA*, March 18, 1971, p. 146.

4. Whitehead, Alfred North, *The Aims of Education*, Macmillan Company, New York, 1921.

5. "Serious Protest Found in 18% of High Schools," *Education USA*, March 2, 1970, p. 145.

6. Roszak, Theodore, *The Making of a Counterculture*, Doubleday and Company, Inc., New York, 1969.

7. *Time*, March 1, 1971, pp. 97-99.

8. "Graduates and Jobs: A Grave New World," *Time*, May 24, 1971, pp. 49-57.

9. Illich, Ivan, *Deschooling Society*, Harper and Row, New York 1971.

10. Silberman, Charles E., *Crisis in the Classroom*, Random House, New York, 1970.

11. "103 Annual AASA Convention in Atlantic City," *Education USA*, March 1, 1971, p. 139.

12. "News Front," *Education USA*, May 3, 1971, p. 194.

13. "Frustrated Principals Seek New Role," *Education USA*, February 16, 1970, p. 133.

14. Spears, Dr. Harold, "Accountability—Menance or Mania," paper delivered at the 1971 convention of AASA, Atlantic City.

15. "News Front," *Education USA*, November 2, 1970, p. 50.

16. Slater, Philip E., *Cultures in Collision*, Beacon Press, New York, 1970.

17. Cf. Clark Spurlock, Education and the Supreme Court. Urbana, Illinois: *University of Illinois Press*, 1955.

18. John C. Hogan, "The Role of the Courts in Certain Educational Policy Formation," *Policy Sciences*, Volume I, No. 3, (Fall 1970), pp. 289-297.

19. John C. Hogan, Analysis of Significant Court Cases which have Affected the Organization Administration and Programs of the Public Schools, 1950-1972, unpublished doctoral dissertation, UCLA, 1972.

20. Coleman, J.S., et al., *Equality of Educational Opportunity*, U.S. Government Printing Office, Washington, D.C. 1966.

21. Reimers, *Schools and Schooling*, Prentice Hall, New York 1970.

References

Kozol, Jonathan, *Death at an Early Age*, Houghton Mifflin Company, Boston, 1967.

Hohl, H., *36 Children*, Signet Book, New York, 1968.

Herndon, James, *The Way it Spozed to Be*, Bantam Books, New York, 1969.

Jencks, Christopher, et al, *Inequality: A reassessment of the effect of Family and Schooling in America*, Basic Books, New York, 1972.

2

Societal Foundations for Change: Educational Alternatives for the Future

Willis W. Harman

To speak of "Educational Alternatives for the Future" implies some vision of the future of the society as a whole. In the work of the Educational Policy Research Center, Stanford Research Institute, we have attempted to construct a comprehensive set of "alternative future histories" from now until the year 2000.[1] (This was accomplished by devising an adequately rich coded description of the state of society and then systematically examining which sequences of these states are feasible for the next 30 years.) The results of this analysis indicate that the vast majority of the "future histories" so constructed are clearly to be avoided if possible. The reasons vary widely—from authoritarian governments to economic collapse, from ecological catastrophe to exhaustion from continuous warfare. The very small percentage of the feasible "future histories" which represent satisfactory states of existence appear to require a drastic and prompt shift in operative values of the society.

Out of this array of "future histories" I would like to select two as contexts within which to compare "educational alternatives for the future." One is essentially the scenario described by Bertram Gross as "Friendly Fascism." The other leads to a "person-centered society" aimed at the qualitative satisfaction of fundamental human needs, spiritual and mental as well as material and physiological. This path, however, is by way of a profound cultural transformation for which, by analogy, we might use the Greek word for religious conversion, *metanoia*: "a fundamental transformation of mind."

Two Possible Futures Compared

Gross describes friendly "techno-urban fascism" as

a managed society ruled by a faceless and widely dispersed complex of warfare-welfare-industrial-communications-police bureaucracies caught up in developing a new-style empire based on a technocratic ideology, a culture of alienation, multiple scapegoats, and competing control networks. [Centralized management and control] would not be limited to the economy: it would deal with the political, social, cultural, and technological aspects of society as well. It would use the skills not only of economists but also of social and natural scientists, professionals, technicians, and assorted intellectuals. The focus of

29

control would be not the economy, but the national society conceived of as a total system operating in the world environment.

Stressing the controllable and nonsentimental, [the technocratic ideology would promote] progress in the form of new technological gadgets for killing people, controlling their behavior, eliminating mental and physical labor, and wasting natural resources. It would expand the principles of R-and-D-ology, i.e., the theory that any problem can be solved quickly, given enough investment of high-quality research-and-development hours with appropriate provisions for controlled testing and evaluation. Materialist 'goodies' in unending kinds and quantities would become the symbols of achievement . . . Every effort to develop a more humanist 'counterculture' would itself be countered by profit-making or bureaucratic takeovers.[2]

Society would be controlled through "selective repression operating through and around the established constitutional system." Order, amid myriad severe social and environmental problems, would be purchased at the cost of decreased liberty. Effective use would be made of indirect control through welfare state benefits, "credentialized" meritocracy, and incentive manipulation of corporations and public authorities. The predominant characteristics of "friendly fascism" can be derived by extrapolation of dominant trends of the past few decades, particularly unlimited economic growth and technological development as paramount social aims, with manipulative stimulation of human wants to provide the motive power behind the aims.

The predominant characteristic of the contrasting "person-centered" society is well stated in the 1960 report of the President's Commission on National Goals:

The paramount goal . . . is to guard the rights of the individual, to ensure his development, and to enlarge his opportunity . . . All of our institutions—political, social, and economic—must further enhance the dignity of the citizen, promote the maximum development of his capabilities, stimulate their responsible exercise, and widen the range and effectiveness of opportunities for individual choice. . . . The first national goals to be pursued . . . should be the development of each individual to his fullest potential. . . . Self-fulfillment is placed at the summit (of the order of values). All other goods are relegated to lower orders of priority. . . . The central goal, therefore, should be a renewal of faith in the infinite value and the unlimited possibilities of individual development.[3]

What was not clearly understood in 1960 and is more apparent now, is that *a fundamental incompatibility exists between these aims and the dominant ethic of the industrial state.* This is the basic paradox of our time, and upon its successful resolution hinges the future of democratic society. We shall examine this topic further in a moment.

Warren Bennis[4] has summarized the nature of the shift from the industrial-state society to the person-centered society:

From	Toward

Cultural values

Achievement	Self-actualization
Self-control	Self-expression
Independence	Interdependence
Endurance of stress	Capacity for joy
Full employment	Full lives

Organizational values

Mechanistic, bureaucratic forms	Organic-adaptive forms
Competitive relations	Collaborative relations
Separate objectives	Linked objectives
Own resources regarded as owned absolutely	Own resources regarded also as society's resources

But such a shift demands attitude shifts that amount to a fundamental cultural transformation. Lewis Mumford has analyzed the basic attitude shifts that would have to accompany conversion to the "person-centered" society. There are, he says,

serious reasons for reconsidering the whole picture of both human and technical development on which the present organization of Western society is based. . . . The deliberate expression and fulfillment of human potentialities require a quite different approach from that bent solely on the control of natural forces. . . . Instead of liberation *from* work being the chief contribution of mechanization and automation, liberation *for* work, for educative, mind-forming work, self-rewarding even on the lowest physiological level, may become the most salutary contribution of a life-centered technology.[5]

The Plausibility of *Metanoia*

There we have the puzzle. Clearly the options open to education are very different in these two future contexts. If we seem reluctantly but inexorably headed for the first, and the second appears unreachable except through a fundamental change of cultural perception, what paths are really open? *Metanoia* cannot be manipulated into being, for the individual or for society. For note that we are talking about pervasive systemic change. When the basic cultural premises, the root image of man-in-society, the fundamental value postulates alter, all aspects of social roles and institutions are affected. Social institutions are constructed with a strong self-preserving characteristic; basic alteration does not take place smoothly nor easily.

Lewis Mumford notes that there have probably been not more than about a half dozen profound transformations of Western society since primitive man. Each of these was accompanied by a change in the "dominant metaphysic," the ruling vision-of-reality, the unquestioned cultural picture of man-in-the-universe. The periods when this metaphysic was in flux tend to be periods of turmoil and social disruption (e.g., the religious wars accompanying the Reformation).[6]

The term "dominant paradigm" is used by T.S. Kuhn to refer to *the basic way of perceiving, thinking, and doing, associated with a particular vision of reality*, largely embodied in unquestioned, tacit understanding transmitted primarily through exemplars. He documents the sequence of phenomena that tend to accompany the breakdown of influence of an old paradigm and its replacement by a new one. Growing awareness of problems which appear to be intrinsic to the old paradigm is one such sign.[7]

In historical retrospect we can see that a paradigm emerged several centuries ago which has since influenced all aspects of Western society. Its general character, sharply differing from the dominant paradigm of the preceding Middle Ages, is suggested by the following words and phrases:

Scientific method	Bureaucratic management
Technological development	Individualism
Industrialization	Democracy
Division of labor	Control over nature
Work ethic	Economic growth
Capitalism	Nationalism

Born out of this paradigm are the fabulous products of modern industrial organization and modern technology. The beginnings of breakdown of the paradigm are dramatically shown in the fact that its successes comprise all the serious social problems of our day. The following table illustrates this. The left hand column lists the achievements of industrial society; the right hand column shows the corresponding problems to which these have led.[8]

"Successes of the Technological Era	Resulting Problems of being "Too Successful"
Prolonging the life span	Overpopulation; problems of the aged
Weapons for national defense	Hazard of mass destruction through nuclear and biological weapons
Machine replacement of manual and routine labor	Exacerbated unemployment
Advances in communication and transportation	Urbanization; "shrinking world"; vulnerability of a complex society to breakdown (natural or deliberate)

Efficiency	Dehumanization of the world of work
Growth in the power of systematized knowledge	Threats to privacy and freedoms (e.g., surveillance technology, "bioengineering"); "knowledge barrier" to underclass
Affluence	Increased per capita environmental impact, pollution, energy shortage
Satisfaction of basic needs; ascendance up the "need-level hierarchy"	Worldwide revolutions of "rising expectations"; rebellion against "non-meaningful work"; unrest among affluent students
Expanded power of human choice	Management breakdown as regards control of consequences of technological applications
Expanded wealth of developed nations	Intrinsically increasing gap between have and have-not nations
Development of prepotent high-technology capability	Apparent necessity of continuous war to use up the output of the "mega-machine"

The problems listed in the right hand column are ultimately unsolvable in the present paradigm precisely because their origins are in the success of that paradigm. Victor Ferkiss, analyzing the unavoidable problems to which the technological ethic leads, concludes that the required "new guiding philosophy" must contain three basic and essential elements. First is what he terms a "new naturalism," which affirms that man is absolutely a part of a nature, a universe, that is always in the process of becoming. The second element, a "new holism," recognizes that "no part can be defined or understood save in relation to the whole." The third, a "new immamentism," sees that the whole is "determined not from outside but from within."[9]

Appearing as though in response to this need for a new guiding philosophy is a "New Age" paradigm, dimly defined as yet but featuring a kind of ecological consciousness that satisfied Ferkiss' three conditions. Whether this seemingly spontaneous emergence of a new outlook is fortuitous coincidence or response to a subliminally perceived need of society is a moot but unimportant point. In either event, the coincidence of the need and the emergence of a possible answer to the need increases the likelihood that we are witnessing the beginnings of a thoroughgoing paradigm shift.

Clues to the nature of the "New Age" premises are to be found in the swelling interest in religious, metaphysical, psychic and arcane literature and discussion groups; in the "consciousness-expanding" activities of the "human potential" movement, ranging from yoga and transcendental meditation to psychedelic drugs and efforts to develop "psychic openings"; in the juxtaposition, in underground newspapers and other activities of "the movement," of revolutionary messages with material on religious, esoteric, and psychic topics.[10] Most significant, as an indication of the growing challenge to the prevailing positivistic premise of conventional science, is the growing interest in "altered states of consciousness."[11]

The Nature of the Emerging Metaphysic

Thus there appears to be in the present situation (a) a *need* for a new dominant paradigm since the natural course of the old one has exhibited an ultimately pathogenic side; (b) a *force* for change evident particularly in, but not confined to, youth's "Great Refusal" to go along with the consequences of the old paradigm; and (c) an *emerging paradigm* which seems potentially capable of resolving the paradoxes and contradictions of the old one.

We have earlier, in the brief description of the "person-centered society," suggested some general characteristics of the contending paradigm as regards cultural and organizational values. Let us look now at the metaphysical side.

Aldous Huxley was one of the first modern writers to suggest that an age-old set of basic assumptions about the nature of man was showing new strength. We shall borrow his term, "The Perennial Philosophy":

Philosophia Perennis—the phrase was coined by Leibnitz; but the thing—the metaphysic that recognizes a divine Reality substantial to the world of things and lives and minds; the psychology that finds in the soul something similar to, or even identical with, divine Reality; the ethic that places man's final end in the knowledge of the immanent and transcendent Ground of all being—the thing is immemorial and universal. Rudiments of the Perennial Philosophy may be found among the traditionary lore of primitive peoples in every region of the world, and in its fully developed forms it has a place in every one of the higher religions. A version of this Highest Common Factor in all preceding and subsequent theologies was first committed to writing more than twenty-five centuries ago, and since that time the inexhaustible theme has been treated again and again, from the standpoint of every religious tradition and in all the principal languages of Asia and Europe.[12]

The basic proposition of the "Perennial Philosophy" is an empirical one, that man can under certain conditions attain to a higher awareness, a "cosmic consciousness," in which state he has immediate knowledge of a reality underlying the phenomenal world, in speaking of which it seems appropriate to use such words as infinite and eternal, Divine Ground, Brahman, Godhead, or Clear Light of the Void. From this vantage point, one's own growth and creativity, and his participation in the evolutionary process, are seen to be under the ultimate direction of a higher center (Atman, the Self of Vedantic writings, the Oversoul).

Ordinary perceptions of one's life and of one's environment are likened to the perceptions of a hypnotic trance.[13] Such phenomena as extrasensory perception, precognition of future events, levitation and other psychokinetic events, "instant" diagnosis and healing, etc., are only extraordinary, not a priori impossible.

The basic assumptions of positivistic science stand in relationship to the Perennial Philosophy much as Newtonian mechanics relates to relativistic physics: they are in no way invalidated for those aspects of human experience to which they are appropriate, but comprise a special case, a limited form of the more general theory. Similarly, the philosophies of materialism and idealism are to each other as the wave and particle theories of light and matter; each fits the world as seen with a particular mode of observation, and a complementary relationship holds between them.

Of course the Perennial Philosophy is not new to Western culture. It is present in the Rosicrucian and Freemasonry traditions. Its symbolism in the Great Seal of the United States, on the back of our dollar bill, is testimony to the role it played in the formation of this country. It shows up with particular clarity in the Transcendentalism of Emerson, the Creative Evolution of Bergson, and the extensive writings of William James; it can be discerned in the background in much of our greatest poetry, art, philosophy, and literature.

Part of society's thus far negative reaction to monistic and Eastern kinds of beliefs as they have appeared in the hippie culture, the drug scene, and numerous cults, has been due to the fear that they would lead to quietism and withdrawal and, therefore, would undermine the social structure. Although it is true that these beliefs have been associated with the Eastern world, there is in fact nothing in the Perennial Philosophy which is contrary to virile and active participation in economic and political affairs. Neither are these premises in any way contrary to a highly technological society; they only say something about the ends to which that technology would be put.

Some Aspects of the New Paradigm

If this claimant paradigm, characterized by (a) a metaphysic asserting *transcendent man* and (b) a *person-centered society*, does indeed become dominant (and, with the general speedup of history, the issue will likely be settled within a decade or two at most), it will—as we have noted—amount to a profound and pervasive systemic change. There will be a "new science," a "new economics," a "new politics," a "new education." Before we look at what this may mean for education we need to look at how the shift would affect some other closely related areas.

Science

Science, in this paradigm, will clearly be understood to be a *moral inquiry*. That is to say, it will deal with what is empirically found to be good for man—in much the same sense that the science of nutrition deals with what foods are wholesome for man. It will place particular emphasis on the systematic exploration of subjective experience, the ultimate source of our value postulates. In this respect it will resemble the humanities and religion, and the boundaries between these three disciplines will become less sharp—as is already presaged in the recent writings of some psychotherapists. Applied science, particularly educational research, will look strongly in the direction of new potentialities suggested by the newly appreciated powers of belief, imagination, and suggestion. To conscious choice and subconscious choice (repression, projection, sublimation, etc.) will be added what might be termed "supraconscious choice"[14] (intuition, creative imagination, choosing "better than we know") —with as much impact upon our policies regarding education, welfare, criminal rehabilitation, and justice as the Freudian concepts had some years earlier. Finally, the new science would become also a sort of "civil religion," supporting the value postulates of the Founding Fathers rather than being neutral or undermining as was the old science.

Institutions

Clearly the "Perennial Philosophy" metaphysic would tend to support effective institutionalization of such values as society serving the self-fulfillment of the individual, equality of justice before the law, individual fulfillment through community, human dignity and meaning, honesty and trust, self-determination for individuals and minority groups, and responsibility for humankind and the planet. However, values do not become operative simply by being deemed "good." Let us look at some arguments that suggest these values might become operative because they work.

As the social system becomes more and more highly interdependent, the need becomes greater for accurate information to be available throughout the system. Just as the modern banking and credit system would not operate smoothly with the low trust level of a warrior culture, so highly complex task operations (such as putting a man on the moon) require a higher level of honesty, openness, and trust than suffice in advertising and merchandising. For quite practical, rather than moralistic reasons, the demanded level of honesty and openness can be expected to increase.

Similarly, as the complexity of societal operations increases, hierarchically organized bureaucratic structures overload communications at the top and discourage entrepreneurship and responsibility-taking lower down. Adaptive organic forms, with relatively autonomous subsystems, seem better adapted to complex tasks and provide more satisfying experiences to the people involved.

In general, the more significant a fraction of the whole is a subsystem, the more important it becomes that its goals be in close alignment with those of the overall system. It would be quite practical to foster (through changes in corporation, tax, and anti-trust laws, credit policies, special subsidies, etc.) the development of profitmaking corporations whose *operative* goals include active response to social problems (as those of nonprofit corporations already do) and fostering the educational growth and development of all persons involved (as the goals of universities already do). In fact, if something like this does not take place the amount of government regulation required for pollution control, fair business and employment practice, resource conservation, etc., can only increase without limit.

In short, the institutionalization of the values of the "person-centered society" would appear to be not only morally desirable, but "good business" for the nation.

Economic System

The portion of the industrial-state paradigm underlying the present operation of the economic system includes such concepts as man as infinite consumer of goods and services (providing his appetites are properly whetted through advertising), profit maximizing and economic growth as pre-eminent goals, and government as master regulator of employment level, growth rate, wage and price stability, and a modicum of fair play. The new paradigm would remind us that the root meaning of "economics" is "home management," and that the planet earth is man's home. Managing the earth, with its finite supplies of space and resources and its delicate ecological balance, and conserving and developing it as a suitable habitat for evolving man, is a far different task than that for which the present economic system was set up.

Furthermore, an economic theory is inevitably based upon a theory of social psychology. If man is not "economic man" in a self-regulating free market, nor an infinite consumer with manipulable motivations, but something quite different, then we need a radical correction to economic theory.

So some changes will take place in our economic institutions and practices, of which we can see only the general directions. One clear need is a network of citizen-participation policy and planning centers at local, regional, and national levels, linked together with a common understanding of the alternatives that lie before the society and some unifying agreement as to the futures to be desired and those to be avoided.

Alternatives for Education

And so at last we come to education. But all that went before was necessary. We had to explore the kinds of futures within which the educational future might have to fit. If, as claimed, we are faced with one particularly significant fork in "the road to the future," we had to see what that implied. If now, as a consequence, we have to cover the implications for education in a most cursory manner, I can only plea that I have been trying to provide a framework for thinking rather than a kit full of answers. Thus we shall deal with only a few aspects of the educational future to illustrate how the broad considerations above furnish new perspective.

Institutions

Whatever future may evolve, as long as it does not involve radical regression in technology and industrialization, it will have to involve effective mechanisms for occupation retraining. But when the demands of a high-technology industrial system are coupled with rising demands for more equitable sharing of economic and political power—which more and more implies knowledge power, the power of education—a far more radical restructuring of educational functions is implied. There will have to be a solution to what we might term the "recycling" problem—an effective way for the discards of the system, those labeled "technologically disemployed," "unemployable," "dropout," "poor," "delin-quent," "criminal," "deviant," and "mentally ill," to cycle around and have another try, stigma-free and with the kind of support and educational oppor-tunity best suited to their individual needs. Our basic moral commitments demand no less, and the society can afford no less.

It is not clear that this problem can be solved within educational institutions as we have known them. Perhaps a multiplicity of institutional forms will be required, including new kinds of collaborative arrangements between educational institutions and industrial and commercial organizations. The emergence of new types of profit-making corporations with diversified goals, as suggested above, might reduce the danger of educational objectives being distorted by the pressures of business.

Federal Role

Providing adequate and effective paths for re-education and re-entry as outlined above implies strong support and leadership from the federal government. There are a number of other reasons to anticipate an increasingly strong federal role in education. (In "friendly fascist" America this would involve strong centralized management; in the "person-centered society" funds and planning assistance would be available from the government but initiative and management would be localized.)

In the first place, gross local and regional economic variations persist, and geographical mobility continues to increase. A person is likely to obtain his educational experience in several different parts of the country, and to live much of his life elsewhere than where he got his schooling. Thus equality of educational opportunity can be approached only if the federal government collects the greatest part of the revenue and performs a redistributing function. (The form of taxing plays a part here too. The nature of the funding source inevitably influences the nature of the funded activity. Thus a progressive income tax source is more likely to lead to equalized distribution of educational opportunity than is a regressive tax source such as local property taxes.)

More compelling is the severity of the problems faced. The present system is being found wanting on two important counts: it fails to achieve an equitable distribution of power, wealth, and justice, and it fails to preserve and develop a habitable (in a broad sense) physical and social environment. The survival of the nation depends upon its making an adequate response to these challenges. Since education must perforce play a key role in that response, it must be a vital element in the overall national policy.

Accountability

The word "accountability" is heard with increasing frequency in discussions of the future of education. Of course, where there is expenditure of public funds there has always been accountability. What is new is that we are no longer satisfied with the old criteria (student-days in school, successes and failures at passing norm-based tests, etc.) nor the results (labeling of clients as "failures," contributing to caste structure of society, institutional rigidities and stultification in the educational system).

In one familiar version, accountability implies accounting in terms of behaviorally defined objectives agreed upon by the society and its delegated officials. In this form, it tends to be associated with individualized curricular management (IPI, PLAN, etc.). Diagnostic tests, modality preference and cognitive style determination, criterion-referenced tests, etc., enable the teacher to place the child on a continuum and to prescribe the next appropriate educational experience, to choose the mode of instruction to fit the individual, and continually assess progress. Management information systems, performance-guaranteed contracts, Program Planning and Budgeting system, and the like all contribute to overall effectiveness in achieving the chosen behavioral objectives. It sounds like progress, but it could lie directly on the charted path to "friendly fascism."

On the other hand, the pressures of growing consumerism, insistence on self-determination, fear of manipulation by those with expertise, push for a different concept of accountability. This version refers to the authority of the basic principle on which the nation was founded, that society is ultimately accountable to the individual. It includes emphasis on "experimental schools" within the system and voucher-supported options outside, support of broad humanistic educational goals, and the principle of consumer choice. It rejects the factory-inspired quality-control model and puts its trust, rather than in expertise, in the ultimate ability of the consumer to choose wisely. Evaluations take such forms as independent audits and "consumer reports."

Perhaps no other issue within education will reflect so faithfully the larger societal issue of "Which future?" as the issue of accountability.

Organization

This same rising force of self-determination will push forward a social organization analogous to that of a living organism, with relatively self-determining units depending on the larger whole for certain services (e.g., revenue collection and distribution, research and development) and directions—hierarchies being functional, fluid, and non-invidious, the whole bound together by shared goals and values. Educational organization in the person-centered society will foster self-directed, self-appropriated learning. The educating and evaluating functions will be separated to reduce threat-competition (as contrasted with game-competition). Increasing use will be made of aides and of students teaching students. This is partly because of the inherently rising relative cost of education (which comes about because technology will not raise educational productivity to the same extent that it will raise output per worker in other areas such as manufacturing) and partly because of the educational value of being in the teacher role. Compulsory schooling as a basic policy may well undergo some modification as non-school educational opportunities become more plentiful.

Should the overall societal path go instead in the "friendly fascism" direction, the trend in the educational system will be toward a more tightly controlling organization, although the control may be exerted in very subtle ways.

Curriculum

If the society does indeed undergo *metanoia*, one of the most obvious ways in which the transformation will be manifested will be in the curriculum. But the curriculum will recognize, first of all, that only a fraction of learning takes place in the formal educational system. Robert Hutchins describes "the learning society" as one that will have transformed "its values in such a way that learning, fulfillment, becoming human, had become its aims and *all its institutions were directed to this end.* This is what the Athenians did . . . They made their society one designed to bring all its members to the fullest development of their highest powers. . . . Education was not a segregated activity, conducted for certain hours, in certain places, at a certain time of life. It was the aim of the society. . . . The Athenian was educated by the culture, by Paidea."[15]

A predominant theme for the formal portion of education in the "learning society" will be preparing its members to make a contribution to the overall enterprise—but with a much broader range of activities implied by the word "contribution" than is usually meant by "career education." Learning to create a habitable environment—the development of "ecological consciousness"—will have an important role in education. The basic premises underlying the curriculum will have been changed in accordance with the new paradigm (which in a sense is not so new—the basic educational task fostered by Paidea was "the search for the Divine Center").

But it is not the curriculum of the future that should concern us most, rather, what we have to do to achieve a desirable future and avoid the many undesirable alternatives. Education is undeniably a prime requisite. It is all of us who need to educate ourselves:

1. To emotional as well as intellectual awareness of the ineluctable fact that we are one race, on one planet, and that only we can take responsibility for the fate of both;
2. To the possibility that a drastic shift in basic premises and operative values may be necessary for a tolerable future; and
3. To the awareness that if a change in dominant paradigm does indeed take place, the strains on the social structure will be such as to demand, for successful passage, unusual understanding and dedication.

References

1. Various reports of the Educational Policy Research Center, Stanford Research Institute, including:

Research Memorandum 6747-6, Alternative Futures and Educational Policy; February 1970.
Research Note 6747-11, Alternative Futures: Contexts in Which Social Indicators Must Work; February 1971.
Research Memorandum 6747-10, Projecting Whole-Body Future Patterns— The Field Anomaly Relaxation (FAR) Method; February 1971.

2. Gross, Bertram, "Friendly Fascism: A Model for America." *Social Policy*, Nov-Dec 1970; excerpted in *Current*, February 1971.

3. *Goals for Americans*, pp. 1, 3, 53, 48, 57. Englewood Cliffs, N.J.: Prentice Hall, 1960.

4. Bennis, Warren, "A Funny Thing Happened on the Way to the Future." *Amer. Psych.* vol. 25 no. 7, July 1970, pp. 595-608.

5. Mumford, Lewis, "Technics and the Nature of Man." *Nature*, 4 December 1965, pp. 923-928.

6. Mumford, Lewis, *The Transformations of Man*. New York: Harper and Brothers, 1956.

7. Kuhn, Thomas S., *The Structure of Scientific Revolutions*. University of Chicago Press, 1962. The applicability of Kuhn's concepts to cultural revolutions is explored more thoroughly in the unpublished work of my colleague, Norman McEachron.

8. Mumford, Lewis, *The Pentagon of Power*. New York: Harcourt, Brace, Jovanovich, 1970.

9. Ferkiss, Victor C., *Technological Man: The Myth and the Reality*. New York: George Braziller, 1969.

10. See, for example, Needleman, Jacob, *The New Religions*. Garden City, N.Y.: Doubleday and Co., 1970. Also Roszak, Theodore, *The Making of a Counter-Culture*. Doubleday, 1969.

11. Tart, Charles, *Altered States of Consciousness*. John Wiley and Sons, 1969.

Harman, Willis W. "The New Copernican Revolution." *Jour. Humanistic Psych.*, discusses the significance of new experimental tools for studying physical and physiological correlates of inner states. Fall, 1969 vol. 9, no. 2, pp. 127-134.

12. Huxley, Aldous, *The Perennial Philosophy*. New York: Harper and Brothers, 1945.

13. "There is a traditional doctrine, usually associated with religions but now and then invading great literature, that our present waking state is not really being awake at all. It is, the tradition says, a special form of sleep comparable to

a hypnotic trance in which, however, there is no hypnotist but only suggestion." (A.R. Orage, *Psychological Exercises and Essays*, London, 1965).

Two recent discussions of this doctrine are: Benoit, Hubert, *Let Go: Theory and Practice of Detachment According to Zen*, George Allen and Unwin London, 1962.

Pearce, Joseph C., *The Crack in the Cosmic Egg*. New York: Julian Press, 1971.

14. Pitirim Sorokin's study *The Ways and Power of Love* (Beacon Press, 1954) is a pioneering effort by a noted sociologist to initiate a systematic study of supraconscious processes.

15. Hutchins, Robert, *The Learning Society*, New York: Praeger, 1968.

**Part II:
Policy Issues Related to
School District Inputs**

3

Constitutional Aspects of Equality of Educational Opportunity

Harold Horowitz

United States Court of Appeals Judge J. Skelly Wright, deciding the case of *Hobson v. Hansen*[1] in 1967, concluded his opinion with what he called a "Parting Word":

It is regrettable, of course, that in deciding this case this court must act in an area so alien to its expertise. It would be far better indeed for these great social and political problems to be resolved in the political arena by other branches of government. But these are social and political problems which seem at times to defy such resolution. In such situations, under our system, the judiciary must bear a hand and accept its responsibility to assist in the solution where constitutional rights hang in the balance.

The "great social and political problems" in *Hobson v. Hansen*, in "an area so alien" to the court's expertise, involved the operation of the District of Columbia public schools. The "constitutional rights" which hung in the balance were the asserted rights of the plaintiff children to equality of educational opportunity in the District of Columbia school system. Judge Wright wrote an opinion in *Hobson v. Hansen* in which, in over 100 printed pages, he analyzed in the greatest detail the administration of the District of Columbia's schools and concluded that in a number of respects those schools were being operated in violation of the plaintiffs' constitutional rights to equality of educational opportunity. Judge Wright's "Parting Word" reflected a concern that the judicial process ideally should not be the point for decision of issues of educational policy such as those which arose in *Hobson v. Hansen*, and that courts should not become too deeply involved in the day-to-day administration of school systems. But in recent years the courts have indeed become focal points for change, or attempts at change, in educational policy, in legal actions based on the concept of equality of educational opportunity. This paper describes these cases and the underlying issues of educational policy and educational research which the cases raise.

The constitutional provision on which this litigation has been based is the equal protection clause of the Fourteenth Amendment: "No State shall . . . deny to any person within its jurisdiction the equal protection of the laws." If a state, or legal subdivision of a state, provides a public school system the argument is that the educational opportunity must be made available to all children within

47

the limits of the "equality" which the equal protection clause requires. If one child receives significantly better educational opportunity than another in the public schools the basis is laid for a contention of denial of the constitutional right, though, as will be seen in the discussion below of de facto segregation, that is not the end of the constitutional analysis. All legal standards which have the consequence of classifying people and their legal rights create inequalities—for example, certain qualifications, such as minimum age or demonstrated competence, must be met in order to be permitted to vote or to drive a car or to obtain a license to engage in a particular calling; some people pay income taxes at a higher rate than do others; some human activities are proscribed by law and others are not. The difficult task for the judge is to decide when specific inequalities in the way that government treats people become denials of equal protection of the laws. Recent and current litigation involving public education poses these problems of interpretation of the equal protection clause in varying and challenging ways.

The education litigation can conveniently be placed in three overlapping categories: inequality in educational oportunity arising from racial segregation of students; other inequalities in educational opportunity within a single school district, such as teacher quality, curricular offerings, and similar inputs into the educational process; and inequalities in educational opportunity among school districts within a state.

Racial Segregation

The prime example of the application of the equal protection clause to invalidate state or local educational policy is, of course, *Brown v. Board of Education* (1954)[2], which held invalid, as a denial of equal protection of the laws, assignment of children to public schools based on their race (de jure segregation). The Supreme Court found "amply supported by modern authority" the finding of a lower court that compulsory racial segregation of children denoted "the inferiority of the Negro group," that this "sense of inferiority affects the motivation of a child to learn," and that such segregation therefore "has a tendency to [retard] the educational and mental development of Negro children and to deprive them of some of the benefits they would receive in a racial [ly] integrated school system." Because of the psychological harm caused by compulsory segregation the black children received an inferior educational opportunity as compared with that received by the white children. "Separate educational facilities are inherently unequal," the Court concluded.

The Supreme Court has yet to decide the constitutionality of de facto segregation in public schools—the condition of racially (or ethnically) concentrated school populations which is the product of a neighborhood school assignment policy superimposed on racially (or ethnically) separated housing patterns, in situations where there is no recent history of de jure school segregation. There have been conflicting decisions by lower federal courts and state courts on this issue. (Judge Wright decided in *Hobson v. Hansen* that de facto segregation did deny the plaintiffs equality of educational opportunity.) Does adherence to a neighborhood school policy—i.e., classification of children for school attendance on the basis of where they live—in such circumstances provide the minority child with a lower quality educational opportunity? There is considerable dispute whether *Brown v. Board of Education* settles that question: did *Brown* reach the conclusion that *all* segregation, de jure and de facto, causes the psychological harm referred to by the Court? Plaintiffs in current de facto segregation cases endeavor to go beyond the social psychology conclusions in *Brown*, turning to more recent social science research on the relationship between the racial makeup of a school and the achievement (on standardized tests) of the children. Though the 1966 H.E.W. report, Equality of Educational Opportunity (the Coleman Report), was equivocal on this issue, the United States Commission on Civil Rights report in 1967, *Racial Isolation in the Public Schools*, found significant relationships between achievement and the racial makeup of a child's school, the black child performing better in a majority-white setting.[3] The Coleman Report found a significant relationship between achievement and the socio-economic status of a child's classmates, the lower SES child performing better in a majority-higher-SES setting. This finding is important in the de facto segregation context because of the disproportionate segments of racial and ethnic minorities in the lower SES ranges; racial and ethnic concentrations in public schools because of housing patterns tend then to be synonymous with socio-economic concentrations.

A critical element in applying the equal protection clause in the de facto segregation case turns, then, on proof of the harm from de facto segregation— i.e., the comparative quality of educational opportunity offered to minority students in the school settings which result from a neighborhood attendance policy. Questions such as the following become pertinent: What are the appropriate measures of the quality of educational opportunity offered children—achievement, personality development, tangibly measurable elements in the educational program, preparation for life? How soundly can social science correlate racial or ethnic makeup of the student body with whatever measure of educational opportunity is settled upon? More specifically, what is the soundness of the conclusions on these issues in the Coleman Report and the *Racial Isolation* report? What would be the impact on comparative quality of educational opportunity of all children in a district if the neighborhood-school concept were abandoned? Do the social and psychological consequences of current trends toward decentralization and community control of schools significantly lessen the harmful impact on the minority child from attending a de facto segregated school? Is the serious injury to lower-SES children from de facto socio-economic segregation now so clearly established as to make a compelling case that there is a denial of equal protection of the laws in assigning children to schools in a manner which results in that form of segregation? To answer these questions inputs from social science research are required.

The de facto segregation case differs from *Brown v. Board of Education* in another respect, aside from whatever differences there may be in the nature and proof of injury to the minority child. In *Brown* the schools assigned children on the basis of race, and there were no persuasive arguments to justify that method of assignment as a means of achieving some legitimate governmental purpose. In the de facto segregation case assignment is based on place of residence, and the neighborhood school concept does serve varying purposes—safety of children, bringing the school and parents closer together, lessening travel time for children. Where pursuance of such governmental purposes can be shown, proof of harm to some children from a neighborhood school attendance policy may not alone be sufficient to establish a denial of equal protection of the laws. A fundamental aspect of the concept of judicial review of the constitutionality of actions of the legislative branch of government emerges: to what extent, in applying constitutional limitations on governmental action, should the Supreme Court, removed from direct responsiveness to the people, review public policy judgments made by elected representatives of the people? This basic question about the role of the Supreme Court is reflected in current differing judicial views about the application of the equal protection clause. Some justices express the position that a legislative classification does not violate constitutional requirements of equality if there is some "reasonable" or "rational" basis for the classification. Other justices find in the equal protection clause a requirement that if an inequality created by a legislative classification infringes upon a "fundamental interest" of those disadvantaged by the classification, the classification will be valid only if there is something more than a reasonable or rational basis, i.e., there must be a "compelling" basis for making the classification. It is this type of question which is part of discussion of how "activist" the Supreme Court is, or should be.

A de facto segregation decision by the California Supreme Court in 1963, *Jackson v. Pasadena City School District*,[4] illustrates how these considerations apply in the context of a specific education case. There the court concluded that "The right to an equal opportunity for education and the harmful consequences of segregation require that school boards take steps, insofar as reasonably feasible, to alleviate racial imbalance in schools regardless of its cause." School boards could not simply ignore the inequalities in educational opportunity which were the result of a neighborhood attendance policy, but in view of the purposes served by such a policy their obligation to refrain from imposing those inequalities went no further than to make use of whatever "reasonably feasible" steps were available to them. With this approach to the issue, any constitutional distinction between de jure and de facto segregation tends to disappear—the failure to use reasonably feasible steps, including bussing, to lessen racial imbalance, may, in purpose and effect, be indistinguishable from officially proclaimed segregation of the pre-*Brown* variety in the South. For by failing to use the reasonably feasible alternative the district is deliberately opting for more, rather than less, segregation. With this type of resolution of the constitutional aspects of de facto segregation, researchers and administrators in education have an indispensable contribution to make to the judicial process, not only on the question of the harm caused by such segregation, but also on the question of the measures available to a specific district to ameliorate that harm while at the same time substantially advancing at least some of the purposes of a neighborhood attendance policy.

Other Inequalities Within a Single District

There is a relatively long history to judicial inquiry into the equality of educational opportunity offered children with respect to seemingly measurable tangible inputs to the educational process by a school system. This was the focus of whatever school litigation there was in the South before *Brown v. Board of Education*, testing whether racially separate educational opportunity was in other respects "equal" opportunity. Currently, there are cases raising the question whether children in one school in a district are provided educational opportunity equal to that provided children in other schools with respect to such factors as teacher quality, expenditures, curriculum, facilities, and the like. (Judge Wright found such unconstitutional inequalities in the District of Columbia schools in *Hobson v. Hansen*.) There are difficult questions here. Do differences in such factors from school to school establish inequality of educational opportunity? Is it necessary to show differences in achievement of children correlating to such differences in these factors, or is there some other way to relate these factors to the quality of education offered? The Coleman Report found no significant differences in achievement related to such factors, with the exception of teacher quality. How does one measure the quality of teachers for this purpose? The Coleman Report stated that the teacher characteristics which had the highest relationship to achievement were the teachers' educational backgrounds and their scores on a verbal skills test. Comparisons are frequently made among schools of the experience, tenure status, and graduate degrees of teachers, but are these sound measures of teacher quality? Are attitudes of teachers more closely related to achievement and other educational development of children than are other attributes of teachers? Again the demonstration in litigation of unequal educational opportunity for some children may be dependent upon the inputs of educational research.

One aspect of *Hobson v. Hansen* should be emphasized here, because of the potential significance of the doctrine stated by the court. The track system, i.e., ability grouping, in the District of Columbia schools was found by Judge Wright to deny equality of educational opportunity. One reason for his conclusion was that the tests by which children were classified for the different tracks were inadequate to the task because the tests were culturally biased. "Rather than reflecting classifications according to ability, track assignments are for many students placements based on status." This question then follows: Can educational psychology provide methods for ability grouping which would survive judicial scrutiny such as that made in *Hobson v. Hansen*? Judge Wright found another constitutionally controlling defect in the track system. " ... [A] nother significant failure to implement track theory ... is the lack of adequate remedial and compensatory education programs for the students assigned to or left in the lower tracks because of cultural handicaps." Judge Wright was here referring to another measure of equality of educational opportunity—the adequacy of response to the differing educational needs of the students. Children in the lower tracks had special educational needs, and those children were denied equality of educational opportunity if their needs were not responded to to the same extent that other children's educational needs were. Again there are basic educational questions implicit in the constitutional inquiry: To what extent can the educational capacity and needs of children be determined? To what extent can "compensatory education" programs effectively respond to differing educational needs?

Inequalities Among School Districts Within a State

Current litigation is adding another dimension to the application of the equal protection clause to public education—expansion of the geographical area within which there must be equality of educational opportunity from the individual school district to the entire state. The Fourteenth Amendment speaks to the states, and the argument is that there are constitutional limits to the inequalities in educational opportunity among children within a state which can be imposed because a state chooses to structure public school administration on a decentralized district basis. The current litigation makes this contention with respect to the substantial differences in expenditure per child from district to district which can be found in many states, as a product of reliance on the local property tax as a primary source of school financing. The California Supreme Court has held, in *Serrano v. Priest*,[5] that, because educational opportunity is a fundamental interest and because the wealth of school districts is so significant a factor in determining expenditures per student, inequalities caused by this method of school finance violate the constitutional principle. The equal protection contention is also being made currently with respect to racial imbalance in some school districts as compared with neighboring districts, seeking alleviation of such imbalance across school district lines.[6]

The injury complained of in the school finance cases is that some children in the state have considerably more spent on their education than is spent on others, and that these great differentials in spending per child mean that some children are receiving a significantly lower quality of educational opportunity than are other children. Again we encounter a social science question: Do differences in expenditure levels establish differences in quality of educational opportunity? Should it be necessary to show a relationship to achievement on standardized tests in order to establish that spending two or three times as much per child in one district as compared with another district means that the children are receiving significantly different qualities of educational opportunity? It may be—and social science may perhaps have something to say on the question—that the maintenance of a system in which substantially more public funds are spent for the education of children in some school districts than in others is, as Professor Karst suggests, in itself "an insult . . . a continuing reminder to the students in the . . . poor . . . school that society does not think their aspirations should reach" as high as the aspirations of the children in the wealthy school.[7] In short, the system may effectively create socio-economic castes, with consequent injury, analogous to the pre-*Brown* racial caste system. Messrs. Coons, Clune, and Sugarman, in their germinal work, *Private Wealth and Public Education*, say (pp. 26, 30) on this matter:

The statutes creating district authority to tax and spend are the legal embodiment of the principle that money is quality in education. . . . If dollars are not assumed to buy education, whence the justification for the tax? . . . .
. . . the basic lesson to be drawn from the experts at this point is the current inadequacy of social science to delineate with any clarity the relation between cost and quality. We are unwilling to postpone reform while we await the hoped-for refinements in methodology which will settle the issue. We regard the fierce resistance by rich districts to reform as adequate testimonial to the relevance of money. Whatever it is that money may be thought to contribute to the education of children, that commodity is something highly prized by those who enjoy the greatest measure of it. If money is inadequate to improve education, the residents of poor districts should at least have an equal opportunity to be disappointed by its failure.

The primary response to these contentions is that organization of public school administration and finance on a district basis within a state advances important governmental purposes, revolving about the values in local government and local self-determination on such educational policy issues as the proportion of community wealth which should be devoted to public education. This is analogous to the contention of school boards in de facto segregation cases that a neighborhood school attendance policy so advances public purposes as to make that policy permissible even though one consequence is that some children receive a lower quality educational opportunity than do others. The "reasonably feasible" standard used by the California Supreme Court in *Jackson v. Pasadena City School District*, a de facto segregation case, suggests an anaology for possible disposition of the equal protection problem raised in the school finance cases: in view of the harm to children in poorer school districts the state must, as a minimum, adopt any reasonably feasible alternative method to school finance which would lessen the inequalities in educational opportunity. Such an approach would require inputs from those expert in school administration and finance: What ways are there to structure school finance within a state which would permit meaningful pursuance of the goals of local determination of policy matters, but with less adverse consequences to children in poorer districts with respect to the comparative amounts of money spent on their education?

* *

As has been indicated in this discussion, social science data can be critical in litigation involving alleged unconstitutional inequality of educational opportunity. These data pertain to the most basic questions about education: How does a child learn? What is the impact on learning of different school inputs and different school and community environments? These are the types of questions which led Judge Wright in *Hobson v. Hansen* to comment in his "Parting Word" that the court was compelled to "act in an area so alien to its expertise." These are questions as to which the law looks to social science in the field of education. At the present time social science does not have, and may never have, unequivocal answers to these questions. The ultimate decisions by the courts on the issue whether equal protection of the laws has been denied are decisions as to societal values, as embodied in the Constitution. Social scientists have the opportunity to contribute effectively to the process of making these value judgments.

Notes

1. 269 F. Supp. 401 (1967), *aff'd sub. nom. Smuck v. Hobson*, 408 F.2d 175 (D.C. Cir. 1969).

2. 347 U.S. 483 (1954).

3. David K. Cohen, Thomas F. Pettigrew, and Robert T. Riley, "Race and the Outcomes of Schooling." In Mosteller and Moynihan, *On Equality of Educational Opportunity*, ch. 7.

4. 59 Cal. 2d 876, 382 P.2d 878, 31 Cal. Rptr. 606 (1963).

5. 5 Cal. 3d 584, 487 P.2d 1241, 96 Cal. Rptr. 601 (1971). The author is one of counsel for plaintiffs in the *Serrano* case.

6. See *Bradley v. School Bd. of City of Richmond* 338 F. Supp. 67, (E.D. Va. 1972).

7. Karst, *Serrano v. Priest: A State Court's Responsibilities and Opportunities in the Development of Federal Constitutional Law*, 60 *Calif. L. Rev.* 720 (1972).

Bibliography

J. Coons, W. Clune, III, S. Sugarman, *Private Wealth and Public Education* (1970) (contains an extensive bibliography of educational and legal materials). Cambridge, Mass.: Harvard University Press.

Equality of Educational Opportunity (*Harvard Education Review* 1969).

J. Hogan, *The Role of the Courts in Certain Educational Policy Formation*, The Brief (Phi Delta Phi Quarterly), Vol. 65, No. 3, p. 190 (1970).

D. Cohen, *Defining Racial Equality in Education*, 16 UCLA Law Review 255 (1969).

President Nixon's Statement on Desegregation, *New York Times*, March 25, 1970, pp. 26-27.

United States Commission on Civil Rights, *Racial Isolation in the Public Schools* (1967). Washington, D.C.: U.S. Government Printing Office.

United States Department of Health, Education, and Welfare, *Equality of Educational Opportunity* (The Coleman Report, 1966). Washington, D.C.: U.S. Government Printing Office.

A. Wise, *Rich Schools, Poor Schools: The Promise of Equal Educational Opportunity* (1968). Chicago: University of Chicago Press.

J. Guthrie, G. Kleindorfer, H. Levin, R. Stout, *Schools and Inequality* (1971). Cambridge, Mass.: M.I.T. Press.

N. St. John, *Desegregation and Minority Group Performance* 40 Rev. of Education Res. 111 (1970).

On Equality of Educational Opportunity (F. Mosteller and D. Moynihan, eds., 1972). New York: Random House.

4 Heritability and Teachability

Arthur R. Jensen

It has been said that the heritability of learning ability or of intelligence is irrelevant to teachability, or as the *Bulletin of the ERIC Information Retrieval Center on the Disadvantaged* (1969, 4, no. 4) printed in boldface: "Teachability is not a function of heritability." In support of this statement we see it pointed out that a child or a group of children show some response to training, and this is held up as evidence against the heritability of intelligence or learning ability.

Heritability (h^2) is a technical term in genetics which refers to the proportion of the population variance in a phenotypic characteristic or measurement that is attributable to genetic variation. It has also been called the coefficient of genetic determination. It can take any value from 0 to 1. It is not a constant but differs for different traits, different measurements, and in different populations. Its value can be estimated by a number of methods in quantitative genetics. Like any population statistic, it is subject to measurement error and sampling error. Since it is based essentially on the analysis of variance, it can tell us nothing at all about the causes of the particular value assumed by the grand mean of the population. It only analyzes the variance (or squared deviations) *about* the grand mean. And it tells us what proportion of this total variance is *genetic* variance and what proportion is *non-genetic*, i.e., due to environmental factors of all kinds and to errors of measurement. Most estimates of the heritability of IQ in the European and North American populations on which we have good data fall in the range from .60 to .90 and most of these estimates are in range from .70 to .80 (not corrected for test unreliability).

The fact that IQ has high heritability surely does *not* mean that individuals cannot learn much. Even if learning ability had 100% heritability it would not mean that individuals cannot learn, and therefore the demonstration of learning or the improvement of performance, with or without specific instruction or intervention by a teacher, says absolutely nothing about heritability. But knowing that learning ability has high heritability does tell us this: if a number of individuals are all given *equal* opportunity—the same background, the same conditions, and the same amount of time—for learning something, they will still differ from one another in their rates of learning and consequently in the amount they learn per unit of time spent in learning. That is the meaning of heritability. It does not say that individuals cannot learn or improve with

57

instruction and practice. It says that given equal conditions, individuals will differ from one another, not because of differences in the external conditions but because of differences in the internal environment which is conditioned by genetic factors. "Teachability" presumably means the ability to learn under conditions of instruction by a teacher. If this is the case, then it is true that heritability has nothing to do with teachability. But was this ever really the question? Has anyone questioned the fact that *all* school children are teachable? The important question has concerned *differences* in teachability—differences both among individuals and among subgroups of the population. And with reference to the question of *differences*, the concept of heritability is indeed a relevant and empirically answerable question.

We have heard it said that "teachability is not inversely related to heritability." Such a statement simply ignores the central fact that heritability deals with differences. The degree to which equal conditions of teaching or instruction will diminish individual differences in achievement *is* inversely related to the heritability of the "teachability" of the subject in question, and various school subjects probably differ considerably in heritability.

The fact that scholastic achievement shows lower heritability than IQ means that more of the variance in scholastic achievement is attributable to nongenetic factors than is the case for IQ. Consequently, we hypothesize what the sources of the environmental variance in scholastic achievement are, and possibly we can manipulate them. For example, it might be hypothesized that one source of environmental variance in reading achievement is whether or not the child's parents read to him between the ages of 3 and 4, and we can obviously test this hypothesis experimentally. Much of the psychological research on the environmental correlates of scholastic achievement have been of this nature. The proportion of variance indicated by $1 - h^2$, if small, does in fact mean that the sources of environmental variance are skimpy under the conditions that prevailed in the population in which h^2 was estimated. It means that the *already existing* variations in environmental (or instructional) conditions are not a potent source of phenotypic variance, so that making the best variations available to everyone will do relatively little to reduce individual differences. This is not to say that as yet undiscovered environmental manipulations or forms of intervention in the learning or developmental process cannot, in principle, markedly reduce individual differences in a trait which under ordinary conditions has very high heritability. By the same token, low heritability does not guarantee that most of the nongenetic sources of variance can be manipulated systematically. A multitude of uncontrollable, fortuitous microenvironmental events may constitute the largest source of phenotypic variance in some traits.

The heritability of individual differences and of group differences in scholastic performance in the total population are therefore relevant if we are at all interested in the causes of these differences. To say that heritability is trivial or irrelevant is to say also that the complement of heritability, $1 - h^2$, or the proportion of variance attributable to non-genetic or environmental factors is also trivial. To dismiss the question of heritability is to dismiss concern with the causes of educational differences and their implications for educational practices. As I read it, what most educators, government officials, and writers in the popular press who discuss the present problems of education are in fact referring to is not primarily dissatisfaction with some *absolute* level of achievement, but rather with the large group *differences* in educational attainments that show up so conspicuously in our educational system—the achievement gaps between the affluent and the poor, the lower-class and the middle-class, the majority and the minority, the urban and the suburban, and so on. Educational *differences*, not absolute level of performance, are the main cause of concern. Whether we like to admit it or not, the problem of achievement differences today is where the action is, where the billions of dollars of educational funds are being poured in, where the heat is on, and where the schools are being torn apart. Are we not trying to understand more about the causes of these differences? But as Carl Bereiter (1970, p. 298) has commented: "It is necessary to avoid both the oversimplification that says if there are genetic group differences nothing can be accomplished through educational improvement and the oversimplification that says if group differences in IQ are environmentally caused they can be eliminated by conventional social amelioration. The possibility that cultural differences are related to heredity, however, adds force to the need for schools to come to grips with the problem of providing for cultural pluralism without separatism or segregation. This may well be the major policy problem facing public education in our time."

It is mistaken to argue that heritability has no implications for the probable effects of environmental intervention. Since $1 - h_i^2$ (h_i^2 is h^2 corrected for attenuation) is the proportion of trait variance attributable to environmental factors, the square root of this value times the *SD* of the "true score" trait measurement gives the *SD* of the effect of existing environmental variations on the particular trait. For IQ this is about six points; that is to say, a shift of one *SD* in the sum total of whatever nongenetic influences contribute to environmental variance (i.e., $1 - h_i^2$), will shift the IQ about six points. (There is good evidence that environmental effects on IQ are normally distributed, at least in Caucasian populations [Jensen, 1970b, 1971].) Thus the magnitude of change in a trait effected by changing the allocation of the existing environmental sources of variance in that trait is logically related to its heritability. This applies, of course, only to existing sources of environmental variance in the population, which is all that can be estimated by $1 - h_i^2$. It can have no relevance to speculations about as yet nonexistent environmental influences or entirely new combinations of already existing environmental factors. With respect to IQ, I believe Bereiter (1970) states the situation quite correctly: "What a high heritability ratio implies, therefore, is that changes within the existing range of environmental conditions can have substantial effects on the mean level of IQ in the population but they are unlikely to have much effect on the spread of individual differences in IQ within that population. If one is concerned with relative standing of individuals within the population, the prospects for doing anything about this through existing educational means are thus not good. Even with a massive redistribution of environmental conditions, one would expect to find the lower quarter of the IQ distribution to be about as far removed from the upper quarter as before" (p. 288). Bereiter goes on to say: "A high heritability ratio for IQ should not discourage people from pursuing environmental improvement in education or any other area. The potential effects on IQ are great, although it still remains to discover the environmental variables capable of producing these effects."

Reaction Range of IQ

Heritability can be understood also in terms of what geneticists refer to as the reaction range of the phenotypic characteristic. In the case of intelligence, for example, this is the range through which IQ varies in the population due to nongenetic influences. It is best expressed in terms of probabilities under the normal curve. There is good reason to believe that the *effects* of nongenetic factors on IQ in the population are normally distributed in the IQ range above 60 (Jensen, 1970b). If the heritability of IQ is .80, say, then we can picture the phenotypic reaction range, and the total distribution of environmental effects on IQ, as shown in Figure 4-1. The shaded curve is the normal distribution of IQs in the population. If we remove the 80 percent of the variance due to genetic factors and leave only the 20 percent of variance due to nongenetic factors, we see in the unshaded curve the resulting total distribution of IQs for identical genotypes that express phenotypic IQs of 100 in average environmental conditions. You can see that this distribution ranges from about IQ 80 to IQ 120. (The unshaded curve's variance is only 20% of the shaded curve's variance.) This is the reaction range of IQ in populations in which the heritability of IQ is .80. Figure 4-2 shows the converse situation. Again, the shaded curve is the actual distribution of phenotypes. The unshaded curve is the distribution of genotypes when the environment is held constant or identical for all individuals. Under these conditions, the absence of any environmental variation shrinks the total variance by 20 percent. As Bereiter pointed out, this makes relatively little difference in the total distribution.

Going back to Figure 4-1, it should be emphasized that the reaction range shown here does not result entirely from what we may think of as "environment." Thus, I use the term nongenetic rather than environmental. By definition, for the geneticist what is not genetic is environmental. But environmental variance includes many more or less random effects with unknown, unpredictable, or (as yet) uncontrollable causes. Even identical twins reared together are

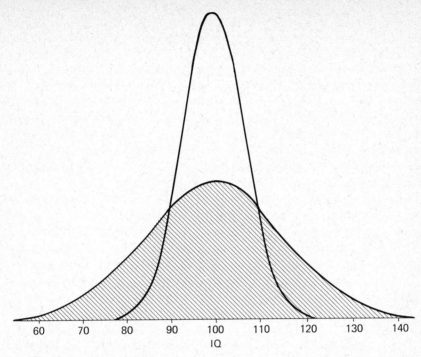

Figure 4–1. Comparison of Normal Distribution of IQs and Hypothetical Distributions with Genetic Variance Removed. Note: Shaded curve is distribution of IQs in population. Unshaded curve is hypothetical distribution if all genetic variance (when $h^2 = .80$) is removed.

not phenotypically identical. How realistic would it be to hope that all members of the population could be subject to as little environmental variance as identical twins reared together? The manipulable or equalizable aspects of the environment probably effect much less of the IQ variance than is suggested by our depiction of the total reaction range in Figure 4-1.

The largest IQ differences that have resulted from very extreme manipulations of the environment—extremes that very likely fall outside the limits of the middle 99 percent of the distribution of naturally occurring environments—have shown IQ changes of some 20 to 30 points. These changes have been observed only in very young children, with few, if any exceptions.

The important experiment of Dr. Rich Heber illustrates this reaction range concept of mental development. He has compared two groups of genotypically similar children in the Milwaukee ghetto, one group reared from birth in what may well be the lowest 1 or 2 percent of environmental conditions found in our society and the other group reared experimentally in the most mentally

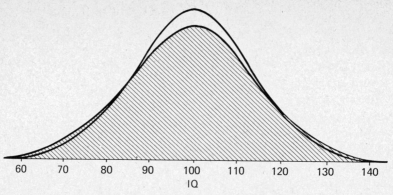

Figure 4–2. Comparison of Normal Distribution of IQs and Hypothetical Distribution with Environmental Variance Removed. Note: Shaded curve is distribution of IQs in the population. Unshaded curve is hypothetical distribution if all environmental variance were removed (when $h^2 = .80$).

stimulating environment that psychologists know how to devise; it is beyond the scale of naturally occurring environments. These two groups of children are now about five or six years old. Heber finds a magnitude of IQ differences between the groups of some 20 to 30 points, which is about what one might predict from our estimate of the reaction range of IQ when the heritability is .80. The Heber results have recently been held up in the popular press as evidence that genetic factors are of negligible importance, and some writers have even pointed to the Heber experiment as a refutation of "jensenism." Yet, interestingly enough, the results are within the range that would have been predicted from a genetic model assuming a heritability of .80.

The famous old study by Skodak and Skeels (1949) is repeatedly subjected to the same kind of misinterpretation by environmentalists who would like to deny the importance of genetic factors in causing intellectual differences. The Skodak and Skeels study is usually held up as an example of evidence which supposedly contradicts the high heritability of intelligence. The fact that the adopted children in the Skodak and Skeels study turned out to have considerably higher IQs than their biological mothers is thought to constitute a disproof of the conclusion from many heritability studies that genetic factors are more impor-tant than environmental factors (in the ratio of about 2 to 1) in the causation of individual differences in IQ. (Another way of saying this is that the heritability of intelligence is about .80, i.e., about 80 percent of the IQ variance is attributable to genetic factors. The 20 percent of the variance due to environ-mental differences can be thought of as a normal distribution of all the effects of environment on IQ, including prenatal and postnatal influences. This normal distribution of environmental effects has a standard deviation of about 7 IQ points since the total variance of IQ in the population is $15^2 = 225$ and the 20 percent of this which is attributable to environment is .20 (225) = 45, the square root of which gives $SD = 6.71$.) Is there anything in the Skodak and Skeels data that would contradict this conclusion? Skodak and Skeels based their study on 100 children born to mothers with rather low IQs (a range from 53 to 128, with a mean of 85.7, SD of 15.8). The children were adopted into what Skodak and Skeels described as exceptionally good, upper-middle class families selected by the adoption agency for their superior qualities. Of the 100 true mothers, 63 were given the 1916 form of the Stanford-Binet IQ test at the time of the adoption. Their children, who had been reared in adoptive homes, were given the same test as adolescents. The correlation between the mothers' and children's IQs was .38. Now, the *difference* between the mothers' IQs and the children's IQs is not really the relevant question. Yet it is on this point that the interpretation of this study has so often gone wrong. What we really want to know is, how much do the children differ from the IQs we'd predict from a genetic model? Using the simplest model, which assumes that the children represent a random selection of the offspring of mothers having a mean IQ of 85.7 and are reared in a random sample of homes in the general population, the children's average predicted IQ would be 96. In fact, however, their average IQ turns out to be 107, or 11 points higher than the predicted IQ. If 20 percent of the IQ variance is environmental, and if one standard deviation of environmental influence is equivalent to about 7 IQ points, then it might be said that the Skodak and Skeels children were reared in environments which averaged eleven-sevenths or about 1.6 standard deviations above the average environment of randomly selected families in the population. This would be about what one should expect if the adoption agency placed children only in homes they judged to be at least one standard deviation above the average of the general population in the desirability of the environment they could provide. From what Skodak and Skeels say in their description of the adoptive families, they were at least one standard deviation above the general average in socioeconomic status and were probably even higher in other qualities deemed desirable in adoptive parents. So an eleven-point IQ gain over the average environment falls well within what we should expect, even if environmental factors contribute only 20% of the IQ variance. But this 11 IQ points of apparent gain is more likely to be an over-estimate to some extent, since these children, it should be remembered, were selected by the agency as suitable for adoption. They were not a random selection of children born to low IQ mothers. Many such children are never put out for adoption. (Most of the children were illegitimate, and as indicated in Leahy's (1935) study, illegitimate children who become adopted have a higher average IQ than illegitimate children in general or than legitimate children placed for adoption.) Even so, it is interesting that Skodak and Skeels found that the 11 adopted children whose true mothers had IQs below 70 averaged 25 points lower than the 8 adopted children whose true mothers had IQs above 105. There are also certain technical, methodological deficiencies of the Skodak and Skeels study which make its results questionable; these deficiencies were trenchantly pointed out many years ago in critiques by Terman (1940, pp. 462-467) and McNemar (1940). In summary, the Skodak and Skeels study, such as it is, can be seen to be not at all inconsistent with a heritability of .80 for intelligence.

Heritability and Individual IQs

Heritability is said to be a population concept because its value cannot be determined independently of the population. That is to say, it is a statistical construct. But does this mean that it is irrelevant when we consider an individual measurement, such as a score on an IQ test? No. The reliability of a test score is also a statistical construct, being the proportion of "true score" variance in the population of obtained scores. Now, just as the square root of a test's reliability coefficient tells us the correlation between obtained scores and true scores, so the square root of a test's heritability tells us the correlation between obtained scores (i.e., the phenotypes) and "genetic values" (i.e., genotypes) on the trait being measured. ("Value" refers here to a scaled quantity; it implies no "value judgment.") Without an absolute scale (as is the case for practically all psychological measurements), these values must be expressed merely as deviation scores, i.e., as deviations from a population mean. For the "genetic value" to have any valid meaning, it must be expressed (and interpreted) as a deviation from the mean of the population in which the heritability was estimated and also in which the individual in question is a member. Given these conditions, we can determine the standard error of a test score's "genetic value," analogous to the standard error of measurement. (The analogy is not perfect, however, since true scores and measurement errors are by definition uncorrelated, while genetic (G) and environmental (E) components may be correlated. But this is a soluble problem. The covariance of G and E can be independently estimated and may or may not be included in the estimates of h^2, depending upon the interpretation one wishes to give to h^2. Roberts (1967, pp. 217-218) has suggested that the environment should be defined as affecting the phenotype independently of the genotype. Thus, if individuals' genotypes influence their choice of environments, the environmental variation resulting therefrom would be considered a part of the total genetic variance.) It is simply $SE_G = SD \sqrt{1 - h^2}$, where SE_G is the standard error of the genetic value, SD is the standard deviation of the test scores, and h^2 is the heritability (not corrected for attenuation due to test unreliability). For IQ, assuming $SD = 15$ and $h^2 = .75$, the standard error of the genetic value is 7.5 IQ points. This can be interpreted the same as the standard error of measurement. It means that 68% of our estimates of individual's genetic values will differ less than 7.5 points from this phenotypic IQ, 95% will differ less than 15 (i.e., $2 SE_G$'s), and 99.7% will differ less than 22.5 points ($3 SE_G$'s). In other words, the probability is very small that two individuals whose IQs differ by, say, 20 or more points have the same genotypes for intelligence or that the one with the lower IQ has the higher genetic value. The individual's estimated genetic value, $\hat{G}_i$, expressed as a deviation score, is $\hat{G}_i = h^2 (P_i - \overline{P}_P)$ + $\overline{P}_P$ where P_i is the individual's phenotype measurement (e.g., IQ), and $\overline{P}_P$ is the population mean.

The statement that an individual's test score is within, say $\pm x$ points of his "true score" with a probability p is no less probabilistic than saying his test score is within $\pm x$ points of his "genetic value," with a probability p. In the individual case, of course, we may be able to take account of a variety of other information in addition to the individual's test score in order to obtain a more accurate assessment. Such adjustments in individual assessments, as Burt (1958) has indicated, can increase the heritability of the scores and consequently reduce the standard error of estimate of individual genotypic values. The use of less culture-loaded tests could have a similar effect.

Heritability and Group Differences

I have been falsely accused of claiming that the high heritability of IQ inevitably means that the mean differences in IQ between social class groups and racial groups must be due to genetic factors. I have never made this incorrect inference. What I have said is this: While it is true, indeed axiomatic, that heritability *within* groups cannot establish heritability *between* group means, high *within* group heritability increases the a priori likelihood that the *between* groups heritability is greater than zero. In nature, characteristics that vary genetically *among* individuals within a population also generally vary genetically *between* different breeding populations of the same species. Among the genetically conditioned traits known to vary between major racial groups are body size and proportions, cranial size and cephalic index, pigmentation of the hair, skin, and eyes, hair form and distribution on the body, number of vertebrae, fingerprints, bone density, basic metabolic rate, sweating, fissural patterns on the chewing surfaces of the teeth, numerous blood groups, various chronic diseases, frequency of dizygotic (but nonmonozygotic) twinning, male/female birth ratio, ability to taste phenylthiocarbomide, length of gestation period, and degree of physical maturity at birth (as indicated by degree of ossification of cartilage). In light of all these differences, Spuhler and Lindzey (1967) have remarked ". . . it seems to us surprising that one would accept present findings in regard to the existence of genetic anatomical, physiological, and epidemiological differences between the races . . . and still expect to find *no* meaningful differences in behavior between races" (p. 413). The high within groups heritability of certain behavioral traits, such as intelligence, adds weight to this statement by Spuhler and Lindzey.

In fact, it is quite erroneous to say there is no relationship whatsoever between heritability *within* groups and heritability *between* group means. Jay Lush, a pioneer in quantitative genetics, has shown the formal relationship between these two heritabilities (Lush, 1968, p. 312), and it has been recently introduced into the discussion of racial differences by another geneticist, John C. DeFries (in press). This formulation of the relationship between heritability *between* group means (h_B^2) and heritability *within* groups (h_W^2) is as follows:

$$h_B^2 \; \simeq \; h_w^2 \; \frac{(1-r)\rho}{(1-\rho)r}$$

where:

h_B^2 is the heritability *between* group means.

h_w^2 is the average heritability *within* groups.

r is the intraclass correlation among *phenotypes* within groups (or the square of the point biserial correlation between the quantized racial dichotomy and the trait measurement).

ρ is the intraclass correlation among *genotypes* within groups, i.e., the within-group genetic correlation for the trait in question.

Since we do not know ρ, the formula is not presently of practical use in determining the heritability of mean group differences. But it does show that if for a given trait the genetic correlation among persons within groups is greater than zero, the between group heritability is a monotomically increasing function of within groups heritability. This is illustrated in Figure 4-3, which shows between groups heritability as a function of within group heritability for various values of the within-group genetic correlation when the mean phenotypic difference between the two groups involved is one standard deviation.

As I have pointed out elsewhere, other methods than heritability analysis are required to test the hypothesis that racial group differences in a given trait involve genetic factors and to determine their extents (Jensen, 1970c).

Analysis of Group Mean Differences

It may be instructive to express the magnitude of the differences between group means in terms of *within-group* environmental effects on the trait in question, which can be estimated from heritability analysis. For illustrative purposes I shall use the heritability value for IQs obtained from the combined studies of

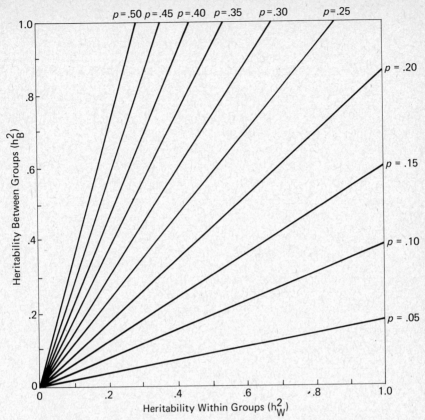

Figure 4–3. Heritability Between and Within Groups for Different Within Group Genetic Correlations. Note: Heritability between groups as a function of average heritability within groups for different values of within-group genetic correlation (ρ) for two populations which differ phenotypically by one standard deviation.

identical twins reared apart (Jensen, 1970b). For the sake of simplicity in this illustration, I will assume the same heritability in white and black populations. This is not a necessary assumption and in practice we would obtain estimates of heritability in both populations. At this point I am focusing only upon the logic of a particular kind of analysis rather than making a case for the particular quantitative values involved. Also, I assume that the total variance is the same in both populations and that the environmental effects on IQ are normally distributed in both populations. This can be shown to hold true in the twin samples in which heritability was determined, but in practice would of course have to be empirically determined in both populations.

Figure 4-4 shows this kind of analysis. The top figure shows the total distribution of IQs in two populations with means of 85 and 100, respectively. The standard deviation, σ, in each group is 15 points. The middle set of curves show the shrunken distribution of IQ when the genetic variance in each population is eliminated. Thus, while the groups differ phenotypically by 1σ (upper curves), they differ in terms of total environmental effects on IQ by 3.2σ. The standard deviation of environmental effects (with error of measurement removed) within groups is only 4.74 IQ points. But this represents the total nongenetic or environmental effect, much of which is "microenvironmental," i.e., unsystematic and unsusceptible to systematic control. If we regard environmental differences *within* families, such as birth order effects, and the like, as largely constituting this source of unsystematic microenvironmental variance, we can estimate it by appropriate methods and eliminate it statistically, leaving only the distribution of *between*-families environmental effects on IQ. This has a standard deviation of 3.35 IQ points and, as shown in the lower curves of Figure 4-4, the population mean difference can be expressed as a difference of 4.5σ of between-families environmental effects. These are the effects we are most likely to have in mind when we talk about changing environments. The between-families environmental effects are the systematic environmental differences we associate with socioeconomic status, nutritional conditions, child rearing practices, cultural advantages, and the like. It can be seen here that these effects as estimated from twin studies account for only a small part of the within-population variance (about 12%), and that if one were to explain all of the 15 IQ points differences entirely in terms of this source of environmental effects, it would have to be granted that the populations differ on a scale of these effects by 4.5σ. This is an enormous difference, implying almost no overlap between the two populations in the distribution of systematic environmental effects on IQ. A warranted conclusion would be that it is highly improbable that the group mean difference is entirely attributable to the environmental variations that make for differences between separated twins reared in different families. To argue otherwise would require us to believe that on a scale of environmental effects the average black is reared under conditions 4.5σ below those of the average white twin. If we call the latter's environment about average for the white population, we would conclude that the *average* black environment is 4.5σ below this level, that is, something below the 0.003 percentile of systematic environmental effects on IQ in the white population. This strongly suggests that if one is to explain the average 15 point black IQ deficit in wholly nongenetic terms, it will probably be necessary to posit some environmental factors other than those we normally think of as the environmental factors affecting intelligence in the white population. Moreover, if the heritability of IQ is not appreciably different in the black and white populations, these hypothesized

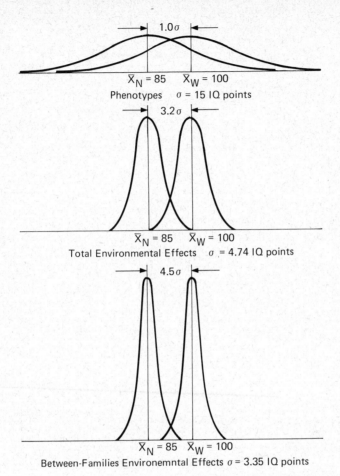

Figure 4–4. IQ Distributions with Genetic and Environmental Effects Removed. Note: The top curves represent two IQ distributions each with $\sigma = 15$ IQ points and the means differing by 15 points or 1 σ. The middle set of curves show the effect of removing all genetic variance, leaving only the total environmental variance; the means then differ by 3.2σ of total environmental effects. The lower curves show the effect of removing both the genetic and the within-families environmental variance, leaving only between-families environmental variance; the means then differ by 4.5σ of between-families environmental effects. The area under all curves is the same.

environmental effects responsible for the lower average black IQ would have to be assumed to produce little or no variance *within* the black population, unless one wanted to assume that virtually none of the environmental proportion of IQ variance *within* the black population was attributable to the same kinds of environmental effects that contribute to environmental variance in the white population. Such an entirely cultural explanation would seem to make the black population too incredibly different. The amount of genetic difference that would have to be hypothesized to explain what we already know is quite small as compared with the fantastically great environmental and cultural differences between the American black and the white populations that must be hypothesized in order to maintain a wholly nongenetic theory. The average amount of genetic difference that would have to be hypothesized to explain the data is about the same as the average difference in genotypic IQs between ordinary siblings in the same family. Do parents view this as such an awful difference among their own children? Yet this is about the amount of difference that would need to be hypothesized by a genetic theory for all that we now know about black-white IQ differences to be accounted for. How else essentially does science advance our knowledge than by trying out various hypotheses for how well they accord with the evidence?

The storm of criticisms that have been leveled at me has been a result of my expressing serious *doubts* that this racial IQ difference is entirely explainable in terms of culture-bias in tests, unequal educational opportunities, social discrimination, and other environmental influences. My position is that there is now sufficient evidence to seriously question the 100 percent environmental theories of the mean white-black intelligence difference. Are there any responsible scientists today who claim that this position can be ruled out on the basis of evidence or ruled out a priori by any principle of genetics? How many scientists today express little or no doubt that all of the racial IQ difference is attributable to environment? And on what evidence do those who claim no doubt base their certainty? I have not found any 100% environmental theory which can explain the facts or which stands up when its major premises are critically examined in the light of evidence. Therefore, I regard this issue scientifically as an open question which can be eventually answered in a scientific sense only if we are willing to consider all reasonable hypotheses. It is a reasonable hypothesis that genetic factors are involved in the average white-black IQ difference, and my study of the research evidence bearing on this question leads me to believe that a preponderence of the evidence is more consistent with a genetic hypothesis, which, of course, does not exclude the influence of environment.

Heritability in the Black Population

Unfortunately, we still have no adequate estimates of the heritability of intelligence in the black population, although two interesting studies have made a beginning in this direction (Nichols, 1970; Scarr-Salapatek, 1971). The statistical problems and the nature of the data in both studies make their results quite tentative, but essentially they found that the heritability of the mental test scores are about the same in the black and white samples or possibly slightly lower in the black group, and definitely lower in the lower social classes of both racial groups. Scarr-Salapatek's results have been misrepresented in some popular accounts (e.g., *Psychology Today*, March 1972, p. 20) as refuting my position. Nothing could be further from the truth. In fact, one of the main points about black-white differences that I made in my *HER* (1969) article finds impressive support in Scarr-Salapatek's study. Scarr-Salapatek emphasizes the point that the heritability of the mental tests is less in her lower social class groups of both races than in the middle-class groups. This fact she apparently interprets as being consistent with an explanation of the mean black-white IQ differences in terms of environmental factors such as cultural deprivation. She states: "The lower mean scores of disadvantaged children of both races can be explained in large part by the lower genetic variance in their scores" (p. 1293). She adds: "If most black children have limited experience with environmental features relevant to the development of scholastic skills, then genetic variation will not be as prominent a source of individual phenotypic variation; nor will other between-family differences such as SES [socio-economic] level be as important as they are in a white population" (p. 1294).

The data shown in Scarr-Salapatek's Table 3 (p. 1288), however, make this interpretation extremely questionable. These data allow comparison of the mean scores on the combined aptitude tests for black children whose parents' level of education and income are both *above* the median (of the black and white samples combined) with the mean scores of white children whose parents' education and income are both *below* the common median. The lower status white children still score *higher* than the upper status black children on both the verbal and the non-verbal tests. Although non-verbal tests are generally considered to be less culture-biased than verbal tests, it is the non-verbal tests which in fact show the greater discrepancy in this comparison, with the *lower* status whites scoring higher than the *upper* status blacks. But in this comparison it is the upper status black group that has the higher heritability (i.e., greater genetic variance) on both the verbal and non-verbal tests. Thus the lower heritability which Scarr-Salapatek invokes to infer that blacks' generally poorer performance is attributable to environmental deprivation applies to the lower status white group in this particular comparison. Yet the lower status white group out-performs the upper status black group, which has the highest heritability of any of the subgroups in this study (see Table 9, p. 1292).

Is this finding more difficult to reconcile with a strictly environmental explanation of the mean racial difference in test scores than with a genetic interpretation which invokes the well-established phenomenon of regression toward the population mean? In another recent article in *Science* (1971, p.

1226), Scarr-Salapatek clearly explicated this relevant genetic prediction, as follows:

Regression effects can be predicted to differ for blacks and whites if the two races indeed have genetically different population means. If the population mean for blacks is 15 IQ points lower than that of whites, then the offspring of high-IQ black parents should show greater regression (toward a lower population mean) than the offspring of whites of equally high IQ. Similarly, the offspring of low-IQ black parents should show less regression than those of white parents of equally low IQ.

In other words, on the average, an offspring genetically is closer to its population mean than are its parents, and by a fairly precise amount. Accordingly, it would be predicted that upper status black children should, on the average, regress *downward* toward the black population mean IQ of about 85, while lower status white children would regress *upward* toward the white population mean of about 100. In the downward and upward regression, the two groups' means could cross each other, the lower status whites thereby being slightly above the upper status black. Scarr-Salapatek's data (Table 3) are quite consistent with this genetic prediction. Scarr-Salapatek's finding is not a fluke; the same phenomenon has been found in other large-scale studies which I pointed out in my *HER* (1969) article (pp. 83-84).

Controlling for Social Class

In the past year two widely publicized studies, one by George W. Mayeske and the other by Jane Mercer, have claimed that racial differences in intelligence and scholastic achievement can be explained entirely in terms of the environmental effects of the lower socioeconomic status of blacks in the United States. They showed that by statistically controlling a large number of social variables associated with socioeconomic status, they were able to "explain" practically all of the achievement gap between blacks and whites. This procedure is what I have termed the "sociologist's fallacy." It is based on the unwarranted and untenable assumption that all the socioeconomic and environmental variables on which the racial groups have been matched or statistically equated are direct *causal* factors, when in fact they are merely *correlates* of IQ. If some part of the SES difference within racial groups has a genetic basis, then statistically equating racial groups on social class equates them also to some degree on the genetic factors involved in intelligence. Indeed, it is theoretically conceivable that if one equated racial groups on a large enough number of *correlates* of IQ, one could statistically eliminate all of the IQ difference between them. But it would prove nothing at all about the *causes* of the mean IQ difference between the total populations. Many environmental indices are undoubtedly correlated with genotypes. Educational level of the parents, for example, is often included as an environmental variable affecting the child's development. But it almost certainly includes also some genetic component which is common to both the parents and their children. If the environmental variables used for statistical control account for more of the IQ variance *within* racial groups than the complement of the heritability (i.e., $1 - h^2$) within the groups, then it is virtually certain that the environmental indices also reflect correlated genetic factors. Controlling SES thus partials out too much of the difference between the racial groups. Matching for SES, in short, matches not only for certain environmental factors but also for genetic factors as well. It is interesting also that when such matching is carried out, it is noted that the average skin color of the black groups becomes lighter in the higher SES categories, indicating that genetic factors covary with SES, for whatever reason. Genetic SES intelligence differences are firmly established within the white population. Matching black and white groups on SES, therefore, is certain to minimize genetic as well as environmental differences. For this reason, studies that control for SES are probably biased in favor of the environmentalist hypothesis and can contribute nothing to elucidating the nature-nurture problem.

Several lines of evidence support with a high level of confidence the conclusion that social classes, on the average, differ to some degree in the genetic factors involved in intellectual development. Social classes may be viewed as Mendelian populations that have diverged genetically. When the population is stratified into five or six socioeconomic status (SES) categories, mainly according to occupational criteria, the mean IQs of the *adults* so classified, from the highest SES category (professional and managerial) to the lowest (unskilled labor), span a range of some 30 to 40 points. The standard deviation of IQs *within* SES groups averages about 9 or 10 points for the adult population, as compared with $SD = 15$ for the whole population. Children born into these SES groups, on the other hand, show a mean IQ difference, from the lowest to the highest class, of only 20 to 30 points; and the SD *within* classes for children is about 13 or 14 IQ points, which means there is almost as much IQ variation among children *within* social classes as we find in the total population.

The cause of the higher degree of correlation between SES and IQ among adults than among children is the high level of social mobility in each generation. In England and in the United States, more than 30% of the adult generation are found to be of a different SES than that of their own parents (Burt, 1961; Gottesman, 1968; Maxwell, 1969). In each generation some individuals move up in SES and some move down. Those who move up have higher IQs, on the average, than those who move down.

Since the heritability, h^2, (i.e., the proportion of genetic variance) of IQ in the total population is between .70 and .80, and since the correlation between phenotypes and genotypes is the square root of the heritability, it follows that the IQ estimates genotypic intelligence with a reliability of between $\sqrt{.70}$ and $\sqrt{.80}$, i.e., between about .84 and .89 (Jensen, 1967; 1969). Conversely, the reliability with which IQ measures the *non*-genetic component of intelligence variation is $\sqrt{1 - h^2}$, or between about .45 and .55. If only nongenetic factors determined individuals' SES, then the maximum correlation that could exist between SES and IQ would be in the range of .45 to .55. In fact, however, the correlations generally found are between .30 and .50 for children and between .50 and .70 for adults (depending largely upon how fine-grained the SES measure is). Now, if the correlation between IQs and genotypes is between .84 and .89, and the correlation between IQ and SES is between .50 and .70, the correlation between SES and genotypes must be greater than zero. To maintain a strictly environmental hypothesis, at the very least one would have to assume that only the environmental component of intelligence played a part in persons' educational and occupational attainments (the chief determinants of SES). If we admit no genetic component in SES differences in IQ and still admit the high heritability of IQ, we are logically forced to argue that persons have been fitted to their SES (meaning largely educational and occupational attainments) almost *perfectly* according to their environmental advantages and disadvantages, which constitute only 20 to 30 percent of the variance in IQ; and it would have to be argued that persons' innate abilities, talents, and proclivities play no part in educational and occupational selection and placement. This is a most unlikely state of affairs.

Consider other, more direct, evidence.

1. Adopted children show only about half as much dispersion in mean IQ as a function of SES of the adopting parents as that of children reared by their own parents (Leahy, 1935).
2. Children reared from infancy in an orphanage, with no knowledge of their parents, show nearly the same correlation between their IQs and their fathers' occupational status (graded into five categories) as children reared by their own parents (Lawrence, 1931).
3. Most of the IQ difference between siblings reared together is attributable to differences in genetic inheritance. (The genetic correlation between siblings is about .5 to .6.) When siblings who are reared together move into different social strata as adults, it is the sib with the higher IQ who is more likely to move up and the sib with the lower IQ who is more likely to move down the SES scale (Gibson, 1970).
4. Sons whose IQs differ most from their father's IQ are more likely to change SES, the higher IQs moving up, the lower moving down (Young & Gibson, 1963). Waller (1971) found a correlation of 0.368 ± 0.066 between the father-son disparity in IQ (both tested as school children) and father-son disparity in SES as adults, when only the middle three of five SES classes were considered (since in Classes I and V mobility is restricted to only one direction).
5. Genetically identical twins who were separated in infancy and reared apart

in homes of different SES (over a range of six categories, from professional to unskilled), differ on the average by only 1 IQ point per each SES category difference, with a total range of about 6 IQ points difference between the highest and lowest SES categories (Burt, 1966). Compare this difference, in which genetic factors play no part, with the difference of 20 to 30 IQ points generally found between children in the lowest and highest SES classes.

All this evidence is highly consistent with a model of social mobility in which the genetic factors involved in mental ability, through the processes of segregation and assortment, become selected into somewhat differing gene pools in various social and occupational classes.

Environmentalist Hypotheses

Those environmentalist hypotheses of the black-white IQ difference which have been most clearly formulated and are therefore subject to empirical tests are the only ones that can be evaluated within a scientific framework. The most frequently cited environmentalist hypotheses which are sufficiently clear to put to an empirical test and which already have been put to a test have not proven adequate to the explanatory function they were intended to serve. A number of lines of such evidence casts serious doubt on purely environmental and cultural theories of the racial IQ difference.

Negative Correlations Between Environment and Ability

A number of environmental factors which correlate positively with mental ability *within* various population groups have been shown to correlate *negatively* with IQ differences *between* certain groups. On all of the many measurable factors which environmentalists have invoked to explain the black-white IQ difference, both American Indians and Mexican-Americans have been found to be much more disadvantaged than Negroes. Yet on non-verbal intelligence tests (which are more fair for bilingual groups such as Mexicans and Indians) and in scholastic performance, Indians and Mexicans significantly outperform blacks. This finding is neutral with respect to a genetic theory, in the sense that no prediction could have been derived from genetic principles; but it contradicts those environmental theories that invoke measurable environmental factors known to correlate with IQ within population groups as the cause of the lower black IQ. The only attempts of environmentalists to rationalize these findings have invoked highly speculative cultural and attitudinal factors which have not yet been shown to be correlated either with IQ or with race.

Culture-biased Tests

Intelligence tests can be rank-ordered according to certain generally agreed upon criteria of their cultural loading. Within a given culture, tests are better described as differing in *status fairness*. Environmentalists who criticize intelligence tests usually give as examples those tests which are most obviously loaded with what is presumably white, middle-class factual knowledge, vocabulary, and the like, as contrasted with more abstract figural material such as compose Raven's Progressive Matrices and Cattell's Culture-Fair Tests of *g*. Yet it is on the latter type of tests that blacks perform most poorly, relative to whites and other minority groups. Disadvantaged minorities, such as American Indians and Mexican-Americans, perform on tests showing different degrees of status bias in accord with the environmentalist hypothesis. Blacks do the opposite. "Translation" of tests such as the Stanford-Binet into the black ghetto dialect also does not appreciably improve scores.

The scholastic and occupational predictive validity of IQ tests is the same for blacks as for whites, and item analyses of tests showing large average group mean differences do not reveal significant differences in rank order of item difficulty or in choice of distractors for error responses. Test-taking attitudes and motivational factors appear unconvincing as an explanation of the group difference in view of the fact that on some tests which make equal demands on attention, persistence, and effort, such as various memory tests, blacks do perform quite well relative to whites. When various diverse tests and test items are ordered in terms of the degree to which they discriminate between blacks and whites, the one feature which is common to the most discriminating tests and items is the conceptual and abstract nature of the test material, or the degree to which they accord with the classic definitions of the psychological nature of *g*, the general factor common to all complex tests of mental ability.

In 1968 I proposed that the heritability of a test be considered as one objective criterion of the test's culture-fairness or status fairness (Jensen, 1968). Since then, M.B. Jones (1971) also has advocated the use of heritability as a criterion in psychological test construction. I also suggested that one might test competing genetic and environmental hypotheses of a particular group difference by comparing the performance of the two groups in question on tests which differ in heritability. The environmental hypothesis should predict a smaller mean difference between the groups on those tests with the higher heritability than on tests with lower heritability; a genetic hypothesis would predict just the opposite. So here we have the possibility of strong inference, since the two competing theories are pitted against each other in yielding opposite predictions.

To see the rationale of this kind of hypothesis, consider the fact that various mental tests differ in their sensitivity to environmental influences. For example, a test which is very sensitive to reflecting environmental influences will show smaller differences between genetically dissimilar and unrelated children who have been adopted and reared together in the same home than between genetically identical twins who have been separated in infancy and reared apart in different homes. Such a test which strongly reflects environmental influences has low heritability. On the other hand, a test with high heritability (or low sensitivity to environmental effects) will show larger differences between unrelated children reared together than between identical twins reared apart.

In order to obtain statistically reliable estimates of the environmental sensitivity of tests I used siblings rather than twins, because siblings are much more plentiful. We identified all siblings in grades K to 6 in an entire California school district. A variety of 16 mental tests of abilities and achievement, many of them standard tests, were administered to the eight thousand children in the study, and the correlations among siblings (r_s) were obtained on each test. Now we know that if only genetic factors were involved in the test variance, the sibling correlation should be very close to .50. (This is the sibling correlation, for example, for number of fingerprint ridges, which, we know, are virtually unaffected by environmental factors.) Any departure of the correlation from .50, above or below, therefore, is an indication of environmental variance. So we can employ as an index of environmental influence, E, on test scores the absolute difference from .50 of the obtained sibling correlation, thus $E = | r_s - .50 |$. This E index was obtained for white siblings and for black siblings. Next we obtained the mean white-black difference on each test, and to put the differences all on the same scale of standard scores, the mean difference was divided by the standard deviation of the tests' scores in the white sample. Thus, on every test the mean white-black difference was expressed in white standard deviation units. We then obtained the correlation and regression lines of the mean difference on the environmental sensitivity index for whites and for blacks. An environmentalist hypothesis should predict a positive correlation. In fact, however, the correlations are negative and statistically significant in both the white and Negro groups. The negatively sloping regression lines are shown in Figure 4-5. The correlation between the black and white values of the E index is .71 ($p < .01$). This means that the various tests are quite similar for whites and blacks in the degree to which they reflect nongenetic influences. The correlation between the black-white difference and the E index is $-.80$ ($p < .01$) for whites and $-.61$ ($p < .01$) for Negroes. Clearly, the results are more in accord with a genetic hypothesis than with a cultural hypothesis as an explanation of the mean white-black differences on the various tests. It should be noted that in general the scholastic achievement tests are more sensitive to environmental influence than the standard intelligence tests.

Is this finding merely a result of the particular selection of tests used in this study? I doubt it. The essential design has been replicated by Nichols (1970) at the University of Minnesota. Nichols used an entirely different battery of tests comprised mostly of the various subtests of the Wechsler Intelligence Scale for

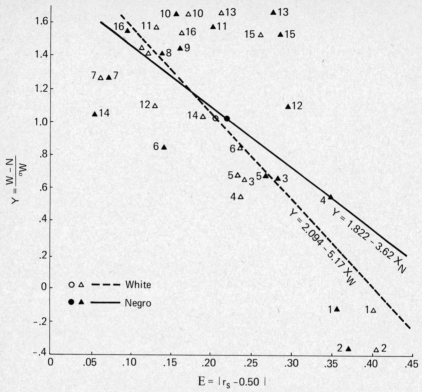

Figure 4-5. Regression of Black and White Differences on Environmental Index for Various Ability Tests. Note: The regression lines (for whites and Negroes) showing the mean white-Negro difference in white sigma units (Y) on 16 ability tests (numbered 1 to 16) as a function of the absolute difference from 0.50 of the sibling correlation for each test (X). Circles indicate the bivariate means; triangles indicate the various tests, which are numbered as fellows: 1. Making X's (Neutral instructions); 2. Making X's (Motivating instructions); 3. Memory – Immediate recall; 4. Memory – After repetition; 5. Memory – Delayed recall; 6. Figure Copying; 7. Lorge-Thorndike IQ, Levels I and II (Pictorial); 8. Lorge-Thorndike, Verbal IQ; 9. Lorge-Thorndike, Nonverbal IQ; 10. Stanford Achievement: Word Meaning; 11. Stanford Achievement: Paragraph Meaning; 12. Stanford Achievement: Spelling; 13. Stanford Achievement: Language (Grammar); 14. Stanford Achievement: Arithmetic Computation; 15. Stanford Achievement: Arithmetic Concepts; 16. Stanford Achievement: Arithmetic Applications.

Children as well as several other tests (e.g., Bender-Gestalt, Illinois Test of Psycholinguistic Abilities, Draw-A-Man, and three scholastic achievement tests). Nichols used black and white sibling correlations to obtain an estimate of heritability for each test; this corresponds closely to the complement of our E index, i.e., $1 - E$. So in Nichols' study the genetic hypothesis would predict a positive correlation between the racial difference (again expressed in standard deviation units) and the heritability of the tests. The correlation obtained by Nichols was +.67 (the average for whites and blacks). The correlation of socioeconomic status differences with heritability was +.86, which is consistent with the hypothesis of a high degree of genetic variance in SES differences in mental abilities. Two independent large-scale studies, therefore, have yielded results that are strikingly more consistent with a genetic than with an environmentalist hypothesis. I know of no other way that scientific investigation can proceed in this field at the present time than by testing a variety of hypotheses in this fashion, one by one, and sizing up the converging lines of evidence. I have examined the most often repeated environmentalist hypotheses in the light of relevant evidence. I can here only briefly summarize some of my observations. All the points made in these summaries are fully documented in my forthcoming book, *Educability and Group Differences.*

Language Deprivation

This is an unconvincing explanatory hypothesis in view of the fact that blacks perform best on the most verbal parts of intelligence tests and poorest on the least verbal materials. All other disadvantaged minority groups within the American population show the opposite trend. Children who are born deaf are the most verbally deprived subjects we can study. They show marked verbal deficits on intelligence tests. Yet they perform at an average level on nonverbal tests, thus showing a pattern of abilities opposite to that of blacks.

Another important difference between low SES children and children who are verbally deprived because of deafness is that while the former begin to lag in linguistic and intellectual development after beginning school, the latter show a gradual catching up to the average level as they progress in school—it merely takes them longer to acquire information because of their severe sensory handicap. But once it is acquired, normal mental development ensues. A study of the developing conceptual capacities of the deaf concluded ". . . the differences found between deaf and hearing adolescents were amenable to the effects of age and education and were no longer found between deaf and hearing adults. Dissociation between words and referents, verbalization adequacy, and (conceptual) level of verbalization were not different for deaf and hearing subjects. Our experiments, then, have shown few differences between deaf and hearing subjects. Those found were shown to fall along a normal developmental line and

were amenable to the effects of increased age and experience, and education"
(Kates, Kates, & Michael, 1962, pp. 31-32).

Poor Motivation

There is no consistent evidence that blacks are less motivated in a test situation
than are other groups. Some groups (e.g., Indians) whose general educational
aspirations and self-concepts are poorer than those of blacks actually perform
better on tests and in school. Also, on performance tests specially devised to
maximize the influence of motivational factors and to minimize the test's
dependence upon abstract or complex cognitive functions which would involve
g, blacks do not perform significantly below whites. The "expectancy" or
"self-fulfilling prophecy" theory has not been empirically demonstrated, and
when put to proper tests it has failed to be substantiated.

Non-cognitive Tests

Certain perceptual-motor tests such as choice reaction time and pursuit motor
learning (which has a very high heritability) show large black-white differences
even under very highly controlled experimental conditions, and the results are
independent of the race of the tester. Moreover, the magnitude of the racial
difference has been shown to be related to the degree of white admixture in the
black sample as assessed by physical indices. If genetic racial differences in
behavioral tests other than intelligence tests are admitted, by what principle can
one exclude the same possibility for types of tests labeled as measures of
intelligence? There is no reason why intelligence tests should be categorically
excluded from the possibility of showing genetic race differences when such
differences in other physical and behavioral traits can be found.

Nutritional Deficiencies

The fact that severe malnutrition, especially protein deficiency, during prenatal
development and in infancy and childhood can impair mental as well as physical
growth is not at issue. Studies from the nutritionally most deprived segments of
populations in Africa, Mexico, and South America would support this conclusion. There are no data, however, which would support the hypothesis that
malnutrition contributes any appreciable fraction to the average black-white IQ
difference. In black communities where there is no evidence of poor nutrition,
the average black IQ is still about 1 *SD* below the white mean. When groups of
black children with IQs *below* the general black average have been studied for

nutritional status, no signs of malnutrition have been found. Physical evidence of malnutrition found to be correlated with lower IQs in studies conducted in Africa, Mexico, and Guatemala have not been found even in the poorest and lowest IQ segments of the American black population. On the basis of present evidence, the hypothesis that lower average black IQ is due to poor nutrition is not tenable.

The nutritional and health care status of Indian children, as indicated by much higher rates of infant mortality, is much poorer than that of blacks; yet Indian children in the first grade in school (age 6) have been found to score about one *SD* above blacks on nonverbal ability tests.

Prenatal and Perinatal Disadvantages

The higher rate of fetal loss and infant mortality in the black population may indicate disadvantages related to prenatal health care of the mother and undesirable conditions attending birth. These conditions prevail in the poorer segment of the black population and probably contribute to the incidence of neurological handicap among black children. All of the causes of high fetal loss, however, are not understood, for there are some relatively disadvantaged populations which have shown lower rates of fetal loss than is found in the white majority—Orientals, for example. There is now evidence that the degree of genetic heterogeneity of the fetus' ancestors is directly related to the probability of fetal loss, and thus genetic factors may be involved even in this seemingly environmental phenomenon. Disadvantaging forms of birth trauma such as anoxia, low birth weight and prematurity are reflected in subnormal perform-ance on infant tests of perceptual-motor development. But large representative samples of black children show no depression of scores on these tests and generally perform at slightly higher levels than middle-class white children. Prenatal and perinatal factors, though differing in black and white populations, do not begin to account for such phenomena as the six times higher rate of mental retardation (IQs below 70) in the black than in the white population. Unless one hypothesizes the existence of genetic factors, in the vast majority of cases the causes of the mental retardation must be categorized as "unknown" or "unidentified."

Educational Implications

At present, neither I nor anyone else, I'm afraid, has any more than rather general notions concerning the educational implications of the wide range of apparent differences in educability in our population. Since the heredity-environment issue is not likely to reach a general consensus among qualified scientists for quite some time to come and after much more genetical and psychological research has been completed, it is probably wise for educators to assume an openly agnostic position with regard to the genetic issue as it involves racial differences, at the same time recognizing that whatever may be the causes of the difference, we do not at present know of any measures or methods within the power of the schools that will appreciably or permanently diminish either individual or group differences in intelligence or scholastic achievement. There is fundamentally, in my opinion, no difference, psychologically and genetically, between individual differences and group differences. Individual differences often simply get tabulated so as to show up as group differences—between schools in different neighborhoods, between different racial groups, between cities and regions. They then become a political and ideological, not just a psychological, matter. To reduce the social tensions that arise therefrom, we see proposals to abolish aptitude and achievement testing, grading, grade placement, special classes for the educationally retarded and the academically gifted, neighborhood schools, the classroom as the instructional unit, the academic curriculum, and even our whole system of education. There may be merit in some of these proposals. But I think they are too often aimed at covering up problems rather than coming to grips with them. We can urge doing away with classification and groups, and enforce laws against racial discrimination in educational opportunities and employment and housing; we can and must insist upon considering only persons' individual characteristics rather than their group membership as a basis for educational treatment and in social relations in general. Well and good. I trust there is no disagreement on this. What we may not accomplish by these means, however, is equality of performance in school or in the acquisition of certain skills deemed valuable by society and rewarded accordingly. If we repeatedly look for the causes of differences in ability to acquire an educationally valued skill such as reading, for example, in the external environment and are hard put to find a convincing explanation there, but we also refuse to consider any other than external factors as possible causes of these differences, perhaps we only sow the seeds of a kind of social paranoia—a need to find strictly external causes to blame for the observed differences.

To seek the answers to these questions and yet to worry about their far reaching implications: surely this is the scientist's moral dilemma. I don't claim to have the solution.

In terms of what we now know in educational research and in terms of what seems immediately feasible, I would suggest further consideration of three main educational approaches. They are not at all mutually exclusive. (The desirability and necessity of eliminating racial discrimination and of generally improving the environmental conditions and educational and occupational opportunities of all disadvantaged persons in the population are taken for granted.) These approaches have nothing to do with race *per se*, but are concerned with individual differences in those characteristics most relevant to educability. Their success in improving the benefits of education to black children, however, may depend in part upon recognizing that racial differences in the distribution of educationally relevant abilities are not mainly a result of discrimination and unequal environmental conditions. None of the approaches that seems to me realistic is based on the expectation of the schools' significantly changing children's basic intelligence.

Seeking Aptitude X Training Interactions

This means that some children may learn better by one method than by another and that the best method may be quite different for different children, depending on their particular aptitudes or other personological characteristics. It implies that the same educational goals can be accomplished to the same degree for children of different abilities provided the right instructional variations are found. This is merely a hope, and the relevant research so far gives little basis for optimism that such aptitude X training interactions will be found which can overcome to any marked degree the importance of IQ level for educability. But since this type of research has been underway only a few years, it is much too soon to discount the possibilities it may turn up—especially if one expects not miracles, but only positive, if modest, benefits from this approach.

Greater Attention to Learning Readiness

The concept of developmental readiness for various kinds of school learning has been too neglected in recent educational trends, which have been dominated by the unproved notion that the earlier something can be taught to a child, the better. Forced early learning, prior to some satisfactory level of readiness (which will differ markedly from one child to another), could cause learning blocks which later on practically defy remediation. The more or less uniform lock-step sequencing of educational experiences may have to be drastically modified for the benefit of many children, but the recent massive insistence on "earliness" and equality of educational treatment of all children has militated against large-scale research on the implications of readiness for children with below-average educability within the traditional school system.

Greater Diversity of Curricula and Goals

Public schools, which aim to serve the entire population, must move beyond narrow conceptions of scholastic achievement to find a greater diversity of ways for children over the entire range of abilities to benefit from their schooling—to benefit especially in ways that will be to their advantage when they are out of school. The academic goals of schooling are so ingrained in our thinking and our values that it will probably call for radical efforts to modify public education in ways such that it will maximally benefit large numbers of children with very limited aptitude for academic achievement. I believe that a well-intentioned but misconceived social egalitarian ideology has prevented public education in the United States from facing up to this challenge.

The belief that equality of educational opportunity should necessarily lead to equality of performance, I believe, is proving to be a false hope. It is the responsibility of scientific research in genetics, psychology, and education to determine the basis for realistic solutions to the problems of universal public education. Though it may be premature to prescribe at present, I venture the prediction that future solutions will take the form not so much of attempting to minimize differences in scholastic aptitudes and motivation, but of creating a greater diversity of curricula, instructional methods, and educational goals and values that will make it possible for children ranging over a wider spectrum of abilities and proclivities genuinely to benefit from their years in school. The current zeitgeist of environmentalist equalitarianism has all but completely stifled our thinking along these lines. And I believe the magnitude and urgency of the problem are such as to call for quite radical thinking if the educational system is truly to serve the whole of society. We have invested so much for so long in trying to equalize scholastic performance that we have given little or no thought to finding ways of diversifying schools to make them rewarding to everyone while not attempting to equalize everyone's performance in a common curriculum. Recommendations have almost always taken the form of asking what next we might try to make children who in the present school system do not flourish academically become more like those who do. The emphasis has been more on changing children than on revamping the system. A philosophy of equalization, however laudable its ideals, cannot work if it is based on false premises, and no amount of propaganda can make it appear to work. Its failures will be forced upon everyone. Educational pluralism of some sort, encompassing a variety of very different educational curricula and goals, I think, will be the inevitable outcome of the growing realization that the schools are not going to eliminate human differences. Rather than making over a large segment of the school population so they will not be doomed to failure in a largely antiquated elitist oriented educational system which originally evolved to serve only a relatively small segment of society, the educational system will have to be revamped in order to benefit everyone who is required by the society to attend school. It seems incredible that a system can still survive which virtually guarantees frustration and failure for a large proportion of the children it should intend to serve. From all the indications, public education in such a form will not much longer survive.

But we should not fail to recognize that to propose radical diversity in accord with individual differences in abilities and interests, as contrasted with uniformity of educational treatment, puts society between Scylla and Charybdis in terms of insuring for all individuals equality of opportunity for the diversity of educational paths. The surest way to maximize the benefits of schooling to all individuals and at the same time to make the most of a society's human resources is to insure equality of educational opportunity for all its members. Monolithic educational goals and uniformity of approaches guarantee unnecessary frustration and defeat for many. On the other hand, educational pluralism runs the risk that social, economic, ethnic background or geographic origin, rather than each child's own characteristics, might determine the educational paths available to him. The individual characteristics appropriate for any one of a variety of educational paths and goals are to be found everywhere, in every social stratum, ethnic group, and neighborhood. Academic aptitudes and special talents should be cultivated wherever they are found, and a wise society will take all possible measures to insure this to the greatest possible extent. At the same time, those who are poor in the traditional academic aptitudes cannot be left by the wayside. Suitable means and goals must be found for making their years of schooling rewarding to them, if not in the usual academic sense, then in ways that can better their chances for socially useful and self-fulfilling roles as adults.

References

Bereiter, C., Genetics and educability: educational implications of the Jensen debate. In J. Hellmuth (Ed.), *Disadvantaged child.* Vol. 3. *Compensatory education: a national debate.* New York: Brunner-Mazel, 1970, pp. 279-299.

Burt, C., The inheritance of mental ability. *Amer. Psychol.*, 1958, *13* 1-15.

Burt, C., Intelligence and social mobility. *British Journal of Statistical Psychology*, 1961, 14, 3-24.

Burt, C., The genetic determination of differences in intelligence: A study of monozygotic twins reared together and apart. *Brit. J. Psychol.*, 1966, *57*, 137-153.

DeFries, J.C., Quantitative aspects of genetics and environment in the determination of behavior. In E. Caspari (Ed.) *Future Directions of Behavior Genetics*, in press.

Gibson, J.B., Biological aspects of a high socioeconomic group. I. IQ, education, and social mobility. *Journal of Biosocial Science*, 1970, 2, 1-16.

Gottesman, I.I., Biogenetics of race and class. In M. Deutsch, I. Katz, & A.R. Jensen (Eds.) *Social class, race, and psychological development?* New York: Holt, Rinehart, & Winston, 1968, pp. 11-51.

Jensen, A.R. Estimation of the limits of heritability of traits by comparison of monozygotic and dizygotic twins. *Proceedings of the National Academy of Sciences*, 1967, 58, 149-156.

Jensen, A.R., Another look at culture-fair tests. In *Western Regional Conference on Testing Problems, Proceedings for 1968*, "Measurement for Educational Planning." Berkeley, Calif.: Educational Testing Service, Western Office, 1968, pp. 50-104.

Jensen, A.R., How much can we boost IQ and scholastic achievement? *Harvard Educational Review*, 1969, 39, 1-123.

Jensen, A.R., Race and the genetics of intelligence: A reply to Lewontin. *Bulletin of the Atomic Scientists*, 1970, 26, 17-23.(a)

Jensen, A.R., IQs of identical twins reared apart. *Behavior Genetics*, 1970, 1, 133-148. (b)

Jensen, A.R., Can we and should we study race differences? In J. Hellmuth (Ed.), *Disadvantaged Child*, Vol. 3: *Compensatory Education: A National Debate.* New York: Brunner/Mazel, 1970, pp. 124-157. (c)

Jones, M.B., Heritability as a criterion in the construction of psychological tests. *Psychological Bulletin*, 1971, 75, 92-96.

Kates, Solis L., Kates, W.W., & Michael, J., Cognitive processes in deaf and hearing adolescents and adults. *Psychological Monographs*, 1962, 76, whole No. 551.

Lawrence, E.M., An investigation into the relation between intelligence and inheritance. *British Journal of Psychology*, Monograph Supplement., 1931, 16, No. 5, p. 80.

Leahy, Alice, M., Nature-nurture and intelligence. *Genetic Psychology Monographs*, 1935, 17, 241-305.

Lewontin, R.C., Race and intelligence. *Bulletin of the Atomic Scientists*, 1970, 26, No. 3, 2-8. (a)

Lewontin, R.C., Further remarks on race and the genetics of intelligence. *Bulletin of the Atomic Scientists*, 1970, 26, No. 5, 23-25. (b)

Li, C.C., A tale of two thermos bottles: properties of a genetic model for human intelligence. In R. Cancro (Ed.) *Intelligence: Genetic and environmental influences.* New York: Grune & Stratton, 1971, pp. 162-181.

Lush, J.L., Genetic unknowns and animal breeding a century after Mendel. *Transactions of the Kansas Academy of Science*, 1968, 71, 309-314.

Maxwell, J., Relative influences of social class and IQ on children's education and occupation. *International Newsletter* (Educational Testing Service, Princeton, N.J.), Issue VIII, December, 1969, pp. 5-6.

McNemar, Q. A critical examination of the University of Iowa studies of environmental influences upon the IQ. *Psychological Bulletin*, 1940, 37, 63-92.

Nichols, P.L., The effects of heridity and environment on intelligence test performance in 4 and 7 year old white and Negro sibling pairs. Unpublished doctoral dissertation. University of Minnesota, 1970.

Roberts, R.C., Some concepts and methods in quantitative genetics, In J. Hirsch (Ed.), *Behavior-genetic analysis*. New York: McGraw-Hill, 1967, pp. 214-257.

Scarr-Salapatek, Sandra, Race, social class, and IQ. *Science*, 1971, 174, 1285-1295.

Scriven, M., The values of the academy (moral issues for American education and educational research arising from the Jensen case). *Review of Educational Research*, 1970, 40, 541-549.

Skodak, Marie, & Skeels, H.M., A final follow-up study of one hundred adopted children. *Journal of Genetic Psychology*, 1949, 75, 85-125.

Spuhler, J.N., & Lindzey, G., Racial differences in behavior. In J. Hirsch (Ed.), *Behavior-genetic analysis.* New York: McGraw-Hill, 1967, pp. 366-414.

Terman, L.M., Personal reactions of the Yearbook Committee. In Whipple, G.M. (Ed.) *Intelligence: Its nature and nurture*, 39th Yearbook of the National Society for the Study of Education. Part I, 1940, pp. 460-467.

Waller, J.H., Achievement and social mobility: Relationships among IQ score, education, and occupation in two generations. *Social Biology*, 1971, 18, 252-259.

Young, M., & Gibson, J., In search of an explanation of social mobility. *British Journal of Statistical Psychology*, 1963, 16, 27-36.

5

Community Influence upon School District Policy: Building Responsiveness in Urban School Districts

The real world of school politics indicates that regardless of what theoretical definition of influence scholars develop, community influence to a large extent lies in the eyes of the beholder. And for all practical purposes, community influence upon school district policy has little meaning for the poor, the disenfranchised and the nonwhite in most urban school districts. This should come as little surprise to anyone who has viewed district policy through the eyes of community people. To residents of the inner city the question of influence is not academic. The issue is a vital one, for influence on school policies is integrally related to the preservation of cultures and the achievement of equal opportunity in the greater society. The question to ask, therefore, is not whether communities influence district policy, but how community influence can be reinstated in the large city school district.

Several observers of inner city school policy-making conclude that one of the greatest barriers to influence being exercised by the community is the very manner in which school districts are organized. Instead of districts organized to respond to community demands (i.e., to be influenced), one finds districts organized according to classical bureaucratic models which insulate district personnel from the influence of community needs and desires. The most popularly proposed solution to this state of affairs is to decentralize the district policy-making structure. As a result, decentralization has become one of the more emotional educational issues of our time, and more than ever, needs a measure of dispassionate scrutiny.

The debate over centralized-decentralized school districts is not entirely new. In fact, as Robert Bendiner has commented, "until two or three years ago the progress of American education was often measured in the distance its systems had come from the small, provincial district of the nineteenth century, from the concept of the neighborhood school as the basis of American education." During the past two decades well over three-fourths of the school boards and their districts were eliminated. There is merit to the observation that we seem to be coming full circle regarding the question of school district size and quality of educational services.[1]

Common sense dictates that decentralization will be no panacea for the dearth of community influence in the inner city; there are no panaceas in this area. On the other hand decentralization may provide sufficient improvements in the policy-making structure of large urban school districts to facilitate the actualization of community influence. What are these improvements, if any?

What will be the concomitant disadvantages of decentralization? What follows is hopefully a dispassionate attempt to find answers to these questions by bringing to bear contemporary research and by offering an evaluation of the impact of decentralization on school districts. Keep in mind, however, that there will be no easy answers to the problems of urban school districts, although there may be better answers than those previously submitted.

Contemporary Research and School District Responsiveness

Contemporary research offers some explanations on the subject of school board responsiveness. Although there is a paucity of data available on the effect of demand stress on the policy structure of the schools, some evidence is available. What happens to school boards under demand stress from their communities? What, in fact, explains the current unresponsiveness of large city school districts to their communities? The research available to date seems to reveal, at least, three major propositions which attempt to answer the above questions, and explain the phenomena so common today to the urban citizen.

The Legitimation Proposition

The first proposition simply suggests that school boards under demand stress become legitimizers of the current district policy and follow the judgment of their administrative staff.[2] The legitimation proposition directly brings into question the representative role of the board member. Does the school board member represent the views of his constituents in the determination of policy, or does he merely legitimize policy already arrived at by the district's "professional" staff? While several school board studies argue that social background, methods of selection, organizational participation, occupation and other similar factors provide linkages with the community which determine a board member's behavior while conducting school business, more recent research indicates other factors intervene between these characteristics and actual performance. For example, one body of research shows much of the policy of the district made in the day-to-day activities of administrators, not by board members. It has been shown to a considerable extent that board members under pressure often seek and rely on the advice of the superintendent and staff. Also, through the control of agenda and information superintendents can (1) define and assign priorities, (2) define alternative solutions, and (3) quite frequently choose between the alternatives.[3] To be sure, these are not meager powers.

There seems to be some plausibility, based on a number of investigations, in the contention that as demand stress increases, boards become "further released from community stress and more exposed to administrator values."[4] If further support of this proposition is forthcoming, one might raise very serious questions about the substantive nature of board representation. If board members are in reality little more than rubber stamp legitimizers of past policies, then a crucial element of citizen representation has been lost in large city school districts. Ultimately one must find ways of reinstituting this representation or continue to witness widespread discontent in these districts.

Societal Change Proposition

Another group of studies provides a basis for the second proposition. This proposition predicts that in communities undergoing rapid and/or abrupt changes in their contextual conditions, school district policy makers will experience extreme demand stress with which they will be unable to cope effectively. Ultimately, changes in board membership and superintendent turnover result.[5] The "societal change proposition," adapted from the studies of Laurence Iannaccone's students at Claremont, sets up a sequence of events. First, demographic changes lead to changes in community values. Secondly, competition for control over the community policy structure occurs as groups representing the emerging value orientation attempt to realign community decision-making. As newer value orientations seek representation on local governmental bodies, involuntary turnover of governmental officials through incumbent losses at local elections results. Finally, shortly after members of the school board are replaced and new members are perceived to be more representative of newer value orientations, the superintendent is asked to resign.[6]

If the Iannaccone rationale is accurate in describing the present problem of influence in urban school districts, several implications arise regarding the solution of that problem. The sequence of events articulated in the Iannaccone rationale probably extend over a period of several years causing a time lag between the expectations of local communities and the efforts of policy makers to accommodate these expectations. The societal change proposition suggests that the longer this time lag, the more conflict and tension can be expected within school districts. Furthermore, if only pockets of a district change in demographic composition, the involuntary turnover of governmental officials at local elections may never occur until the pockets of new value orientations increase to such a size as to control elections. The upshot of the Iannaccone rationale for community peoples is that influence upon district policy will come in time, but not very soon. It seems frightfully clear that the ever-widening gulf between the credibility of the schools' policies and the educational needs of subcommunities within the larger community can only lead to disillusionment, discontent and despair. Indeed, such a volatile mixture can quickly lead to the threat of or actual violence.

The Responsiveness Proposition

Citizen demands are by no means articulated to educational policy-makers by uniform methods or, for that matter, through predetermined or regular channels. Demands are articulated in a variety of ways with the ultimate objective of being converted into binding decisions. Accordingly, the final proposition to emerge from a perusal of contemporary research suggests that much of the responsibility for the incapacity of local policy makers, particularly boards and superintendents, to respond to client demands lies with the very nature of the present bureaucratic structure of large local school districts.[7]

New directions in research on the politics of education focus on the antecedents and attributes of demands, the processing of demands, and the effects demands have on the adaptability of local school districts. One study reveals that board meeting time is consumed primarily by adjudication functions, such as settling disputes and holding hearings over conflicting demands from competing community groups.[8] Another study of a large city school district documents the magnitude of school board responsibility in responding to demands. A total of over 1600 demands were found placed before the school board in a single year, out of which fewer than 60 were acted upon by the board. Additionally, four months were required for this central policy making body to respond to each of the 60 demands.[9]

Even more pertinent to the responsiveness proposition is a case study of two medium sized cities which sought an answer to the question, "What reasons do board members give for not responding to the demands of citizens in the community?"[10] This study is mentioned because the responses of the school board members may be more pervasive than one realizes in the school districts of this country. Moreover, the members' responses capture the interrelationship which exists among all three propositions set forth. A listing of how most board members accounted for their lack of responsiveness follows:

1. The demands of community organizations are irrelevant to providing a good education of the children.
2. Because of the limited role each community organization plays in the overall community, school district policy cannot be adapted to their independent needs.
3. Due to the disruptive tactics of many community organizations, it is clear they are irresponsible, unfair, antagonistic and their demands should be ignored.
4. Community organizations are not legitimate. They do not accurately reflect the entire community.[11]

Although the responsiveness studies mentioned here are by no means exhaustive of the efforts of many in the field, they do illustrate the contemporary dilemma of the school district policy-maker who finds himself, and his colleagues, under demand stress. An additional complication is provided by this administrative bureaucracy in large school systems. Often well-intentioned individuals who would be more than willing to engage in participative decision making find their efforts thwarted by an entrenched bureaucracy. More than one would care to admit, one finds school districts built around a structure conceived a few hundred years ago and allowed to grow by simply enlarging the structure's span of control and adding new departments, offices, and bureaus. Even the well-intentioned find it virtually impossible to provide new and adaptive channels for regulating the flow, yet responding adequately to a wide range of community needs and desires.

The Case For Decentralization

It may be instructive summarily to review the information supplied by contemporary research to the dilemma of restoring influence to communities. Research studies reveal the school board, as the legal arm of the state, behaving as a legitimizer of professional and bureaucratic norms when under the stress of community demands. Additionally, research indicates a time lag between changes in societal values and changes in school district policy. Finally some interesting research into responsiveness portray professional administrators and lay board members incapable of responding to community demands due to the heavy resistance of the structure they supposedly control.

Although there is evidence to support the three propositions articulated here, admittedly more research is needed to test their validity. However, if there is some currency in what little is known to date, serious questions must be asked about how school district policies can become more representative; about how the ever widening gulf between changing community values and school district policies can be diminished; and about how school systems can be restructured so that districts can respond to, accommodate, and handle the demands of their environment. Such questions permit less and less time for academic debate. As Seymour Lipset contends, when the channels of communication constrict the expression of wants or dissatisfactions, the result is often more intensive forms of political action, frequently invoking more abrasive tactics and violent expressions of protest.[12] The task at hand is to assess current proposals of decentralization against these questions.

Before entering upon this assessment, however, the utility of viewing the school district as a political system should be pointed out. A school district like all political systems comprises legalized structures, roles, and processes through which preferences or values are authoritatively determined for society. A district assumes a sense of stability through time. It has boundaries over which interchanges are made between demands and decisions, and also between resources and support for those decisions. Finally, because of the inter-dependence which exists between the school district and its environment, if the district is to survive it must be responsive and adaptive to changes in the surrounding society and within the system itself.[13] These ingredients are comparable to all political systems, and underline the importance of looking at the political phenomena of school districts in terms of activities and processes, rather than directing attentions entirely to the more formal, legalistic and institutional interpretations. Viewing the school district as a political system, therefore, provides a measure of objectivity about structure of policy-making. If a tightly centralized structure could adequately fulfill the qualifications of a responsive, vital political system, there would be little reason to oppose such a structure. The same holds for a decentralized structure.

The political system perspective of school district policy-making provides one additional important advantage. The school district may be considered a political system within a political system, a mirror within a mirror, which must reflect only images received from the outer system. Like the mirrors, the school district as a political system can only act upon a part of the total environmental image. This phenomenon of the inter-relatedness of political systems suggests a useful point at which one might begin to expect ameliorative effects of proposed or actual reforms. Reforming or reinstating influence in inner city school policy formulation, for instance, *may* improve educational efforts but it *neither* has to *nor* can do so in the absence of any other reforms in the larger political system. For example, decrying decentralization because it fails directly to change teacher training programs would be mere absurdity according to the political systems approach. Far more appropriate a criterion for assessing decentralization as a proposal or actual reform would be estimating the amount of indirect impact it might have in the larger political system.

The Forms of Decentralization

Decentralization can mean many things to many people. The basic concept behind decentralization simply is to break up the large, inflexible school bureaucracies into smaller districts which would be more accessible to the communities served. Categorized within this basic concept, however, are several variations of decentralization. One type does not actually involve any direct structural change. Instead this variation encourages the school system to make greater attempts to involve the community by organizing community planning councils, citizen advisory committees, and more informal parent-teacher confer-ences.[14]

Many would argue, however, that more direct structural change is necessary.

The more radical spokesmen of this point of view argue for a redistribution of the concentration of power which now lies in the hierarchical nature of school bureaucracies. This power, they argue, should not be used to legitimize existing practices. More conservative spokesmen argue for a redistribution of the concentration of power but only to more numerous smaller hierarchical bureaucracies.[15] Both forms of structural decentralization would involve breaking the gigantic urban school district into many smaller ones; the two are distinguished by their participative emphasis. According to both forms, however, each district would be responsible for hiring and firing teachers, raising its own finances and developing its own curriculum.

Another proposed method decentralizes only certain aspects of school administration; for example, redistributing authority for formulating curriculum goals and hiring of teachers, while keeping other responsibilities such as the budget and construction under a central authority.[16] Under this system one basically assumes that school districts can be broken into more responsive units while still retaining the advantages of a more centralized system.

One final approach may serve either as a temporary measure for increased responsiveness or as a permanent means for structural redesign.[17] This arrangement sets up parallel institutions such as community action agencies, which work with the existing school structure. These new institutions have the potential of greater flexibility. In turn, these institutions could create coalitions of interested community organizations. The end result envisions a newer agency created from the coalition which would maintain enough vitality to make the older alliances of power ineffectual.

In sum, decentralization can take many forms—all of which can be modified, combined or adjusted to fit the particular needs and limitations of a given community. But what substantive improvements in the area of community influence will accrue if any of these forms are adopted?

Criticisms and Counter-Arguments

There is no rationale for beginning this assessment with negative predictions of the impact of decentralization schemes. But there is some merit to considering the real and imaginary drawbacks to these schemes, and then comparing such drawbacks with possible positive effects.

Criticisms of decentralization usually conclude with the argument that by setting up smaller jurisdictions within the community

1. great inequities in money distribution would develop;
2. ethnic solidarity would be destroyed by gerrymandering;
3. segregation would be more strongly entrenched;
4. community conflict would increase since decisions would be localized;

5. too much power would be held by parochial interests thereby destroying minimum standards now existing;
6. substantive reform would be hampered since, in the past, educational innovation has rarely come from the grass roots; and
7. too many limitations would be placed upon teachers since local pressures could be too binding.[18]

Upon closer scrutiny most of these criticisms can either be answered or resolved by certain structural provisions. For example, money could be raised and distributed by a central agency. Laws could be passed which limit gerrymandering. The argument of increased segregation is not compelling since the present system has done little to decrease segregation. Indeed, the reverse has occurred, for segregation has increased. In fact, there may be validity to the contention that true desegregation and equality in education can only come about by first building a strong cohesion among various ethnic communities and by improving the quality of their schools.

There are several good arguments countering the complaints of parochialism and the fear of control by radical groups. The Bundy Report in New York City suggests, for example, that rather than decentralization resulting in parochialism, it should create a greater sense of community identity, and, consequently, eliminate the feelings of powerlessness which breed radicalism.[19] Other scholars have voiced similar opinions. Though community conflict may be increased, the level of participation will also increase—thus activating new elements of the community which could offset any tendency toward unresolvable power struggles.

Possible intimidation of teachers by the community need not be the case. Communities and teachers can learn to work together. The possibility of such a cooperative relationship may even be furthered by the fact that communities would have a greater say in the selection of teachers. Accordingly, teachers would be selected, one would assume, because they would be more amenable to community values and desires. One can and should expect, nevertheless, the teacher unions to perceive decentralization as a direct threat to their organization's solidarity and job security. Gittell's description of the New York experiment substantiates the resistance of the teachers and supervisory staff.[20] If acceptance by the professional is to be considered in the decentralization proposal, that proposal will have to reinforce the tenure system and protect present conditions of employment. How serious a restriction this is to improving community influence and district responsiveness through decentralization is a debatable proposition.

Finally, an answer to the charge that innovation has very seldom come from the community is primarily imbedded in the problem of the inflexibility of the school bureaucracy. To assume that people who have never had an opportunity for grass roots participation are never quite ready for participation is neither reasonable nor justifiable. There is no better way to engage in developing innovative educational programs responsive to local needs than to practice participation.

Some Positive Effects of Decentralization

An adequate assessment of decentralization has to include more than consideration of the criticisms of such a plan and rebuttals to those criticisms. An analyst must be able to find clear direct and indirect payoffs from such a proposal. Benefits could accrue from implementation of a decentralization scheme in large urban areas. For instance,

1. Decentralization could make schools more responsive and eliminate feelings of powerlessness in ghetto communities. In turn, it could bring many fresh, new ideas into the system.
2. Because decentralization has the strong political support of many ghetto and barrio communities—particularly the political support of militants—it has a higher probability of success in the central city.
3. Although historically decentralization has been most unsatisfactory due to financial inadequacies, it can be less expensive and more efficient than a highly centralized system. Experiments with small, localized schools have shown this to be true.
4. Decentralization could improve community-professional relations. The main purpose of the Bundy report and its plans for decentralization was to "reconnect all the parties with an interest in the public schools of New York so that each will have more constructive power, and so that contact with each other will center on cooperation, instead of suspicion or recrimination."[21]
5. Decentralization could help remove much of the authority from existing bureaucracies which have in the past only supported the status quo. As Dr. Marilyn Gittel states, "only minor procedural changes can be expected from the present educational system given the distribution of power within it. This power can be redistributed only through a thorough reorganization that will dislodge the central headquarters staff from its almost complete control of policy."[22]
6. Decentralization could create healthy competition among schools which would keep a constant pressure for change and innovation.

Though decentralization can make many valuable contributions towards solving the crisis in the schools, it cannot solve all problems if it is used as the sole solution. First, many problems reflected in the schools are deeply rooted in our society and cannot be solved merely by decentralizing different school districts. Education can only offer a limited contribution to the solution of some of these problems. Secondly, though some studies show increased parental involvement in schools increasing student achievement, other studies show little conclusive evidence of such occurrences. New programs undoubtedly will have to be instituted in conjunction with decentralization to realize positive results in student achievement. Furthermore, true to historical experience, actual power may not be redistributed at all when boundary lines are redrawn. The school bureaucracy which has evolved over the past century is not about to relinquish its power. In the past, coalitions strong enough to combat the school bureaucracy have not existed.

Is Decentralization the Answer?·

Whether decentralization is the answer to the ills created by large, unresponsive urban school districts largely remains to be seen. But whether it might be a fruitful direction for beginning to respond to these ills can be inferred from this analysis. Historical perusal warns that decentralization is not an untried remedy. On the other hand, the concept of historical fallacy reminds one not to confuse two perhaps distinguishable decentralization proposals. Current proposals for decentralization attempt to control for undesirable effects experienced in past decentralization efforts. For example, many proposals attempt to foresee financial troublespots and gerrymandering dangers. Even more to the point, in unresponsive districts current decentralization schemes often involve more than size manipulation of districts. Such schemes speak to the need of changing old participation patterns by subverting the notion that the professional knows best.

In response to the three research propositions attempting to explain lack of community influence, decentralization, as currently proposed, offers some interesting change possibilities. Decentralization has a reasonably good chance of reducing the legitimization functions of board members, of reducing the time lag which characterizes value differences in communities undergoing rapid population shifts, and of increasing the responsiveness of board members to community demands. More importantly, decentralization has the potential of generating hope in communities disgusted and demoralized as a result of such conditions. Hope aligned with real change can be a powerful tool for revitalizing the schools and the communities.

Expecting too much of decentralization, however, can lead to serious miscalculations and dashed hopes. Though decentralization can be an important tool in arresting power from the gigantic school bureaucracies, it can only be effective if it is part of a much greater plan of reform. David Rogers in *110 Livingston Street* offers an example of such comprehensively planned reform of the nation's educational structure.[23] Roger's plan includes tactics such as pressing for rapid and radical decentralization, organizing parents in poverty areas through training programs aimed at developing necessary skills, improving teacher education, and setting up parallel structures to put existing structures out of business. Roger's plan is noteworthy because of its systemic perception of the problems of education and its coordinated approach to change. If urban minority communities will ever again enjoy influence upon school district policies, massive, broad-based approaches will be critical factors in attainment of that influence.

A national sense of urgency about the responsiveness of large institutions of all types to all segments of public opinion summons the educator's attention to the large urban school district. Surely, the urgency of the matter places a prodigious obligation on the educational researcher and practitioner. If decentralization "is to be the answer" much research is needed both prior to and in conjunction with the implementation of various reform alternatives. Looked upon as a comprehensive "political process," rather than merely as a structural redesign, political systems analyses of decentralization alternatives would appear to have merit. Clearly, such analyses are needed of the variety of structural goals each decentralization plan seeks to achieve, and even more apparent is the need for assessments of the extent decentralization helps the large urban school district adapt to contemporary educational needs. The researcher, on the one hand, must seek the root causes of the internal wounds of the large urban school districts. He must work jointly with the practitioner, on the other hand, to assist in the structural redesign of our schools and school systems to create more accountable and responsive processes.

Notes

1. Robert Bendiner, *The Politics of Schools: A Crisis in Self-Government* (New York: Harper & Row, 1969), p. 177.

2. Norman D. Kerr, "The School as an Agency of Legitimation," *Sociology of Education,* 38 (1964), p. 38.

3. David W. Minar, *Educational Decision-Making in Suburban Communities,* Cooperative Research Project No. 2440 (Evanston: Northwestern University, 1966), pp. 48-56.

4. Jay D. Scribner, "The Politics of Educational Reform: Analyses of Political Demands," *Urban Education,* 4 (1970), pp. 348-374.

5. Laurence Iannaccone, *Politics in Education* (New York: Center for Ap-Research in Education, Inc., 1967), pp. 82-89.

6. Ibid., pp. 89-98.

7. Scribner, "Politics of Educational Reform," pp. 368-369.

8. H. Thomas James, "School Board Conflict is Inevitable," *The American School Board Journal,* (March, 1967), p. 7.

9. Scribner, "Politics of Educational Reform," p. 369.

10. Robert F. Lyke, "Representation and Urban School Boards," in *Community Control of Schools,* ed. Henry M. Levin (Washington, D. C.: The Brookings Institution, 1970), p. 141.

11. Ibid., pp. 142-151.

12. Seymour Martin Lipset, *Political Man: The Social Bases of Politics* (New York: Doubleday & Co., Inc., 1960), pp. 70-71.

13. For a more complete statement on the school system as a political system see Jay D. Scribner, "Politics of Educational Reform."

14. An article dealing with various forms of decentralization is Marilyn Gittell, "Urban School Reform in the 1970's," *Education and Urban Society,* 1 (1968), pp. 9-19.

15. Ibid.

16. See Marilyn Gittell, *Participants and Participation* (New York: Praeger, 1967), p. 60; and Theodore R. Sizer, "The Case for a Free Market," *Saturday Review* (January 11, 1969), p. 93.

17. David Rogers, *110 Livinston Street: Politics and Bureaucracy in the New York City Schools* (New York: Random House, 1968), pp. 249-431.

18. Sizer, "The Case for a Free Market," pp. 34-36.

19. See "Reconnection for Learning," a report prepared by the New York City Mayor's Advisory Panel on Decentralization of the New York City Schools, 1967, often referred to as the "Bundy Report" after the Panel's Chairman, McGeorge Bundy, p. 68.

20. Gittell, *Participants and Participation,* pp. 13-14.

21. McGeorge Bundy, "Reconnection for Learning," p. 69.

22. Gittell, *Participants and Participation,* p. 60.

23. David Rogers, *110 Livingston Street,* pp. 429 and 420.

Bibliography

Almond, Gabriel and Bingham Powell. *Comparative Politics: A Development Approach.* Boston: Little, Brown. 1966.

Altshuler, Alan A. *Community Control: The Black Demand for Participation in Large American Cities.* New York: Pegasus, 1970.

American School Board Journal. "Cubberley Conference: School Boards in an Era of Conflict," *American School Board Journal* 154 (March, 1967), 40 pp.

Bauer, Raymond and Kenneth J. Gergen (eds.). *The Study of Policy Formation.* New York: The Free Press, Chapters 4, 5, and 6. 1968.

Campbell, Roald F. and others. *The Organization and Control of American Schools.* Columbus: Charles E. Merrill Publishing Company, 1970. Chapters XII,XIII, and XIV.

Easton, David. *Systems Analysis of Political Life.* New York: John Wiley. 1965.

Fantini, Mario. "Community Participation," *Harvard Educational Review,* XXXVIII (Winter, 1968), pp. 160-175.

Fink, Lawrence and Raymond Ducharme, Jr. *Crisis in Urban Education.* Waltham, Massachusetts: Xerox College Publishing, 1971.

Fuchs, Estelle. *Pickets at the Gate.* New York: The Free Press, 1966.

Gittell, Marilyn. *Participants and Participation: A Study of School Policy in New York City.* New York: Praeger Publishers, 1967.

Gittell, Marilyn. "Urban School Reform in the 1970's," *Education and Urban Society,* I (November, 1968), pp. 9-20.

Kerr, Norman D. "The School Board as an Agency of Legitimation," in Alan Rosenthal *Governing Education: A Reader on Politics, Power and Public School Policy.* New York: Anchor Books of Doubleday & Co., Inc., 1969. pp. 137-172.

Kirst, Michael and Edith Mosher. "Politics of Education," *Review of Educational Research.* Washington, D.C.: AERA, Vol. 39, No. 5, pp. 623-640. 1968.

Lutz, Frank W. *Toward Improved Urban Education.* Worthington: Charles A. Jones Publishing Company, 1970. Chapters 8 and 9. 1970.

Lyke, Robert F. "Representation and Urban School Boards," in Henry Levin (ed.) *Community Control of Schools.* Washington, D. C.: Brookings Institution, 1970. pp. 138-168.

Rosenthal, Alan (ed). *Governing Education: A Reader on Politics, Power, and Public School Policy.* New York: Doubleday & Company, Inc., 1969. Part II.

Schrag, Peter. *Village School Downtown: Politics and Education—A Boston Report.* Boston: Beacon Press, 1967.

Scribner, Jay D. "The Politics of Educational Reform: Analysis of Political Demands," *Urban Education* (Beverly Hills: Sage Publications), Vol. IV, No. 4, pp. 348-374. 1970.

Sizer, Theodore R. "The Case for a Free Market," *Saturday Review,* January 11, 1969. A special issue on "Education in the Ghetto."

Wirt, Frederick M. "Theory and Research Needs in the Study of American Educational Politics," *The Journal of Educational Administration.* Vol. VIII, No. 1, pp. 53-87. 1970.

6

Teacher Militancy: An Analysis of the Strike-Prone Teacher

Harmon Zeigler

How militant are teachers? To ask this question is to open a Pandora's box of definitional problems. We hear, for example, that teachers—both the NEA and AFT variety—are seeking a larger voice in decision making. In this sense, their demands are not unlike those of students in higher education. Yet, if such demands are "militant," the methods typically are not. We have yet to see teachers engaging in the physical destruction that characterizes student unrest; and certainly the teacher's movements have typically been far less intense.

The Strike as an Indicator of Militancy

In spite of the temptation to spill a great amount of ink seeking an appropriate definition of militancy, I propose to take the easy way out and focus upon a single—indisputable—manifestation of militancy: the strike. Given the impressive formal and informal sanctions against striking, I suggest that this behavior is, for teachers, as extreme as a student riot, even though in private industry strikes are a relatively mild form of protest.

If we take the occurrence of strikes as a crude indicator of teacher militancy, then militancy is indeed on the rise. According to the National Education Association, strikes were virtually unknown at the beginning of the 1960s. Fewer than five strikes per year occurred from 1960 to 1964. From 1964 the number of strikes increased gradually until about 35 per year were taking place. This modest increase was replaced in 1967-68 by a sudden upsurge: 114 strikes were recorded (NEA, 1968). These figures hardly suggest that strikes are becoming a way of life for teachers, but they do indicate that certain changes are taking place in education. After all, strikes by public employees are outlawed in many states. Even more impressive—a point to which I will return—the professional norms of teaching are not conducive towards going on strike. Given the legal and informal sanctions against strikes, I feel some justification in arguing that the willingness to go on strike is a good indication of militancy.

The research reported in this article was conducted as part of the research and development program of the Center for the Advanced Study of Educational Administration at the University of Oregon, under the sponsorship of the Cooperative Research Program of the U.S. Office of Education.

The Data

I want to address myself to the question: what kind of teachers are apt to go on strike? In pursuing this task, I will draw upon data collected within the context of a larger study of political socialization of American high school students. During the spring of 1965, interviews were held with a national sample of social studies teachers to whom the students in the sample had been most exposed during grades ten through twelve. A total of 317 teachers were interviewed, 286 of whom were public school teachers. Because public school teachers operate in milieu with a different set of expectations than do their counterparts in nonpublic schools, the latter are excluded from this analysis.

Inasmuch as the teacher sample is not a sample of the universe of all teachers, we should be very explicit about how the sample was determined. The investigators in the socialization study desired a sample of social studies teachers that would reflect the number and variety of course hours taught the sample of students. Decisions about the relative value of various levels of depth coverage—number of students per teacher—were achieved by means of a selection scheme. In a number of small schools an obvious choice existed, since there was only one main social studies teacher. In order for another teacher to be chosen in these schools, he had to have taught at least three students. Among the other schools, automatic selection went to the top two teachers in terms of the number of sample students taught. Additional teachers were chosen by assigning scores that gave most emphasis to coverage of a wide number of sample students and next most for achieving depth coverage of the sample students. A concise definition of the sample is that it represents those social studies teachers bearing the heaviest load of teaching during grades ten through twelve for a national sample of twelfth graders.

The Acceptance of Strikes

The main limitation of the sample is that it includes only high school social studies teachers. In general, these teachers are more "liberal" than their counterparts in other disciplines. To be explicit, they are *more* inclined to view the strike as a legitimate form of protest (Zeigler, 1967, p. 116). Nevertheless, there is some justification in using the sample, precisely *because* it represents the hard-core activists among teachers. According to those teachers, strikes are not a very promising form of endeavor. Given the opportunity to respond to a variety of forms of political expression, strikes come resoundingly in last place. The line of questioning that elicited appropriate norms of behavior went as follows:

Now I would like to ask you some questions about something that a teacher might do in the community and the classroom. I will mention something that a teacher might want to do, and would you tell me if you think a teacher should or should not feel free to do this, assuming that the teacher wanted to?

Eleven activities are cited; the proportions indicating that a teacher should feel free to engage in particular activity are presented in Table 6-1.

Table 6-1
Porportion of Social Studies Teachers Agreeing that a Teacher Should Feel Free to Engage in Certain Activities

Speak in class in favor of the United Nations	96%
Join a teachers' union	88
Serve as party precinct worker in pre-election activities	87
Run for political office	83
Belong to the NAACP or CORE	81
Speak in class for or against civil rights movement	76
Publicly criticize local government officials	68
Allow the distribution of anticommunist literature put out by the NAM	63
Allow an atheist to address the class	58
Speak in class favorably about socialism	57
Go on strike to secure higher salaries and other benefits	42
N = 349*	

*This is a weighted N made necessary by the use of unavoidably imprecise estimates used in the construction of the sampling frame. All data reported are derived from this weighted base N.

As we can see from the table, going on strike, with a 42% rate of agreement is the only item with which less than a majority agrees. Whereas strikes are increasing, we can safely assume—given the activist tendencies of social studies teachers—that substantially less than a majority of the teaching population is willing to support strikes. Also, the data is seven years old: perhaps the percentage has increased, but I still doubt if a majority of teachers is ready to take to the pavement. Yet one should not place too much emphasis upon the total number of potential strikers. After all, the turmoil on the nation's college and university campuses—and for that matter the violence in ghettos—has been supported by a minority of the potential participants.

All in all, there is a substantial reservoir of support for strikes among public school teachers. Rosenthal's assessment, although perhaps a bit too general and extreme, may well be accurate in terms of the future if not the present.

Public school teachers, once the docile handmaidens of public education, are no longer quiescent. . . . The "teachers movement" is gaining in strength nationwide, and particularly in large cities. The former widespread, if passive, consensus on the operating rules of the educational game has undergone erosion.

Teachers, or at least their leaders, are beginning to envision a full partnership in the educational enterprise. They are beginning to talk about rights, not privileges, and power, not consultation. Their actions indicate that they mean what they are saying, as they never meant it before (Rosenthal, 1969, pp. 1-2).

Explanatory Variables: Region and Community

There is no need to belabor the point that teachers are becoming more strike-prone. What is more important is the question: what kinds of teachers? In order to answer this, I propose to examine two classes of explanatory variables: community characteristics and occupational variables. The *intersection* of these two kinds of variables will also be examined, because, as will be demonstrated, each has an independent and additive effect upon the attitudes of teachers.

Turning first to community characteristics, we will consider region and community complexity. The choice of these variables is dependent upon our previous work on the behavior of teachers (Jennings and Zeigler, 1970, pp. 439-444).

Sectionalism has always been considered a significant aspect of the American political scene. The most explicit statement of regional values at the mass public level is found in Stouffer's work on tolerance (Stouffer, 1966). Stouffer found that Southerners and Midwesterners were substantially less tolerant of nonconformists or deviant behavior. If we inquire about the extent to which teachers, as smaller subsamples of these larger regional samples, epitomize these regional values, we should find that Midwestern and Southern teachers are less likely to be strike-prone than Western and Eastern teachers. In the analysis we will keep the four conventional regions. (Regional groupings follow Census Bureau classifications: Northeast comprises New England and Middle Atlantic states; Midwest comprises East North Central and West North Central states; South comprises South Atlantic, East South Central, and West South Central states; and West comprises Mountain and Pacific states.)

Similar hypotheses can be argued for the next variable; size and complexity of community. Teachers in large, heterogeneous communities face a relatively tolerant environment and should consequently appear as small images of the environment. Conversely, the smaller, more homogeneous communities, which are the least tolerant, should produce the least strike-prone teachers. Although absolute community size is an obvious measure that could be employed to tap this dimension, we have elected to use a scheme based on the presence and/or nature of the Standard Metropolitan Statistical Area (SMSA) in which the school is located. An advantage to using a SMSA classification is that it incorporates not only population and urban factors in the immediate environment, but also includes social and economic dependencies. Using this measure instead of sheer community size means, for example, that the small town in a large metropolitan area is separated from the small town in a remote, rural area; simply using community size would put these two towns in the same cell. The sample is divided into the twelve most populated SMSAs in the nation (large), other SMSAs not among the twelve largest (medium) and communities not part of any SMSA (non-SMSAs).

For this portion of the analysis, we will draw upon some additional data. In the same school districts in which the 1965 teacher interviews were taken, we returned in 1968 to conduct interviews with school board members and superintendents. Also, the 1968 Survey Research Center election study was used to include several items relating to education. We thus have additional interviews with the mass public. Thus, we are able to include a broad spectrum of opinions in regard to the appropriateness of strikes. Obviously, the three year time difference in the interviews must be taken into account when the findings are examined. To facilitate comparisons, the data will be reported in means, with the higher figure indicating greater tolerance of strikes.

Table 6-2

Willingness to Support Strikes among Mass Public, Teachers, School Board Members, and Superintendents, by Region and Metropolitanism

Region	Mass	(N)	Teachers	(N)	Board	(N)*	Superintendents	(N)
NE	.43	(61)	.41	(97)	.097	(24)	.043	(23)
MW	.22	(98)	.35	(110)	.19	(33)	.22	(33)
S	.25	(180)	.45	(70)	.14	(32)	.062	(32)
W	.31	(34)	.51	(62)	.18	(17)	.080	(17)
Metropolitanism								
Non-SMSA	.25	(229)	.35	(121)	.16	(49)	.11	(49)
Med. SMSA	.27	(107)	.43	(191)	.14	(51)	.11	(51)
Large SMSA	.47	(36)	.67	(28)	.21	(7)	.079	(6)

*N = number of boards rather than number of members.

The data indicates that—not surprisingly—teachers, whatever the region or metropolitan area, are more strike-prone than the general public or members of the educational governing bodies (with the exception of the Northeast, where the mass public is actually more tolerant than teachers). Also, it is usually the case (the Midwest being the sole exception) that the mass public is more tolerant than school boards which, in turn, are more tolerant than superintendents. Obviously, the atmosphere in which teachers' demands are raised becomes more hostile as the environment becomes more immediate. It is frequently asserted that teachers strikes are impractical politically because of intense public hostility. However, our data indicate that the general public is, to a substantial degree, more sympathetic than school board members and superintendents, the latter forming a particularly impregnable roadblock.

Administrative Response: A Digression

It is perhaps understandable that superintendents are so hostile to teachers strikes. They are responsible for the smooth operation of public schools and strikes certainly rock the boat. However, there is more to it than this. American public education is geared toward the concept of the teacher as the *employee*, rather than the professional (Corwin, 1966). It is certainly true that the "official" doctrines of educational administration stress "participation" and "democracy" but the official ideology and the long-established norms are at variance. Essentially, administration recognizes the need to consult with "their" staffs, but find it extraordinarily difficult to think of "their" teachers as exercising independent political judgment. If one reads the numerous journals published by and for school administrators, one gets the impression that teacher militancy is a contagious disease that only an enlightened administrator can cope with. Above all, administrators seem clear in their assertion that they have final authority. Authority is a very important concept in education administration, no matter how much the official ideology has shifted (Goldhammer, et al., 1967). The increase in teacher strikes can be interpreted as a challenge to traditional authority as much as a demand for higher wages, and it is this challenge which contributes so much to the negativism of superintendents. There is a vast distinction between *noblesse oblige* and equal political bargaining, a distinction which has escaped educational administrators.

To illustrate this point, let us digress briefly to another matter. We wish to make the point that there is a strong relationship between a non-militant attitude and perception of administrative support. In Table 6-3, we return exclusively to the teacher sample and present an index of perceived administrative support. Teachers were also asked if they thought they ought to have more to say about how the school was run. As we can see, there is a relation between wanting to have a greater voice and perception of hostility on the part of the administrators. Roughly twice as many of those who do *not* seek more authority score higher on the index of perceived administrative support in comparison to the more activist-oriented teachers. The point is that there is an

Table 6-3

Attitude Toward Teachers' Participation in School Decision-Making and Perception of Administrative Support

| | Perception of Administrative Support | | | |
	Low	Medium	High	N
Teachers should have more to say	36	40	24	201
Teachers should not have more to say	18	35	47	139

association between perception of administrative support and "safe" behavior. Teachers with an activist orientation risk administrative sanction (Jennings and Zeigler, 1969).

We can gain additional insight into the behavior of administrators by returning to Table 6-2. Among both the mass public and teachers, the expected relationships can be found. There is greater support for strikes in the Northeast and West, and in the large cities. However, these relationships are blurred considerably among school board members and especially superintendents. Considering superintendents, their support for strikes is lowest in big cities and in the Northeast, the very area where teachers are likely to be the most militant.

Whereas mass public are relatively tolerant, and teachers relatively militant—in response perhaps to the cultural values characteristic of such areas—superintendent attitudes appear remarkably stable. Strategically, teachers would stand to gain more from appeals to the public than from approaches to a supposedly "enlightened" administrative cadre.

Indeed, structural factors contributing to arbitrary administrative decision making go a long way toward helping us understand the aspirations of teachers. Consider, for example, the tenure system. The more administrative direction, the greater the number of strike-prone teachers. In Table 6-4, we have classified the school district according to the tenure system.

Table 6-4
Tenure Systems and Proportion of Teachers Favorable Toward Strikes

Tenure System	% of Teachers Favorable Toward Strikes	N
1. None	35	84
2. Administrative discretion	71	10
3. Administrative discretion after specified number of years	42	38
4. Automatic after specified number of years	43	207

As the table suggests, it is better to have *no* tenure system than to have one in which administrative discretion is the sole criterion. When this is the case, there is overwhelming support for strikes. The low proportion of teachers favoring strikes in non-tenure systems also suggests the ever present role of administrators. Given the total absence of job security, striking is risky business indeed. The lessons for administrators seem fairly clear: the more unrestrained authority, the greater the militancy of teachers, providing there is a tenure decision to be made. To this conclusion we should add that superintendents typically do *not* view tenure decisions as the responsibility of teachers, tending to restrict collective bargaining agreements, where possible, to salaries and other working conditions.

The Role of Occupational Expectations

In the preceding section, I demonstrated the impact of forces extra-individual in nature. But just as a teacher's perspectives are shaped by his environment, so may he also respond to conditions of his occupational training and career patterns. One such variable is length of time teaching. If we conceive of the occupation as a socializing influence, then it is logical to assume that there is a developing congruence of values between the individual and the occupational role he plays. Even though a person may work to change the occupation to suit his conception, there is a strong tendency to either leave an occupation or adjust to the demands. It is instructive, therefore, to think of a career in terms of its stages (Hall, 1958). Also, as he passes through these career stages, the teacher will learn more clearly what is expected of him (Becker, 1953). Guba and his associates found that such personality characteristics as need for deference and order are substantially more exaggerated in more experienced teachers (Guba, et al., 1963). In view of these findings we can adopt an explicit hypothesis concerning the relationships between length of time teaching and attitude toward strikes: the longer a person remains in the teaching role the less he will sanction strikes.

Having based one variable upon the assumption that a career socializes its occupant after entrance, we base the next upon the assumption that differential patterns of recruitment and training are operative within a career. With this in mind we will examine the undergraduate background of teachers, distinguishing among five majors: education, social studies, history, the social sciences, and "other" subjects. The distinction between social science majors and "social studies" majors is crucial. Among the former are the classic social science disciplines of political science, economics, sociology, psychology and anthropology. Teachers with social studies backgrounds ordinarily majored in that area—as opposed, for example, to English or mathematics—as a specialty in their preparation for a teaching career.

The choice of an education major implies that such students have chosen the most direct route to the classroom. Similarly, the social studies majors come primarily from teachers colleges and divisions. Both are more likely to be profession-oriented than those who elect other majors and different types of instruction. In addition, the education and social studies majors probably begin the acquisition of professional norms at an earlier stage. They encounter less of the "fads and frills" of the usual college communities and are exposed to a more uniform set of values. Thus, Guba, et al., found that teachers college students had developed a need pattern not unlike that of teachers with at least ten years service (Guba, et al., 1963). We, therefore, hypothesize that teachers who majored in education and the social studies will be less strike-prone in comparison to teachers who majored in other fields.

We should also assess the effect of graduate training. It may be argued that having a M.A. versus a B.A. would broaden the teacher's conception of what is legitimate behavior because the teacher will feel more assured of his own status. It is also true that those obtaining an M.A. displayed enough aggressive behavior to earn that degree and may, therefore, be more disposed toward aggressive behavior generally. On the other hand, it might be argued that M.A. holders will be super-representatives of the profession and will consequently be less aggressive.

In addition to these variables we should consider organizational membership (e.g., NEA, AFT or none) and sex. Concerning the former, the NEA has traditionally been more conservative than the AFT with regard to strikes, although the older, larger, NEA has recently become more militant in response to competition from the AFT. While this paper is not the place for a detailed account of the rival philosophies of the two organizations, some brief comments may help us to develop some hypotheses. The AFT official policy is to use the strike when necessary. NEA, while not having an unequivocal no-strike policy, is clearly evocative of a philosophy of cooperation rather than conflict (although NEA local organizations have authorized strikes). It has relied upon the code of ethics to deter strikes by demanding observance of teachers' contracts, and has relied upon professional sanction as a resource in case of an impasse between school board and teachers. Significantly, the NEA welcomes administrators into the organization and has traditionally placed them in top leadership positions (however, teachers are now assuming more formal authority). The AFT excludes administrators from membership (Rosenthal, 1969; Stinnet, 1968). It is relatively simple to hypothesize, therefore, that AFT teachers will be more strike-prone than their counterparts in the NEA. Further, since both teachers organizations can be classified as (within the limitations noted) for and against the strike, we suggest that those teachers without an organizational membership will fall between these two extremes with regard to the appropriateness of strikes.

Once a numerically female-dominated occupation, teaching is becoming less so. However, the residual effects of the female character remains. There has been an increase in the percentage of male teachers, resulting from both an intentional effort to recruit men and lower male turnover rate. Today, men constitute a majority of senior high school teachers. The increase in male teachers should have specific implications for the occurrence of strikes. Men are generally less satisfied with their jobs (Zeigler, 1967). They are expected to play a subservient role to administrators and are paid what is essentially a woman's wage. Male teachers are also trapped in a vocational dilemma. The only avenue for advancement is through administration, yet there are naturally few administrative positions available. These conditions lead us to predict that male teachers will be more strike-prone than female teachers.

In the following table, we have set forth the simple relationships between the above variables and attitudes toward strikes, reserving for later the discussion of the interaction of the variables with each other and with the community linked variables.

Table 6-5
Relationship between Occupational Characteristics and Attitude toward Strikes

	% Favoring Strikes	N
Years teaching		
0-4	32	67
5-9	58	89
10-19	44	100
20 +	29	85
Undergraduate major		
Education	33	18
Social studies	35	84
History	49	104
Social science	47	30
Other	43	82
Education level		
B.A.	37	172
M.A.	47	167
Organization membership		
Neither	63	33
AFT	68	26
NEA	36	274
Both	67	6
Sex		
Male	41	252
Female	45	87

As we can see from Table 6-5, *most* of the hypotheses are supported, the exception being the relation of sex to attitude toward strikes. Increasing experience dampens the ardor of teachers: the longer one teaches the more conservative one becomes, although the association is not monotonic. What happens is that the least and most experienced teachers are more conservative, with the in-between categories, especially those teachers with five to nine years experience being most strike-prone. Whether this pattern comes about because of differential career dropout rates, generational changes in the teaching profession, or the socialization process is not easily resolved with the data at hand. At any rate, there is clearly no argument in support of the traditional folklore that experience and reticence go hand in hand. The "sophomore surge" lends itself to another interpretation. Beginning teachers are unsure of their status and of the norms of the profession. They are thus reluctant to engage in any but the most conservative kinds of behavior. However, as the situation becomes more clearly defined, expressive behavior increases until the conservative influences of the teaching profession take root. It can be argued from these data that the role of teaching is not merely an artifact of age, for if this were the case, the decline should be monotonic. The absence of a monotonic pattern lends credence to our argument that there is a period between uncertainty and the onset of stricter institutional expectations when the militancy of teachers is at its peak.

It was initially hypothesized that the educational background of teachers would affect their behavior primarily because of the process of selective recruitment. The aspirations and motivations of teachers with education and social studies undergraduate major should differ from those with other kinds of majors; and those teachers who have some graduate training should display attitudes fundamentally different from those who had none. An examination of the table indicates that the educational background of teachers is strongly related to their attitude toward strikes. As predicted, education and social studies majors are substantially more restrained in their orientation. By comparison, the history and social science teachers are substantially more militant.

Although it cannot be demonstrated here, our interpretation is that both the major and the type of institution at which the teacher matriculated have a bearing on these differences. To be sure, there are probably self-selection features distinguishing the teacher attending certain schools and adopting certain majors. Our contention is that these differences are likely to be reinforced and elaborated during the college years. Social science and history majors receive more of the liberal arts slant and typically matriculate at liberal arts colleges and universities. Social studies and education majors receive training that reflects the conservatism of the profession and, in addition, are often trained in normals, teacher colleges, and education schools.

What is the effect of graduate training upon attitudes toward strikes? As we can see, there is a connection between level of educational attainment and attitude toward strikes. An immediate question is the relation of educational attainment with attitude toward strikes where other variables—particularly undergraduate major—are taken into account. But for the moment it is sufficient to point out that possessing the M.A. seems to give the teacher more confidence and aggressiveness.

In spite of the growing militancy of the NEA, our data indicate that membership in this organization drastically restricts the existence of a strike-prone attitude. AFT members, non-organization members, and—few as they are—members of both organizations are substantially more tolerant of the strike. The NEA concept of "professionalism"—which should be clearly distinguished from the "militant professional" as outlined by Corwin (Corwin, 1965)—is a fundamental tenet of NEA ideology. The fundamental distinction is one of status versus procedure. According to the NEA, striking is an unprofessional *procedure* because it is one borrowed from the working class, and pits teachers against administrators. According to the AFT, one cannot be professional without authority to exercise their judgment in the area of their competence. The strike is a procedure which will help teachers to attain true professional status. As explained by Selden (1966, p. 69), "When you are in a fight you use the best weapons at your command. Very often the best weapon is to stop work; strike."

What is intriguing is that not only do AFT members appear more strike-prone, but also those who belong to *no* organization are more strike-prone. It might be argued that it is more the negative influence of the NEA than the positive influence of the AFT which is contributing most to the disparity in attitudes.

The Interaction of the Variables

One puzzling aspect of these findings is the absence of a difference in attitude between men and women. We had predicted a more militant stance on the part of men, but such is not the case. However, before we abandon the role of men and women entirely, we should examine the interplay of occupational factors to see if some other factors are muting possible differences between males and females.

Before dealing with this question, a more general statement of the interplay of occupational factors is in order. One question of immediate interest is whether the strong differences according to undergraduate majors are exacerbated or erased by the effects of graduate training. Table 6-6 indicates some opposing patterns. History and social science majors show very little of the liberating effect of an advanced degree (indeed, for history majors the essential pattern is reversed). However, for education majors an advanced degree appears to be quite liberating. In general, a control for highest degree tends to obliterate (at the level of M.A.) the difference between majors. When the education major has acquired an advanced degree, his orientation is quite similar to that of social science and history majors. Perhaps more education increases self-esteem, so that the more educated teacher feels more confident of his worth and more inclined to engage in behavior which will force others to recognize his worth.

Another way of getting at this notion of increased self-esteem is to examine the interaction between length of time teaching and undergraduate major. Contrary to what might be expected, increasing teaching experience extracts a greater toll from the strike-proneness of M.A.s (gamma = −.23) than B.A.s (gamma = −.13). Favorable attitudes toward strikes among M.A.s declines more with experience than it does among B.A.s. Further, while this finding should not obscure the fact that M.A.s are still more generally strike-prone, there are some interesting expectations, as Table 6-6 indicates.

M.A.s actually begin their career with a less favorable attitude toward strikes

Table 6-6
Attitude Toward Strikes and Undergraduate Majors, by Highest Degree Obtained

Undergraduate Major and Highest Degree	% Favoring Strikes	N
Education		
B.A.	0	5
M.A.	47	13
Social Studies		
B.A.	32	53
M.A.	39	31
History		
B.A.	53	50
M.A.	46	54
Social Science		
B.A.	46	11
M.A.	48	19
Other		
B.A.	33	46
M.A.	55	36

than do B.A.s, but undergo a more radical change in attitude. Further, a favorable attitude toward strikes lasts well into the 10-19 year range of teaching experience before suffering a decline. Then there is a more extreme shift in the attitude of M.A.s. Perhaps they begin their career with more expectations—given their investment—than do B.A.s, but become more intensely disillusioned.

In the final portion of the sections dealing with the interaction of occupational variables we will consider the relation of sex to the previously discussed variables, eliminating organizational membership as a control because of the small number of AFT teachers.

It will be recalled that the difference between male and female teachers was slight. However, if we examine the attitudes of teachers controlling for length of time teaching, undergraduate majors and highest degree obtained, more appreciable differences appear. For instance, males who majored in either education or social studies are a good deal *less* strike-prone than females, although the prediction lies in the other direction. In other undergraduate majors, there is no appreciable difference. Further, while—as we know—education and social studies majors are the least strike-prone, this generalization does not hold true for women who have elected these majors. It would seem, then, that the recruitment and socialization process in education schools is particularly debilitating for males.

On the other hand, the acquisition of an advanced degree is more liberating for males than for females. As we can see, the acquisition of a master's degree does virtually nothing to change the perspective of female teachers.

Table 6-7
Attitude toward Strikes of Male and Female Teachers, by Highest Degree Obtained

	Degree			
	B.A.		M.A.	
	% Favoring Strikes	N	% Favoring Strikes	N
Sex				
Male	33	112	47	140
Female	46	61	43	27

Female attitudes are—judging from these data—somewhat more *stable* than male attitudes. They seem to fluctuate less with the job situation. Perhaps the male, with (at least in the majority of cases), more of an investment in the career, the job situation proves to be more significant.

If we examine the effect of the teaching experience upon males and females, this notion is given additional support.

Table 6-8
Length of Time Teaching and Attitude toward Strikes, by Sex

Years Teaching	Male		Female	
	% Favoring Strikes	N	% Favoring Strikes	N
0-4	27	54	55	13
5-9	59	69	57	20
10-19	41	88	58	19
20 +	31	49	27	35
	gamma = .04		gamma = .38	

Here we see that the "sophomore surge" operates only for males. Females begin their teaching careers substantially more strike-prone than males, and persist in this attitude until the last category of teaching experience is attained. The larger gamma correlation for women is reflected, not of less stability in attitude, but rather of the absence of a monotonic pattern. In this table, as in our previous discussion, we find that men respond more to the vagaries of the job situation. Thus, even though they are generally not more strike-prone than females, their responses appear more volatile.

We have now considered two major classes of variables affecting the attitude of teachers toward strikes. Each apparently helps account for differing norma-tive structures, or definitions of proper behavior. But there may be interrelationships between the community and occupational characteristics that confound the apparent contributions of each set of variables. Given the initial sample size, it would be impossible to control simultaneously for even a sizeable subset of the community and occupational characteristics involved. It is possible to take at least a pair at a time, especially those variables that are most likely to be introducing a spurious note to the initial association and those that emerged as the most powerful.

It should be observed at the outset that there are a few large biases with respect to the distribution of any given occupational characteristic along a community characteristic, or vice versa. Among the most notable is the greater incident of social studies and education majors in the South and Midwest and in the medium size and non-SMSAs, and an accompanying greater incident of majors outside these fields in the West and Northeast and in the larger SMSAs. Male teachers are also more likely to be found in the West and Northeast, and in the large SMSAs. Bearing these exceptions in mind, the likelihood of spurious relations is reduced though certainly not eliminated.

It will be recalled that years of teaching was negatively related to a favorable attitude toward strikes. This association holds up when community characteristics are controlled, but there are noticeable differences. For example, according to metropolitanism the gamma coefficients are $-.41$ for large SMSAs, $-.17$ for medium SMSAs, and $-.06$ for non-SMSAs. Thus, the negative sanctions of the community depress the initial associations. On the other hand, there is an additive effect of combining these two variables. It will be recalled that the most strike-prone teachers are those with five to nine years experience and those teachers in large SMSAs. Conversely, the least strike-prone teachers are those with 20 years or more experience and those teaching in non-SMSAs. If we look at the combined effect of these variables we find 86% of the large SMSA teachers with five to nine years experience are strike-prone, compared to 21% of the non-SMSA teachers with 20 years or more experience. These percentages represent the extremes in the distribution.

Variations by region are more erratic but continued to show a negative sign. By the same token, the strong association between region and metropolitanism with support for strikes remains when length of teaching is controlled.

Similar sorts of configurations develop when other sets of controls are involved. However, of particular interest is interaction of sex with community characteristics, because the now familiar stability of female attitudes emerges once more. For the sake of brevity, let us consider the attitudes of male and female teachers by metropolitan area.

Here we see that male attitudes perform quite well according to the expectations, but female attitudes show very little change; indeed the sign of the correlation is reversed. Thus, males become more militant than females only in the urban setting.

Table 6-9
Relation of Community to Attitude toward Strikes, by Sex

| | Male | | Female | |
	% Favoring Strikes	N	% Favoring Strikes	N
Non-SMSA	26	78	50	42
Medium SMSA	44	152	40	39
Large SMSA	72	72	46	6
	gamma = .45		gamma = −.15	

Conclusions and Speculations

From these data we can draw a portrait of the typical militant: a teacher, probably male, teaching in a large metropolitan area for between five to nine years, a member of the AFT, with an undergraduate degree in history or social science and an advanced degree. Such teachers are likely to be the most "professional" in the sense that they want more money and, equally important, they want control over their occupational lives. They want to control who becomes teachers, who awards tenure, who teaches what course, what materials are used, etc. In short, they want the same rights that are normally accorded to other "professionals." It is extremely significant, as Corwin (1970, p. 326) notes, that the most frequent type of dispute in public schools concerned authority problems between teachers and administrators.

The structure of American education is not currently equipped to accept such changes. The school system remains relatively authoritarian, with teacher organizations having less power than other participants in the educational decision making process. Rosenthal's findings are instructive on this point. He writes that teacher power is meager, especially in comparison to mayors, school boards, superintendents or "whoever happens to dominate in a particular policy domain" (Rosenthal, 1969, p. 155). As Rosenthal makes clear, militancy is still so small a part of the attitude structure of the average teacher that teachers' organizations can do little to influence educational policy.

Why this is so is difficult to ascertain. Speculatively, the recruitment and occupational socialization of teachers has left the militants in the minority. The real question is whether the militants—as we have described them—will grow in number and influence. As we have seen, their occupational lives are more hazardous than those of the more quiescent teacher. The militants are a minority, but they are *not* a marginal group. We have provided a portrait of the typical militant. Corwin (1970, p. 327) reports that militants (with some minor exceptions, Corwin's militant and mine resemble each other) are among the most respected teachers, and have the support of many more teachers who are silent, but potentially active. In a sense military teachers are like militant blacks in the ghetto: a small, strategically located, and prestigious minority. If the militants do gain in influence, nothing short of radical restructuring of the educational decisional structure will satisfy their demands.

Several *caveats* concerning the last statement come to mind. First, the quest of the militant teacher for power is—like that of any interest group—a narrow quest. Militant teachers seek—in addition to increased tangible rewards—a piece of the governing action. They do *not* seek (at least organizationally) a larger voice for others (e.g., students). So we should not equate teacher militancy with the broader issues of educational reform (student participation, a more "relevant" curriculum, etc.). Indeed, the teacher militancy movement and the more general reform movement might prove to be in opposition.

It is true that teacher militancy is part of the general assault upon the "system": taxpayer revolts, civil rights demands (and counter-demands), student protests, and the demands for community control. Everybody focuses upon the same target. However, teacher militancy is a quest for teacher *authority*. While fighting a recalcitrant administration for authority, they are likely to view similar demands by other previously disfranchised groups as illegitimate. Teachers reacted negatively to the Ford Foundation proposal to decentralize the governance of New York City's public schools because they viewed it as a threat to their authority. New York City's teachers, organized by the A.F.L., are (comparatively speaking) militant. I doubt that the civil rights organization urging community control *viewed* them as anything less than reactionary.

Teacher reaction to student demands—another threat to authority—has been generally hostile. As Corwin (1970, p. 344) notes: "the more militant teachers appeared to be less oriented toward students and more concerned instead about their colleague's opinions of them. This suggests that the quest for decision-making authority . . . [is] important to even the professionally oriented teachers than is their commitment to students' welfare." In support of these contentions, consider the conservative impact of formal organizations in society. Commenting upon this tendency to resist change, I recently noted: "This is not to suggest that organizations seek to change, but that the change they seek is minimal. If they achieve even a portion of what they wish to achieve, then they have established a stake in the ongoing system and have a rational basis for moderate politics" (Dye and Zeigler, 1970, p. 212). Organizations such as, for instance, labor, typically begin with radical goals but ultimately become more change resistant with success and age. Today's militants who strike terror into the hearts of school boards and superintendents might become part of tomorrow's "establishment," thus starting another cycle of demands and accommodation to demands.

References

Corwin, Ronald G., "Militant Professionalism, Initiative and Compliance in Public Education," *Sociology of Education*, 38 (1965), pp. 310-330.

Corwin, Ronald G., *Staff Conflict in the Public Schools* (U.S. Department of Health, Education, and Welfare, 1966).

Corwin, Ronald G., *Militant Professionalism: A Study of Organizational Conflict in High Schools*, (Appleton-Century-Crofts: New York, N.Y., 1970).

Dye, Thomas R. and Harmon Zeigler, *The Irony of Democracy* (Belmont: Wadsworth Publishing Co., 1970).

Goldhammer, Keith, John E. Suttle, William D. Aldridge, and Gerald Becker, *Issues and Problems in Contemporary Educational Administration* (U.S. Department of Health, Education, and Welfare, 1967).

Guba, Egon G., Philip W. Jackson, and Charles E. Bidwell, "Occupational Choice and the Teaching Career," in W.W. Charters, Jr., and A.L. Gaze, eds., *Readings in the Social Psychology of Education* (Boston: Allyn and Bacon, 1963), pp. 271-278.

Hall, Oswald, "The Stages of a Medical Career," *American Journal of Sociology*, 52 (1958), pp. 327-336.

Jennings, M. Kent, and Harmon Zeigler, "The Politics of Teacher-Administrator Relations," *Education and Social Science*, 1 (1969), pp. 73-82.

Jennings, M. Kent, and Harmon Zeigler, "Political Expressivism Among High School Teachers," in Roberta S. Sigel, ed., *Learning About Politics: A Reader in Political Socialization* (New York: Random House, 1970), pp. 434-453.

National Education Association, "Teacher Strikes and Work Stoppages," January 1940 to July 1968," *Research Memo* (November, 1968).

Rosenthal, Alan, *Pedagogues and Power: Teacher Groups in School Politics*, (Syracuse: Syracuse University Press, 1969).

Selden, David, "Professionalism," in Patricia Cayo Sexton, ed., *Readings on the School in Society* (Englewood Cliffs: Prentice-Hall, 1967), pp. 66-70.

Stinnett, T.M., *Turmoil in Teaching*, (New York: Macmillan, 1968).

Stouffer, Samuel, *Communism, Conformity, and Civil Liberties* (New York: Wiley, 1966).

Zeigler, Harmon, *The Political Life of American Teachers* (Englewood Cliffs: Prentice-Hall, 1967).

7

School Finance Policy for the Next Decade

Erick L. Lindman

School finance policy changes from year to year not so much because better solutions are found for old problems but because the problems change. Society makes new demands upon the schools. Patterns of taxation change and governmental responsibility shifts from one level to another. Perhaps the most significant recent change is the erosion of public confidence in educational institutions which occurred during the decade of the 1960s.

The common school system concentrating upon the three R's and avoiding religious controversy is an indigenous American institution. It sought to serve all the children in the community in one school. The system flourished during a period of intense sectarian religious controversy and did much to overcome the divisiveness of this controversy.

The common schools achieved their mission with notable success. Except for the racially segregated schools in the South and the parochial schools maintained by the Roman Catholic Church, the neighborhood schools dominated American education for more than a hundred years. They were regarded by many as an essential part of the American dream of equal opportunity for all.

Yet today this institution is under continuous attack. Parents blame the schools for the low test scores made by their children. Sociologists conduct surveys and conclude that the schools are ineffective. Courts find the neighborhood schools and the local school property tax to be unconstitutional.

Civil rights groups find the school administrators to be bureaucratic and insensitive to their needs. Economists point out that the public school system is a tax-supported monopoly lacking the stimulation that comes from competition. Devout supporters of church-related schools charge that the godless public schools fail to teach moral and spiritual values to the oncoming generations. This chorus of criticism causes teachers to close ranks and to become more militant, which, in turn, alienates more public school supporters.

This is the condition of the public schools today. If one were to believe the critics, instead of proposing ways to finance their continued operation, it would be more timely to seek sufficient funds for their burial and then proceed to develop a plan to finance a new school system suitable for the 1980s. Whether we anticipate substantial change in the nature of America's schools or whether we expect them to remain much as they have been in the past, in either event we must face up to the school finance policies that will in many respects shape the development of the schools in the decades ahead.

New Demands Upon the Schools

Established state programs for financing public schools are not responding effectively to the new demands placed upon the schools. Perhaps the most fundamental new demand placed upon the public schools since 1954 is that they should lead, not follow, in the development of a racially integrated society. In this role, the schools are fostering a social policy which, in many instances, differs from the social policy advocated and believed in by a substantial part of the adult community. Under these conditions, the divided electorate is less likely to vote taxes for the support of the increasing cost of public schools.

There is also the demand that the public schools broaden their scope of services to compensate for deficiencies in the home and community, and to protect children from parental ineffectiveness and neglect. This has called forth expensive programs in compensatory and remedial education which have proved to be less effective than many had hoped; now their costs seem high in relation to their overall effectiveness.

The demand for collective negotiations by teachers' organizations and the counter demand for teacher accountability by boards of education have placed new strains upon the public school system. A substantial part of the public does not enthusiastically support the idea of unionizing teachers lest the teachers become propaganda agents for organized labor. Under these conditions, people who formerly were enthusiastic supporters of the public schools may become lukewarm in their support.

Then there is a demand for greater participation in the control of schools by community groups, especially by minority groups. This has led to proposals for decentralizing the large city school systems so that parents can be more effective in influencing educational policy.

Finally, there is a demand for more schooling: nursery schools, kindergartens, a longer school year, instruction in the summertime, more post-secondary schools, a greater proportion of students attending colleges and universities, and so forth. The demand for more schooling has contributed to increasing costs, leading to taxpayer resistance and to questions concerning the value and importance of the added amount of schooling.

The stress upon the schools, created by these new demands, has focused attention upon basic weaknesses in public school governance and finance. In reacting to these new demands, school boards' responsibilities clearly exceed their authority, especially when additional funds are needed. To obtain additional funds to meet new demands placed upon the schools, the school board must seek the approval of the electorate or must appeal to state authorities or, in some instances, to city or county authorities. In such cases, the school board is held responsible for the failure of the schools to meet the new demand, but the board is not authorized to provide the needed additional funds.

In the fiscally independent schools of the West, the requirement of a vote of the people to approve higher school tax rates has led increasingly to a vicious circle. Stress and controversy tend to undermine public confidence in the schools and people vote against school taxes. This, in turn, generates more stress and controversy leading to continued lack of confidence in the schools and more defeats in school tax elections.

In the past, the public schools have been successful in appealing to the electorate for the approval of taxes for the expansion and development of the public schools. Recently, the electorate has been less willing to provide the additional taxes schools seem to need. Voter reluctance to authorize taxes for schools may be attributed, in part, to the excessive use of property taxation for public school support, placing the burden for supporting public schools upon local property owners while the benefits of education tend to be dispersed throughout the state and nation.

The Serrano Decision

Local property taxation for public schools is not only under political attack, it is also being challenged in the courts. The Serrano decision, rejecting unequal local support for public schools, provides a rationale for opposing local property taxation for public schools and adds one more challenge to present methods for financing public schools.

After reviewing disparities among school districts in assessed value of taxable property per pupil and the effects of California's foundation program for supporting public schools, the California Supreme Court points out that:

Above the foundation program minimum ($355 per elementary student and $488 per high school student), the wealth of a school district, as measured by its assessed valuation, is the major determinant of educational expenditures.

The Court then declares:

The foundation program partially alleviates the great disparities in local sources of revenue, but the system as a whole generates school revenues in proportion to the wealth of the individual district.

This statement of the Court seems to invalidate the foundation program concept as it is used in nearly all of the fifty states. For, in most states, the disparities in local sources of revenue are only partially offset by state aid, and local school districts are permitted to supplement the equalized revenues included in the foundation program with unequal local supplements derived from unequal local revenue sources. Such supplements, the California Court declared, make the "quality of a child's education a function of the wealth of his parents and neighbors." Since education is a "fundamental interest," discrimination based upon wealth violates the equal protection clause of the Fourteenth Amendment.

If this finding of the California Supreme Court is sustained, the foundation program concept, which has dominated public school finance for fifty years, can no longer be used. As we search for remedies, it is well to be aware of the strengths, as well as the weaknesses, of the foundation program concept.

Under the foundation program, equalization of public school support was sought by *gradually improving* the status of schools in the less-wealthy school districts without *reducing the quality* of school programs in the wealthy school districts. Such a process is well adapted to the inevitable compromises of the legislative process. Moreover, the school programs in the wealthy districts set the pace and create pressures for improving the basic program in all schools. But the process of equalization of school support has been *too gradual* in California and in most states. The California Supreme Court decision reflects impatience with the pace of the movement toward equalization.

On the other hand, partial equalization of financial support reflects one of the essential compromises upon which public schools rest—a balance between statewide equality of schools, on the one hand, and local option to strive for excellence on the other. Most Americans accept equal opportunity for all children and youth as a worthy, high-priority goal, but they want equality without uniformity or mediocrity. Moreover, as members of local communities, many want local control, so that they can modify the school program to meet local needs and strive to have better public schools.

The traditional American resolution of this inherent conflict has been to establish a statewide standard program for public schools and then permit local school systems to supplement this program from local tax sources. Using these local funds, the local school board could pay higher salaries to teachers, maintain smaller classes, employ more counselors, or establish kindergartens, etc. The state standard program provides the equality, and the local supplement provides the opportunity to pursue excellence.

In principle, this compromise between statewide uniformity, on the one hand, and local option, on the other, has worked reasonably well. Its acceptance depends upon the maintenance of a reasonable balance between the quality of public schooling guaranteed for all children and youth in the state, and the quality of schooling provided in the best local school systems in the state. If this gap is small, and if the state standard program is adequate, the compromise is generally accepted.

The justification for the statewide standard program to assure equal educational opportunity requires little elaboration. It is regarded as self-evident. One might challenge the standard program concept on the grounds that it implies uniformity of education, instead of equal access to suitable education. In practice, however, the state standard program is usually defined in terms of educational resources, or expenditures per pupil, allowing considerable local option in how these resources are used by the local school board.

The case for local supplementation of the state standard program is not so self-evident, since it contributes to inequalities among local school programs. It is only if one accepts the proposition that these inequalities provide an element essential for progress and improvement in public schools that the argument for local option becomes apparent. Most of the improvements in public schools, over the years, have been initiated as local supplemental programs in city school systems, financed from the local property taxes. For example, kindergartens were first introduced in a few city school systems. Now, in many states, including California, kindergartens are included in the state-financed program for all children throughout the state. Thus, the power to provide local tax funds to supplement the state standard program has been a vehicle through which community aspiration for better schools generated school improvement. After these improvements have been in effect for a few years, and their effectiveness generally accepted, they have often been included in the state standard program for all children.

The argument for local supplementation of the state standard program rests, primarily, upon the need for a vehicle through which improvements and innovations can be made, but an obvious weakness of this approach is that local tax resources are not equally available to all local school systems. Some have concentrations of valuable taxable property, and a relatively low tax rate produces ample funds for costly local supplemental programs. Others have no taxable industrial property and residents with only modest taxable incomes, requiring prohibitively high tax rates to finance these same supplementary programs.

Since virtually any local tax—property, income, or sales—would produce unequal amounts per pupil, the use of local non-property taxes are also proscribed by the Court's decision. The Court does not discuss inequalities in expenditure rates per pupil, which result from the unwillingness of local school boards, or the electorate, to approve higher school tax rates. Presumably, inequalities in expenditure rates per pupil, due to voter preferences, equally violate the equal protection clause of the Fourteenth Amendment.

In analyzing the options under the Serrano decision, it is necessary to identify, quite precisely, three distinctly different degrees of state participation in the financing and operation of public schools. These three basic patterns may be summarized as follows:

The foundation program approach has been the dominant guiding principle of public school finance for some fifty years. Under this principle, a basic or minimum level of public school support is defined by the state and assured for each local district. State funds are added to the proceeds of a prescribed local school tax rate, so that the sum of these two amounts produces the state-guaranteed level of school support. Under ideal conditions, this approach results in equal support for the basic program in all school districts of the state and requires for this program a uniform local property tax rate.

Authority to supplement the state basic program from local tax sources, however, produces inequalities in school operating funds, reflecting not only the willingness of school districts to levy additional taxes for school purposes, but also differences in the value of taxable property per student. The foundation program approach seeks to establish an equal basic program, but permits unequal supplementation of this program by local school districts.

Complete state support of public schools implies elimination of authority to supplement the state-established program from local tax sources. Under this approach, the state basic program would be increased to an adequate level, and the local school board would be required to operate schools within its allotment of state funds.

Such a plan would, of course, eliminate inequalities in school programs which are due to inequalities in the school property tax base and to the willingness of school districts to levy higher taxes for school purposes. Inequalities resulting from other causes, however, would be unaffected by this change.

State operation of public schools would substantially reduce the operational responsibilities of local school boards. An expanded State Department of Education would employ teachers, assign them to local schools, purchase and distribute school supplies, etc. School boards, if retained, would serve in an advisory capacity and as a communication link between the State Department of Education and the citizens in each community. Their powers and responsibilities, with respect to the adoption of budgets and tax rates, would, of course, disappear.

Under the state operation plan, school tax rates would be fully equalized and the school program would be more nearly equal. Undoubtedly, some communities would be more fortunate in the quality of teachers and school administrators assigned to them. Moreover, some might be more successful than others in getting their school needs recognized by the State Department of Education.

Although there are many differences between complete state support and state operation of schools, they have, in common, the elimination of the local school property tax and the equalization of school tax rates.

Perhaps the most obvious result of complete state support, or of state operation of schools, would be the equalization of school tax burdens. Even if the legislature chose to continue property taxes for the support of schools, there would be a uniform statewide school property tax rate. The proceeds from this tax would be combined with other state tax revenues to provide sufficient funds to operate all schools in the state. Since no supplementary funds could be raised from local sources, all taxpayers in the state would contribute for the support of schools on exactly the same basis.

Even more significant for the future of public education would be the elimination of the right of a local community to tax itself to meet school problems unrecognized by the state legislature, or to pursue educational excellence. Especially vulnerable under the full state funding plan would be the large city school systems, whose peculiar needs are often ignored by state legislatures. If the city school systems were denied the right to use local property taxation, they would encounter great difficulty in maintaining their complex and expensive educational programs.

Although there is a basic American preference for local control of governmental services, the local property tax does not win many popularity contests at this time—even if the rival contestants are the sales and income taxes. Under these conditions, a trade may be in the making, sacrificing local pursuit of excellence for a greater statewide equality of educational opportunity. Before such a trade is made, the inherent difficulties of equalizing educational opportunity need to be examined.

Equalization of school tax burdens could be achieved quite simply by placing all school monies in a state fund and eliminating the local property tax for schools. However, the task of equalizing educational opportunity for all children in the state presents a much more difficult problem.

There are several definitions of equal educational opportunity; some of them are:

1. *Equal educational opportunity is achieved if all students are exposed to an identical educational program.* Although the word *equal* suggests *identical* programs, this definition must be rejected. No one would suggest that equal medical service implies the same medical treatment for all patients. Similarly, educational treatments must reflect the needs and talents of students.
2. *Equal educational opportunity is achieved if all schools serving the same grade levels expend the same amount per pupil each year for current purposes, exclusive of pupil transportation.* This definition has been used for the development of most foundation programs throughout the nation. It is inadequate, however, because it fails to recognize unavoidable cost differences encountered in different school districts for different types of students. Suitable education for physically-handicapped children, for vocational students, for students with special talents, and for students in need of compensatory education does not cost the same as that for "average" students.
3. *Equal educational opportunity is achieved if all schools serving the same grade levels have an equal number of pupils per professional staff member, and professional staff members are paid in accordance with a uniform salary schedule.* This definition is essentially a refinement of the second definition and is substantially achieved within the boundaries of school systems. Yet, we are all aware of the limitations of this definition. Even if the racial composition of schools were "balanced," there would still be differences in resources needed to provide suitable education for different students.

4. *Equal educational opportunity is achieved if state funds are allocated among schools, so as to provide additional teaching resources for pupils whose achievement test scores are substantially below established norms.* This definition reflects the growing concern for compensatory and remedial education. It suggests that equality of educational opportunity should be measured by student performance. Such a goal could lead to neglect of students with special talents.

5. *Equal educational opportunity is achieved if all students have equal access to educational programs suited to their needs and talents.* Although this definition is the most difficult to implement, it must guide educational planning in the years ahead. The other definitions have been useful in the past, but they fall short of an acceptable ideal for American education.

In the light of these definitions, would the elimination of the local property tax as a supplementary source of school funds facilitate or hinder the pursuit of equal educational opportunity for all? Such elimination may well facilitate the achievement of equal educational opportunity, as implied by definitions one, two, three, and possibly four; however, implementation of the fifth definition would likely be hindered. Without a local tax to supplement programs financed from state and federal sources, local adaptation of school programs would be difficult. Experimentation with innovative school procedures would be drastically limited if always dependent upon state or federal appropriations.

These facts indicate that if, in the search for educational opportunity, we actually eliminate the right of local school boards to levy a local school tax, we may, indeed, destroy an important dynamic element in the public school system and, incidentally, not achieve very much equalization of educational opportunity of the kind we need in the years ahead—equal access to suitable education.

A Programmatic Approach to School Finance

The foundation program concept which has served America so well for the past four decades is no longer adequate because of its exclusive concern with minimum levels of expenditure and its tendency to obscure the great variety in the scope of educational services needed in local school systems. Moreover, equal school expenditure per pupil is no longer accepted as an adequate definition of equal educational opportunity. Instead, the schools are expected to examine each child's educational needs and provide an individualized program, even though the programs differ greatly in cost.

Under this approach, equal expenditure per pupil is not sought; instead, an effort is made to give all students equal access to educational programs suited to their needs and talents.

If this definition of equal educational opportunity is accepted, then the school finance plan must provide for greater variation of instructional programs within and among school districts. Most of the existing foundation programs fail to provide adequately for needed program variation.

In the development of systems for financing public schools during the decade ahead, optional supplemental programs will play a more important role. In the past, special or categorical aids have been regarded as necessary evils by most school administrators because of the constraints they place on the budgetary process and because of their burdensome administrative concomitants.

Appropriating agencies, however, like their clarity of purpose. Unlike general support, categorical aids seem to assure legislators that, for a relatively small appropriation, substantial program improvement will be achieved. For this reason, categorical aids tend to proliferate.

The problem, then, is to retain their clarity of purpose and avoid their administrative constraints and burdens. This can be achieved by consolidating existing categorical aids into fewer programs with broader purposes.

Moreover, proper emphasis upon the extra costs of supplemental programs should go a long way toward solving the school finance problem of large cities. This emphasis, along with appropriate recognition of the municipal overburden when the local taxpaying capacity of a city school system is determined, should lead to a solution of the problem of financing schools in the urban centers.

In the decade ahead, there will be more emphasis upon evaluation of school programs. For specially aided supplemental programs, the evaluation process will take on a new significance. While the basic program is subject to modification and improvement, it cannot be terminated. However, if a specially aided supplemental program is not producing results in a local school system, the aid for such a program may well be discontinued.

In the past, "process standards" have been established in an effort to assure quality. For example, to be eligible for state aid for special education, school districts are often required to employ a teacher with special training and maintain a prescribed small class size. In the future, evidence concerning "program accomplishments" may replace process standards in determining whether or not state aid for the program is continued. Increased emphases upon cost-effectiveness is expected to become an important element in schol support systems of the 1970s, requiring new techniques and procedures.

These concerns, along with the need to communicate effectively with the state legislature, suggest that the state support for public school systems should be related to identifiable programs that the legislature can understand and evaluate. It is suggested that the programs be as follows:

1. The Standard Elementary Program
2. The Standard Secondary Program
3. Pre-First Grade Education
4. Summer School Education
5. Vocational Education
6. Special and compensatory Education
7. Adult Education

In addition to these seven instructional programs, three student service programs are proposed:

1. Health and Guidance Services
2. Food Services
3. Pupil Transportation Services

For each of these programs, goals and objectives should be formulated along with criteria for assessing the program's effectiveness. For example, the purpose of the summer school education might be: (1) to provide for children who have failed a course an opportunity to make it up during the summer, (2) to provide special advanced instruction for gifted students who show talents for school work substantially beyond that available in the regular school program, and (3) to provide typing for students who want one course in it for personal use. If these are the objectives of a summer school program, then it should be possible to report, at the end of the year, the number of students who completed the courses and how well they did in these courses. With such a report, the legislature should be able to determine whether or not its investment in summer school education is a sound one. Similar objectives should be spelled out for each program.

The allotted amounts may be paid in full from state tax sources, or the cost of each program may be shared between the state and the local educational agency. The cost sharing arrangement is justified not only by historical precedent, but also by the decision making processes involved. If the state-supported educational program is to be essentially the same in all school districts, there is little need for a local contribution. However, if options are offered to school districts calling for increased state contributions, then there is need for a corresponding increase in the local contribution.

It is assumed that the state will define and require a standard or basic elementary and secondary school program in all local educational agencies. In addition, the state will partially support optional programs supplementary to the required standard program.

For example, the standard program might include a 180-day school year and the optional program might be a six-weeks summer session for the purposes already enumerated. Under the cost sharing arrangement, a school district which chose to operate the optional six weeks summer session would be required to contribute part of the additional cost from local tax sources. The rest of the additional cost of the summer session would be contributed from state sources.

This arrangement offers some options to school districts and requires the people in a district which chooses the more expensive options to contribute part of the additional cost. State-wide uniformity is required for the standard program, but not for the supplementary optional programs.

Equalized Matching Grants

An essential tool for implementing a programmatic approach to school finance is the equalized matching or percentage grant. Under this cost sharing arrangement, a matching ratio or reimbursement percentage is computed for each local educational agency, based upon its taxable wealth per student.

The formula used for this purpose is derived directly from the subtracted local share concept, and may take many specific forms. Two formulas for computing the percent of the cost of an optional program to be paid from state sources are shown for illustrative purposes. To simplify the writing of these formulas, a variable, Q, is defined as follows:

$$Q = \frac{\text{Assessed valuation per pupil in a district}}{\text{State average assessed valuation per pupil}}$$

where the ratio of assessed to true value of property has been equalized on a statewide basis.

Thus, for a school district of "average wealth," where the assessed valuation per pupil equals the corresponding state average, Q equals 1.

Using this definition of Q, two equalized percentage grant formulas are shown below:

$$\text{State Percent} = \frac{2 - Q}{2} \tag{1}$$

$$\text{State Percent} = \frac{3 - Q}{3 + Q} \tag{2}$$

It will be noted that, under each of these formulas, the state would contribute 50% of the cost of the optional program to a school district of average wealth. The formulas differ not in the average contribution rates but rather in the extent to which they equalize school property tax rates in school districts which maintain similar programs. This fact is illustrated by the following table:

Table 7-1
Percent of Program Costs Reimbursed by the State Under Suggested Formulas

Value of Q	Percent from State under Formula: 1	2
0	100%	100%
1/4	87	85
1/2	75	71
1	50	50
1-1/2	25	33
2	0	20
3	0	0

In addition to these two formulas there are, of course, an infinite number of other formulas that are possible. The selection of a formula depends primarily upon answers to two questions: (1) What percent of the cost of the program should the state contribute to a school district of average wealth? and (2) How much should the state contribute to school districts which are above average in wealth per pupil?

Under formula 1, it will be noted that a school district in which the assessed valuation per pupil equals twice the state average would receive no contribution from the state. On the other hand, under formula 2, such a school district would be entitled to a state contribution equal to 20% of the approved cost of the supplementary program.

These formulas illustrate possible equalized matching or percentage grant formulas which can be used to share the cost of school programs. This system, including both the mandated standard program and jointly-financed optional programs, provides a broader, more flexible plan for financing schools in the decade ahead. The mandated standard elementary and secondary school programs could be financed entirely from state sources, including funds derived from state-wide property taxes. However, the optional programs should be jointly financed so that the beneficiaries of the more costly programs contribute part of the additional cost from local tax sources.

This plan assures a standard program in every community paid from taxes borne uniformly by all taxpayers in the state. It also authorizes supplemental programs for local option. In either case, the legislature can readily see what the funds are to be used for. This is the kind of state support program needed in the 1970s.

Federal Aids for Public Schools

Since the founding of the Republic, the Federal role in education has been the subject of recurring controversy. While Congress is empowered to "levy and collect taxes . . . for the common defense and general welfare of the United States," education of the people is not one of the enumerated powers of the Federal Government. Accordingly, for many years, there was serious doubt about the authority of the Congress to appropriate funds for the purpose of educating the people of the respective states.

In recent years, this restrictive view of the powers of the Federal Government in the field of education has changed. The general welfare clause has been interpreted broadly enough to permit effective participation in the field of education by the Federal Government. Constitutional authority, however, did not immediately usher in a period of effective participation in education by the Federal Government. Instead, it ushered in a prolonged debate concerning the proper role of the Federal Government in the field of education.

In this debate, advocates of general purpose grants-in-aid were pitted against those who advocated special purposes or categorical aids for education. Prior to 1960, most educators advocated Federal general support for public schools. They emphasized the need for general purpose grants to states to supplement state and local school tax revenues. They sought to minimize Federal direction and control of the educational process.

Despite these recommendations for general purpose grants for public education, Federal participation in education during the past fifteen years has moved sharply toward categorical grants for narrowly defined educational purposes. Although state and local taxpayers contribute more than 90 percent of the cost of operating public elementary and secondary schools, the Federal Government exercises extensive control over various facets of the public school program through an amazingly complex assortment of categorical aids. A recent publication entitled, "Guide to OE-Administered Programs, Fiscal Year 1970," in which the U.S. Office of Education listed 132 programs, reveals how far we have gone down the categorical aid route.

This Federal educational policy was accepted by some as an expediency—hopefully temporary in nature—to get needed Federal dollars started. Efforts to enact laws granting Federal general purpose aid to states for public schools encountered two insurmountable roadblocks—the school segregation issue and the church-school controversy. While it is possible to design Federal categorical aids so that parochial schools receive some benefit, general purpose grants to parochial schools would probably violate the First Amendment to the U.S. Constitution.

To others, however, the new emphasis upon categorical aids for education is not a device for getting around historical roadblocks to general Federal support funds. Instead, it is part of the "necessary revolution in American education." Categorical aids are welcomed as the key to educational change.

Some Federal categorical aid programs are intended to be temporary, but, like temporary buildings, they tend to persist beyond their planned termination dates. Such categorical grants provide a financial stimulant for selected programs or items in the school budget. These grants often provide temporary aid to try out new ideas; they are not expected to become part of the continuing school support program. Title II of the Elementary and Secondary Education Act of 1965 and some of the titles of the National Defense Education Act are of this type.

On the other hand, some categorical grants are intended to finance, on a continuing basis, selected high cost school programs such as vocational education, compensatory education, and school lunches. These Federal grant programs cannot be terminated without curtailing public school programs which contribute to important national goals. The programs supported in this way are usually above average in per student cost and are often related to other concerns of the Federal Government (e.g., vocational education to full employment; compensatory education to the war on poverty).

This distinction between temporary and continuing categorical Federal grant programs suggests what the "next steps" should be. First, definite plans should be made to terminate temporary categorical aid programs and, at the same time, strengthen the general support of public schools so that funds are available to continue the improvements stimulated by temporary categorical aid grants. Second, the continuing categorical grant programs should be consolidated and streamlined, and the distribution of funds should be improved and standardized.

If temporary programs are excluded, it should be possible to consolidate continuing categorical aids into a few major "blocks" such as:

1. Vocational education programs
2. Education of children in low-income families
3. Compensation to schools for Federal tax-exempt property
4. Education of handicapped children
5. Educational research and development

Along with these consolidated continuing grants-in-aid, it is necessary to have a few temporary aid programs directed at specific national problems, such as devising better ways for schools to combat drug abuse among young people. Such temporary grants-in-aid, however, should be held to a minimum because they often lead to inefficient planning and an unjustifiable effort to become permanent.

General Purpose Grants-in-Aid to States for Education

Proposals for general purpose Federal grants-in-aid for public elementary and secondary schools have been presented to the U.S. Congress regularly for more than a third of a century. With equal regularity, the Congress has declined to enact a general support program for public schools. During recent years, however, there has been renewed interest in "block grants" for education as well as proposals to share Federal revenues with state governments. These revenue sharing proposals reflect a general concern that Federal fiscal dominance has led to a highly centralized control of public services. Revenue sharing is intended to strengthen decentralized control of state and local public services.

A Federal grant-in-aid program for the general support of public schools would accomplish most of the purposes sought from revenue sharing programs. But, in addition to accomplishing the fiscal purposes of revenue sharing, Federal general support for public schools would also assure the people of the nation that public schools in all parts of the nation were adequately financed. The case for Federal general support for public schools, therefore, rests first upon the same arguments which support revenue sharing and second upon the national need for adequately financed public schools in all parts of the nation.

The case for revenue sharing is summarized by the Advisory Commission on Intergovernmental Relations in its December 1970 publication entitled "Revenue Sharing—An Idea Whose Time Has Come." In summarizing the case for revenue sharing, the Commission points to need for strengthening the states to preserve the Federal system:

During the days of the Confederation, the federalists sought ways of strengthening the National Government without undue sacrifice of the powers of the State. Contemporary "federalists" are now searching for ways to strengthen the States and localities without undue sacrifice of National goals. Because money and political power are so inexorably intertwined, this search concentrates on developing fiscal mechanisms such as revenue sharing—a means best calculated to use the unquestioned revenue superiority of the National Government to reinforce the advantages of decentralized government.

An increasingly independent economy, a vastly superior jurisdictional reach and a near monopoly of the income tax enable the Congress to raise far more revenue at far less political risk than can all of the State and local officials combined.

The Federal fiscal dominance is attributed in part to elasticity of personal income tax which is the backbone of the Federal revenue collection system:

Because the National Government now collects about 90 percent of all personal income tax revenue, it has virtually "cornered" the revenue producer that is most sensitive to economic growth. For every one percent of growth in the Nation's economy, individual income tax receipts automatically rise by about 1.5 percent. In contrast, most of the State and local tax levies behave rather sluggishly—their 'automatic' growth performance lags somewhat behind economic growth.

In stating the case for revenue sharing, the Commission goes on to say:

In addition to this automatic growth superiority, the National Government enjoys another revenue raising advantage—its freedom from the hobbling fears of interlocal and interstate tax competition. The more limited a government's jurisdictional tax reach, the more apprehensive the government becomes about its relative tax climate. Two great forces are heightening this sensitivity to intergovernmental tax competition—the growing desire of State and local policy-makers to promote economic development and the increasing interdependence of our economy.

These arguments apply to all forms of revenue sharing; when revenue sharing is in the form of general support for public schools, other important national goals are attainable:

1. Each state should be required to use its Federal funds along with state and local funds to assure that every public school in the state is adequately financed.
2. The Federal grant should provide an incentive for adequate state and local tax effort for public school support.
3. A plan for evaluating the effectiveness of various school programs should be part of the state plan for spending Federal general support funds.

To accomplish these purposes, an equalized matching plan for public schools is proposed. Under the equalized matching plan, Federal reimbursement percentages would be computed for each state from a statutory formula, and each state would receive a Federal grant equal to the product of its Federal reimbursement percentage and the amount it expended from state and local sources for public school support during the preceding school year. The Federal reimbursement percentages would be inversely related to the state's per capita income, so that low income states would receive a greater percentage grant.

A suggested formula for computing the Federal reimbursement percentage is:

$$\text{Federal Reimbursement Percent} = \frac{25\%}{\text{State's Fiscal Capacity Index}} - 5\%$$

The Basic Federal Reimbursement Rate of 25% would be established by law, thus determining an overall Federal contribution rate of 20%. The State's Fiscal Capacity Index is the quotient obtained by dividing the state's per capita income by the national average per capita income. For a state with average income per capita, the fiscal capacity index would be 1. Using the above formula and recent information concerning the per capita income for each state, it is possible to estimate the range of Federal reimbursement percentages among the states.

State Fiscal Capacity Indices, based upon personal income per capita for 1969, ranged from .6 in the state with the lowest per capita income to 1.25 in the state with the highest per capita income. The suggested formula would provide Federal reimbursement percentages as follows:

	Fiscal Capacity Index	Federal Reimbursement Percentage
High Income State	1.25	15%
Average Income State	1.00	20%
Low Income State	.60	36%

Under this plan, a state would qualify for its grant by its own effort to support public schools. This approach has a built-in assurance that the state would not reduce its effort. A reduction in state and local effort would result in a decreased Federal payment during the ensuing year. In this sense, the Federal grant would be an incentive for at least maintaining state and local effort for public school support.

The total state and local current expenditures for public schools would be computed for each state each year by first determining the total amount it contributed during the preceding school year for current public school purposes. This total would include amounts for kindergarten, grades 1 through 12, and summer schools. From this total would be deducted amounts contributed by the Federal Government for the current support of these school programs during the preceding year.

Under the equalized matching formula, the total annual Federal contribution for the general support of public schools would be equal to approximately 20 percent of the amount contributed from state and local tax sources. However, it is anticipated that some Federal categorical aids would be continued, making the total Federal contribution for all programs approximately equal to 25 percent of the *total cost of public elementary and secondary schools.*

While these overall amounts are reasonable, they would need to be approached gradually, perhaps over a three or five year period. However, the ultimate goal should be established at the outset, so that orderly fiscal planning is possible.

The equalized matching approach is based upon the assumption that states and local school districts will continue to provide most of the funds needed to operate public schools. Federal funds are supplemental, intended to compensate for deficiencies in state and local school revenues and to provide an incentive for continued state effort to support public schools.

The equalized matching plan has a relatively clear purpose—to share public school costs on an established percentage basis and to provide an incentive for continued state "effort" in the support of public schools from state and local sources. Under this plan, the appropriation process should be less controversial, since the states would "earn" their Federal apportionment by contributing amounts from state and local tax sources. Moreover, the percentage relationship, once established, would not need to be changed each year to reflect changes in the value of the dollar. With such stability, effective local planning would be facilitated.

The chief criticism of the Equalized Matching Plan is that it would provide an incentive which might lead to extravagance in educational expenditures. However, if the maximum state reimbursement percentage is less than 50% and, in high income states, less than 25%, the danger that Federal aid would constitute an incentive for extravagance is minimized. However, an additional constraint upon the equalized matching approach, limiting the effect of extremely high or low state and local effort, may be needed. Under this constraint, no state could receive more than 110% or less than 90% of the national average amount per pupil.

The equalized matching approach to Federal support for public schools is intended to accomplish the goals of revenue sharing and also achieve important national goals for education.

Bibliography

Johns, R.L. and Morphet, Edgar L., *The Economics and Financing of Education*, Prentice-Hall, 1969.

Benson, Charles S., *The Economics of Public Education*, Houghton Mifflin Company, 1968.

National Educational Finance Project, *Dimensions of Educational Need*, National Educational Finance Project, Gainesville, Florida, 1969.

Advisory Commission on Intergovernmental Relations, *State Aid to Local Government*, U.S. Government Printing Office, April 1969.

Schultz, Theodore, W., *The Economic Value of Education*, Columbia University Press, 1963.

Norton, John K., *Dimensions of Educational Finance*, National Education Association, 1966.

American Association of School Administrators, *The Federal Government and the Public Schools*, The Association, Washington, D.C., 1965.

Economic Factors Affecting the Financing of Education, National Educational Finance Project, Volume 2, University of Florida, Gainesville, Florida, 1970.

Part III:
Policy Issues Related to the
Instructional Process

8

Early Education and Child Care

Richard R. Rowe

Interest in Early Childhood Education

Interest in early childhood education is not a new phenomenon in American society. At the turn of the century, philanthropists and educators were advocating the benefits of early education as a way of overcoming the negative effects of parental neglect in the "slums" of our cities. During the Second World War, day care centers, particularly in California, were available to mothers who wanted to participate in the war effort. Nursery schools have been with us for decades for the middle and upper classes who could afford them. Yet, there is no doubt that over the past five years there has been unprecedented interest in early childhood education and child care arrangements outside the home. A number of major factors account for this.

Reasons for the Dramatic Rise in Interest
in the 1960s

The first is the change in the labor force itself. In 1948[1], 18% of the labor force were women. In 1971, it was 42%, a dramatic rise. Again, in 1948, 33% of women with children under the age of 18 were working. Now in 1971, 43% of the women who have children under the age of 18 are working. These changes in the labor force have created a tremendous demand for child care, and a great concern over the way in which children will develop if they are not cared for on a full-time basis by their parents.

A second factor is the demand of minority groups for "equal opportunity"; a demand which the government attempted to meet through the War on Poverty. There seems to be clear evidence that young children who are not given the advantages of a secure, loving, and stimulating environment in their early years have a major problem in formulating and pursuing constructive personal goals later on.[2] The logic of this research led many people to believe that government could foster equality of opportunity by focusing on young children, by giving low-income children a "Headstart."

The third factor is welfare reform. Recent proposals have advocated the "workfare" notion, the idea of getting people off the welfare roles and into

145

jobs.[3] This effort requires subsidized child care arrangements for the children of mothers who will be entering the labor force. The provision of child care is meant to avoid interruption of a woman's work outside the home—to maintain her self-confidence, her skills, and her self-image as a working adult.

The fourth factor is what might be called a generalized anxiety about the overall state of our society. Many people have a sense of "things falling apart" and desire to concentrate on young children, the family and family life. Some believe that if we can give our children good care to begin with, they can do a better job than we have, as they grow up. This is the notion that each succeeding generation provides society with another chance to improve. This point of view is presented with unusual effectiveness in Slater's *Pursuit of Loneliness.*[4]

A fifth factor is in some sense implicit in all of the others; we now have research evidence, and have had for some time, that the early years are crucially important for the emotional and cognitive growth of all children.[5] There is also a growing body of evidence that schooling in the later years may not be powerful enough to overcome deficits, particularly language deficits, that may have occurred in the earlier years.[6]

Responses to the Interest in Early Childhood

What are some of the responses that we have made to this increased interest in how our children are being raised and the increased demand for child care? There is growing acceptance of the notion that society has some responsibility to meet the needs of all young children. In a recent survey in the Commonwealth of Massachusetts, 51% of parents with young children agreed with the statement that "America should change its priorities and put children and family life above everything else." Only 30% agreed with the statement that day care centers are for lower income people.

The federal government began to increase its support for child care in the mid-sixties. Headstart began six years ago, in 1965, as a central feature of the War on Poverty. In 1970 we spent $393,000,000 on Headstart. In 1968, Follow-Through was developed as an attempt to maintain the gains from Headstart. In 1967, Title IV-A of the Social Security Act provided for an unlimited 75% federal reimbursement of costs for state investments in child care—for welfare recipients, potential welfare recipients, and former welfare recipients, all broadly defined. In 1971 this remains one of the most useful pieces of federal legislation for child care, in many ways superior to subsequent proposals. Its open-ended provision and broad coverage have made it possible for some states, such as Michigan, to expand child care enormously. In 1970 Michigan received approximately $200 million in federal aid from this source.

In 1969 the Office of Child Development was established within HEW as a major bureaucratic symbol, and hopefully, more than a symbol, of increased federal recognition of the importance of focusing on children. Mr. Nixon introduced Family Assistance Plan (FAP) legislation which would provide substantial day care funding for working mothers or others in training and rehabilitation programs. In 1971 a number of major bills were introduced in the Congress to provide federal funds in day care. The amount of money authorized by such bills ranges from $400 million to over $5 billion yearly. New bills and revisions of earlier ones appeared almost weekly.

The private sector is also becoming involved. "Sesame Street," at a cost of $8 million in 1970, is a joint private/government effort. Private enterprise has become interested in day care; a number of franchise operations have opened up in response to increased demand, and in anticipation of a major influx of federal funds.

State and local governments are beginning to expand plans for child care; teachers are concerned about how early education may change the elementary and secondary curriculum. There has also been a major increase in child care research, though to date, with the exception of Headstart and Title IV-A of the Social Security Act, there has been no major provision of operational funds for child care.

Two significant concerns about movement toward non-parent child care arrangements require attention. The first concern of many parents and educators is that early education and child care outside the home, particularly for infants, can be harmful to the child; that separation from parents is not a good thing to encourage, especially for very young children. There are two sources for this concern. First, there are the classic studies showing severe deprivation among institutionalized children; these have raised many fears about the effect of any kind of institutional arrangement for children. Soviet and Israeli experience with infant care do not support these deprivation fears, but have not really decreased the widespread concern about the effects of pulling children out of a home relationship too early. Also, many mothers feel that to be a good mother means to take care of children on a 24-hour basis: "If you aren't with your children all the time you can, you are not being a good mother."

The second major opposition to expansion of child care comes from minority groups who see day care and early education as a potential strategy to separate children from their parents. "Re-training children, to break the poverty cycle," is sometimes read as a plan by federal social planners to destroy black and other minority cultures. This is a charge taken very seriously by many minority group people. The desire to preserve and develop distinctive cultural backgrounds with one's children should be viewed as a basic human right to be guaranteed by any governmental child care program which may be developed.

The above outline of the current political-social setting indicates that developments in the field of early education and child care will continue and will grow rapidly in number and scope. But there is little consensus about what should happen. Educators are being asked to give their best answers as to what children and parents need and what kinds of programs are most effective in meeting those needs. At this point so little is known that answers must be speculative.

Current Child Care Arrangements and Attitudes among Parents

Good planning for early education cannot occur without some sense of what is now happening to children and how parents feel about it. Data are scarce, but some indication of the situation can be gained from a 1970 survey of early education in Massachusetts.[7] Parents from 516 families were interviewed in forty-five minute, in-depth, home interviews. Interviews were conducted on evenings and weekends in order to include fathers. Parents were asked first about their current child care practices; second, what kinds of child care and early education they would like to have for their children; and third, about their general attitudes in this area. The few comparisons that can be made with other studies lead to the conclusion that the situation in Massachusetts does not differ greatly from the total national picture. The following are some of the results from that survey.

Child Care Arrangements

Over half of all children in the age range of zero to six years (other than those going to public school systems) are regularly cared for by someone other than a parent, and one-third of all children in that age range are regularly cared for outside of the home. About 75% of all child care takes place in a home setting, as distinct from a formal program in a center outside of a home setting or a parent's taking a child with him to work. About 13% are in public school and less than 10% of pre-school care is in other formal programs such as a day care center or nursery. Thus the overwhelming amount of child care now takes place in a home setting.

Well over half of child care by people other than the parents is not paid for in cash by parents. That is, services are paid for by government or private funds or provided as a gift or through a barter arrangement. The grandmother, the neighbor next door who takes the children this week and then leaves her children the next week, are typical of non-monetized and barter arrangements. Most of those who pay anything pay only very small amounts. Only about 2% of Massachusetts parents pay as much as $20 per week for child care for preschoolers.

Only 20% of child care in centers or other people's homes is more than 20 hours a week. Mothers thus tend to leave their children for short, rather than long, periods of time, although 45% of parents surveyed would like to extend their child care arrangements to more than 20 hours a week. This indicates a large gap between the amount of child care that is available and the amount that parents would like to use. Only 40% of the mothers who take care of their children at home all of the time say they would choose to do so. Again, there is a gap between what is available and what is desirable.

Parents' Attitudes

Parents' reported attitudes about child care make the picture more complex. When parents were asked what arrangements they wanted, only 40% of mothers and fathers said that they would choose to have *no* regular child care other than that which they provide. But when we asked the question, "Do you agree or not agree with the statement, 'a good mother stays home with her children if she doesn't have to work.' " 75% agreed with that statement. Thus, it appears that there are many mothers who want to get out of the home, who don't want to spend as much time caring for their children in their homes as they do, but who feel that this means that she might be a "bad mother." And to the statement, "fathers should take more responsibility for child care than they now do," 80% of the mothers and 80% of the fathers agreed. So there is potential for involving fathers more in child care.

There is a good possibility that the percentage of parents wanting regular child care will rise over the next decade, as more and more women join the labor force. Forty percent of all parents say they would like to have their child taken care of in their home and another 40% in somebody else's home. Only 20% say they prefer some kind of formal center, if they could have their choice and if cost were no factor. The small percentage preferring center care is not surprising. Parents are simply not familiar with child care in centers, which are not now readily convenient or available. There are few options. Parents therefore do not know very much about what the alternatives are, and the well-understood notion of home is comforting to them, especially for the care of infants. We may expect center care to become more desirable as it becomes more available, and more familiar to parents. Moreover, parents do not necessarily know much about the child care arrangements they already use. For instance, 75% of the parents of Massachusetts say that "schools are generally doing a good job." Parents generally feel good about the way *all* schools are being run. But many parents do not know the names of the teachers of their children; they often do not know the names of other children in the school, and frequently cannot describe for you what happens to their child during the day. The degree of satisfaction of most parents with their child care arrangements seems to be most strongly correlated with their own personal convenience, and personal convenience is now generally best served by home care.

Parents overwhelmingly now choose child care programs that are: (1) free or very inexpensive, and (2) close to home. Individual families vary, depending upon family circumstances, as to which of these two factors is most important. However, parents give these two factors highest priority. "Nearness to home," as a high priority, is independent of family income. Thus, it is as important to those who are comfortably well-off as it is for those who have very little money. The third priority that parents consider in choosing a program is having a sufficient number of hours at the right time in the day. According to several surveys it appears that more than half the present demand for child care occurs, at least in part, outside the ordinary 9 to 5, five-day work week.[a] And only fourth is there direct concern for the quality of the care provided. In considering quality, most parents are first concerned with opportunities for socialization— for their children to learn how to get along with other children, second with food and medical care, and third with cognitive development. Items that parents show no special interest in include TV and special toys; they don't seem to think that these are high priority in early childhood education.

Thus parents are most concerned with convenience and expense, and generally have not learned, or have not felt they could learn, much about the content of their children's education. When you ask parents, however, whether or not they would be interested in learning about child care and being more involved with their children, a large parentage say that they think it would be a good thing and would like to pursue it.

Parents were asked whether or not they would participate in parent-education activities, and what topics concern them as parents. A choice of possible topics was offered, from which parents could choose any number of relevant items. As their first choice (52%), parents wanted to know how to help children learn. The second item, picked by 47%, was drug education, although these were parents of children from the ages of zero to six. There was no difference between the response of parents who also had teenagers from those who had only pre-school children. It would appear that all parents today are concerned about the problems of drugs. The third and fourth items on the list, each receiving 37% response, were helping children to grow, and problems with being a good parent. Fifth was problems of discipline, receiving 34% response. Discipline, further down the list than might have been expected, was not reported by parents as a major concern.

Parents say they would welcome opportunities to learn to be better parents, especially if those opportunities were in small neighborhood settings where there could be informal discussion. Fifty-two percent of them said they would attend some sort of seminar or parent education course. TV and books are also of interest, but clearly parents are more interested in small neighborhood discus-

[a]Surveys in Vermont, California and Massachusetts indicate more than half the total demand for child care occurs, at least in part, outside the hours of 7 to 7, five days a week.

sions, parent education, parent-child center types of settings. One conclusion that may be drawn from this is that properly organized parent-child centers, family centers, and community schools have potential for responding to needs of parents; parent education might well be built into most child care and early education settings.

There is also widespread feeling among educators that interest in early childhood should be related to what might be called pre-parent education. Many high school and even junior high school students enjoy taking care of little children and are often highly motivated to learn about being parents and teachers. These students can become involved in child care settings in ways which are mutually beneficial for children and young people—for instance, in centers attached to high schools. Older people too should be involved with children. There is some indication that skipping a generation between child and caretaker has benefits in socialization and in children's health development. As Bronfenbrenner has so aptly pointed out, age segregation is a main feature of contemporary society.[8] Such age-segregation works against the needs of both children and grownups. Thus, one of the things that ought to be given serious consideration in terms of program development within school systems is the kind of center that can involve parents, children, young people, and older people.

This section has presented a general picture of what parents do with their children and what they say they would like to do if they had the opportunity. Verbal responses to hypothetical circumstances are not accurate indicators of how people will actually behave, however, and what parents really want can be discovered only after they have a real opportunity to choose among alternative arrangements.

Child Development Programs—The State of the Arts

What do we know about early childhood which is applicable to education and child care? This is a difficult area. It is easy to cite expert opinion, yet despite years of research on children there is very little we can say with confidence about the ways early education should be organized. Nevertheless, the general social pressures to provide child care and early childhood education require our best guesses at this moment.

It seems clear from the work of Bloom[2], Bruner[9], Piaget[5] and many others that the first four or five years are crucial for healthy physical, emotional, cognitive and social development. The importance of good nutrition in early years is undisputed. Much of the intellectual and emotional development of children occurs during those early years, and some of it may be age-specific. That is, if a child doesn't learn a specific skill during the appropriate stage of development, then he may not be able to learn it later on. In addition, attitudes and emotional patterns learned in the early years are often very difficult to change later. Unfortunately a great deal of the research in this area has focused on the problems of pathology rather than normality, and the problem of generalizing from pathological cases to normal children is always a difficult one. Nevertheless, whether or not early deficits can be made up in later years, it is far more desirable from a human viewpoint, and probably less expensive, to facilitate a child's early development than to provide remedial services later.

Theories Relevant to Child Development Programs

Two groups of general theories of early childhood development are influential, although not necessarily adequate or accurate, in the field today. The first group is reinforcement theory or behavior modification, exemplified by Skinner's behaviorism. This is a system of thought which basically says: positively reinforce the behavior you want, and punish the behavior you don't want. A more recent and helpful amendment to this position is an awareness that undesirable behavior may be inadvertently reinforced by making a fuss over it, or by trying to eliminate it directly. Often direct punishment of behavior that you want to get rid of in fact reinforces and maintains it. So, the modified rule of thumb is: reinforce the behavior you want and reinforce behavior which is incompatible with behavior you do not want.

Reinforcement theory or behavior modification has been translated into programmatic child care principles in the works of Bereiter and others.[10] Their programs include highly structured systems of controlled learning environments with concrete cognitive development objectives specified beforehand and specifically reinforced in a variety of ways—such as tokens and verbal praise. While some of these programs seem to be successful in terms of the objectives that have been set, most of their objectives have been in relatively narrow cognitive terms, and the applicability of these methods to emotional and social objectives is less clear. Despite some serious concerns and drawbacks, the general approach of behavioral modification is winning many adherents, not only in early childhood but in primary eduation and in psychotherapy. One of its most appealing features is the relative success that some programs have had in producing measurable short-term changes in cognitive skills. It has been much more difficult, however, to establish any long-term effects.

The second general field of theory might be called developmental theories. In the area of intellectual development the works of Piaget are influential. Basically, these theories propose that children grow according to a stable pattern of development. The rate that an individual child will go through that pattern of development will vary considerably from child to child, but the stages remain constant. Stages cannot be by-passed, nor can a child be pushed into a stage before he is developmentally ready for it. So the notion that you can teach a child certain highly abstract concepts at a very early age is "wrong because they can't do it." A child may learn how to mimic certain behavior or memorize certain responses, but he won't understand what he is doing nor be able to apply his knowledge in new situations unless he has reached the appropriate developmental stage. Applied to education, this approach relies heavily on the spontaneous eagerness of children to grow as they move through the stages of development. The Montessori method, which as an educational method antedates Piaget's research, is an example of the stages of growth approach, focused on intellectual development.

Other methods are based on a similar theory of stages, but emphasize social and emotional growth. The works of Dewey, the Bank Street School, and the British Infant School model are typical of this approach which has much appeal for many liberal educators. It appears that the social-emotional development programs as currently practiced have been markedly ineffective at overcoming cognitive deficits, particularly for lower income, minority people. This apparent failure is strengthening the appeal of a behaviorist approach, but it also points out the need to move toward new, more adequate theories and practices.

For those wanting a more detailed review of developmental theories and their relationship to early childhood programs, several major reviews are available.[11]

Early Childhood Programs

Children can learn some very complex cognitive tasks at an early age—certainly at a much earlier age than now taught. O.K. Moore is able to teach two-year olds to read and write with typewriters. Children can be trained to develop cognitive skills, reading, writing, arithmetic, much earlier than is usual in the schools. There are many experimental examples of its being done. The crucial questions are (1) what kinds of child care and early education are *desirable* from that point of view of the personal and societal development and (2) in the allocation of resources, what priority should be given to different kinds of progress.

Much of the energy behind current early childhood education centers around the attempt to provide equal educational opportunity to all children, especially those who are poor. Headstart and "Sesame Street" are recent major efforts which have specifically attempted to provide improved educational opportunities in the early years.

Headstart started in 1965 and in 1970 had an operating budget of about $393 million. A major goal was to provide needed nutrition and cognitive and social experiences for children from poor homes. In many cases special attention is given to preparation for elementary school. The recent Westinghouse evaluation which is the most comprehensive evaluation of Headstart to date, has been extensively reported and debated.[12] The study looked at a large number of Headstart centers throughout the country and followed the children through a two or three-year period in order to determine whether the Headstart experience had any effect upon academic performance in first, second and third grades. The data indicate that Headstart programs had little or no uniform effect upon the cognitive achievement of children in elementary schools three years later.

There are examples where positive effects were observed, but these seemed to be due to special circumstances.[13] Despite its modest effects on cognitive development, the program seems to have had major impact in terms of other objectives such as community organization, parent involvement and satisfaction, and employment. The goals of Headstart are concerned not only with academic achievement but also with children's socialization and self-image and with parent and community development. The success of these goals, much more difficult to measure, was not evaluated.

Although as a cognitive development program Headstart has not been demonstrated to be very successful on a large-scale basis, this fact requires careful examination before being used as a basis for making policy decisions about the future of Headstart. Given the methodological difficulties inherent in child care evaluation, the lack of longitudinal studies, and considering alternative strategies available at this time, Headstart and similar early education programs may in fact be excellent child care programs for young children.

One of the dilemmas of Headstart is that in the effort to concentrate scarce funds on children from poverty families Headstart has isolated poor children from children of other socio-economic groups. There is evidence that higher academic achievement in poor children is related to their being in mixed socio-economic groups rather than being only with other poor children.[14] Efforts to combine Headstart children with other children whose parents can pay all or part of the costs of child care should be encouraged. Similar advantages can be gained from integrating into regular child care programs children with special medical or emotional needs. Insofar as possible special needs of all kinds should be met without separating children into permanently isolated groups made up of children with the same special needs. Some separation may be desirable some of the time, but only in extreme cases should we accept a permanent separation of children into groups with the same problems. Separation allows specialized care, is often more convenient for the provider of care, and sometimes less expensive; but it often has the effect of perpetuating a special need rather than satisfying it.

A recent study of "Sesame Street"[15] measured development in those academic skills that the program had specifically aimed at developing. The findings showed a uniform, statistically significant and fairly large increase in reading readiness and math skills for children who watched the program. The amount of increase was correlated with age, with the three-year olds gaining more than the four-year olds and those age four more than those age five. The program was in fact designed for three-year olds, so a decrease of effectiveness with age was expected. Academic scores were also positively correlated with the amount of time spent watching the program. Careful longitudinal studies also need to be undertaken before we will know whether any such program has important long-term effects.

An incidental discovery of this study was the amazing amount of television viewing that goes on. Large numbers of children watch television forty or more hours a week. Some children view all of the "Sesame Street" shows every day and the whole replay on Saturday morning. Moreover, there were very few children in the survey who had never seen "Sesame Street." It has been estimated that in its first year "Sesame Street" was watched by eight million children in the United States.[16]

The evaluation study found, however, that the program is more effective for upper and middle class children than for lower class children. The specific goal of "Sesame Street" when it began had been to increase the skills of lower class children more than of children in other income groups. The program was to concentrate on children in urban environments and minorities, but children in the upper and middle class still gained more.

There is a real problem with the inevitable comparisons that are made between Headstart and "Sesame Street." The evaluative data that are available are not comparable. The research instruments of the two studies cited above were completely different; the Westinghouse Headstart study used some longitudinal data and asked children to recall and use some concepts, while the "Sesame Street" study was not longitudinal and used predominantly recognition tests. And Headstart adherents have criticized "Sesame Street" for being too narrow in its objectives and in its evaluation criteria, pointing out that the broader objectives of Headstart do not easily lend themselves to accurate and objective measurement. Yet many are concerned that the Headstart study showed little evidence of positive results while the "Sesame Street" study showed striking results.

Costs inevitably enter the discussion: it is frequently pointed out that Headstart costs nearly $400 million and "Sesame Street" $8 million. Even though Headstart and "Sesame Street" do have some goals in common, simplistic cost comparisons are highly misleading. Headstart provides half and full-day care with physical exercise, personal attention, food, some medical help, parent involvement and education and so on; many parents are enabled to work. "Sesame Street" had much more limited goals.

There is in fact little evidence at this point that *any* pre-school program has wide-spread compensatory effects. "Sesame Street" may be an exception; this can be better determined when longitudinal data become available. The potential effects of media however should not be underestimated. Both broadcast TV and TV cassettes are likely to play an increasingly important role in education over the next decade.

One tentative conclusion from data on program effectiveness is that school improvement is more strongly correlated with the total amount of time spent in settings with responsive adults than with any particular program component. A pilot study conducted by Handler in Illinois is inconclusive because of the small number of cases studied, but it is suggestive of this hypothesis.[17] It compared a Headstart program which was explicitly "cognitive and compensatory" with a day care center, which was explicitly "custodial." The children were observed two years later in elementary school, matched on socio-economic variables. They found that the day care children were higher in academic achievement than Headstart children. The most reasonable explanation that could be found for these results was that the "custodial" day care program was a full-day program, and the Headstart program much shorter; the greater number of hours in the day care center meant more socialization within a school-like setting than had been provided with Headstart. This seemed to account for the greater academic achievement later on.

The common distinctions between "custodial" and "compensatory" or "developmental" child care have often been used to differentiate between day care centers (custodial) and early childhood education (developmental or compensatory). This kind of distinction is of dubious value although it is used extensively in the political debates over which bureaucracy should control child care programs. In practice, a program's formal label tells one very little about the effects it has on children. It would be more meaningful to distinguish between programs according to variables shown to be related to effects upon children. We are barely beginning to learn systematically about the components of child care programs that have significant desirable effects on children. We know some things about abusive or destructive environments for children but otherwise "quality" labels for particular kinds of child care programs should be eyed askance.

Components of "Quality" Child Care

One of the better attempts to further understanding of the components of quality child care comes from a recently completed study of twenty child care centers and systems around the country.[18] "Quality" of a program was described in various ways: Were the children happy? Was there a "good" classroom climate? Was there a feeling of warmth, and laughter? Were children concentrating on self-directed tasks? Was there an absence of excessive crying, noise, subjectively perceived general anxiety? How did teachers respond to children—warmly? Positively? How often? Ratings on quality were correlated with various program characteristics.

The most clear-cut finding was that the critical variable in "warm" child care is staff, particularly the director. The director of the program appears to be by far the most critical and central element to a successful program. The director sets the tone of the center and has the most influence over the environment in which both teachers and children will operate. Directors often work 50-60 hours a week; a good program requires a tremendous output on the part of the director, and if the director is not willing to work so hard, the quality suffers. It also appears that directors' skills cannot readily be spread over a large number of children. As the number of children in the center increased, a drop in "warmth" was observed. In addition, the supply of committed and talented directors is limited. Thus selection and training of child care administrators is a high priority in planning for an expansion of child care facilities.

With respect to teachers, a crucial variable is the ratio of staff to children. There seems to be no correlation between formal educational qualifications of staff and their performance. A sufficient number of uncredentialed high school graduates can provide the same quality of child care as staff with credentials so long as the center has a good director, well-chosen staff, and inservice training.

Costs and Funding of Child Care

The cost of good child care is high, especially if all inputs are given realistic dollar values. In an urban setting well-staffed child care costs $2000-2500 or more per child in the three-to-five-year age range. This is at least twice as much as the expenditure in typical elementary schools, and is difficult for many people to accept. Some kinds of child care can be provided at lower costs, but it is much more difficult to provide good care.

An analysis of program budgets shows why good child care must be so expensive. First of all, 75-80% of the costs for quality care are in staff. Really good care for children two to five years old generally seems to require an over-all staff ratio of around 1 to 5, or 1 to 7 (teacher-student ratios of 1 to 7, or 1 to 10). Few programs seem to do well with fewer staff. For infants the appropriate ratio drops to about 1 to 3. Some franchisers in day care have the idea that costs can be substantially reduced by using standardized toys, prepackaged lunches and the like. There can be some savings of this type, but they will not substantially affect the basic costs of the program, which are for staff. Staff costs can be reduced in three ways: (1) by underpaying the staff (many centers currently pay their staff below minimum wage); (2) by raising the over-all staff-child ratio to 1 to 7, 1 to 10, 1 to 12, with a probable, consequent drop in quality; or (3) by recruiting volunteers. Most quality centers have a fairly high volunteer contribution. Typically about 25% of the resources of quality centers are from donations or the services of volunteers, with a range from 5% to 70%.

There are probably no significant economies of scale in child care. Larger centers, ones with 70 or 300 children, do appear to cost a little less per child (perhaps 10% less per child), but also seem to deliver less good care, as measured by warmth and responsiveness of staff. The slight economies of scale made possible by fewer administrative staff are often more than offset by reduction in warmth and responsiveness to children.

Nationally, the costs of child care differ greatly due to four factors. One is the cost of living in a specific locality, which vary as much as 100% from place to place. Second is the staff-child ratio. Third is the extent to which special services are provided. Most programs provide more than child care—medical services and various other special services such as parent education and counselling. Fourth is only an apparent difference—some budgets are all in cash, others using the same amount of resources rely heavily on gifts and volunteers.

The Abt Associates study and Westat supply and demand survey[19] both investigated how early childhood programs are paid for. Around the country parents pay less than half of the costs of *formal* child care; a great many do not pay anything, because their children are in programs paid for by government or in informal arrangements with relatives and neighbors. Families below the $4000 poverty level pay less than 10% of the total costs of formal child care facilities used by them. Few families earning less than $9000 a year can pay more than $6-$12 per week per child. Thus substantial subsidies are necessary.

Governments now pay more than half of all formal child care costs—by paying for welfare children, and by direct support of programs. The rest of the resources now being used to provide formal programs come from volunteers, donations, private agencies, churches, etc.

It is difficult to see how good child care operations can become profit-making with most parents able to pay so little. The ordinary sources of profits—economies of scale, automation, product innovations, a captive market either with money, or with no options—do not really exist in child care. In a situation where profits must generally mean unfavorable staff-child ratios (not conforming to Federal Inter-Agency Guidelines), it seems important that planners continue to seek multiple sources of funding and that in particular nothing be done that will have the effect of reducing the current proportion of voluntary inputs in child care.

The present apparent lack of needed facilities exists where private organizations and persons find it hard to put together more than half the costs. Federal, state and local governments cannot easily pay even half the costs of all who need child care. Unless multiple sources of funds and volunteer contributions are available for many more programs, it seems likely that child care will often be of undesirably low quality.

We seem to be moving rapidly toward a time when the general public will assert that every child from birth has a right to certain basic opportunities for developing physically, socially and mentally, and that it is a public responsibility to assist parents seeking help in providing those opportunities. In order to fulfill that responsibility a great deal more must be known about the effects on children of different kinds of experiences. We must also learn how to help children without creating a bureaucracy which stifles the development of innovative programs and absorbs resources before they get to children.

Given the increased demand for child care and given our inability to prescribe any particular set of programs as demonstrably better than any other, the next few years should be a period of developing and evaluating a wide diversity of child care programs. Different types of sponsors, including parent-cooperatives, school systems, and private enterprise, etc., should be supported. Different types of programs should be tried, including not only programs in centers but family day care systems and mixed systems involving family day care and centers working together.

While the initial priority for child care funds should be to help children with special needs, including children from poor families, programs which concentrate children with special needs into separate groups should not be encouraged. Government support should facilitate the development of the widest possible diversity with a minimum of restrictions concerning programs. A system of vouchers which would enable parents to choose whatever type of child care they wish should be extensively tried out as the primary means for subsidizing child care and education.

The responsibility for raising children must ultimately remain with parents and families. We must ensure that the programs which are developed for children strengthen parental roles rather than replace them.

References

1. U.S. Government Census Reports.
2. Bloom, Benjamin S., *Stability and Change in Human Characteristics*. New York: John Wiley & Sons, Inc., 1964.
3. Family Assistance Plan, draft legislation, U.S. Congress, HR-1, 1971.
4. Slater, Phillip E., *The Pursuit of Loneliness: American Culture at the Breaking Point*. Boston: Beacon Press, 1970.
5. Piaget, Jean, *The Origins of Intelligence in the Child*. New York: International Universities Press, Inc., 1952.

Piaget, Jean and Inhelder, Barbel, *The Psychology of the Child*. Translation by Helen Weaver. New York: Basic Books, Inc., 1969.

Bruner, Jerome S., *Poverty and Childhood*. Detroit: Merrill-Palmer Institute, 1970.
6. McCandless, Boyd R., *Children and Adolescents: Behavior and Development*. New York: Holt, Rinehart & Winston, Inc., 1961.

Cazden, C.B., "The Neglected Situation in Child Language Research and Education," *Journal of Social Issues*, 1970, 26, 35-60.

"Equal Educational Opportunity," *Harvard Educational Review*, 38; 1, 1968.
7. Fein, Robert, "Analysis of a Survey of Current Child Care Practices, Parental Needs and Attitudes in Massachusetts." Cambridge, Mass.: Massachusetts Early Education Project. (mimeographed)
8. Bronfenbrenner, U., et al., "Children and Parents: Together in the World." Report of Forum 15, White House Conference on Children, Dec., 1970. (mimeographed)
9. Bruner, Jerome S., op. cit.
10. Bereiter, C., Case, R. and Anderson, V., "Steps toward Full Intellectual Functioning," *Journal of Research and Development in Education*. 1968, 1 (3), 70-79.
11. Evans, Ellis D., *Contemporary Influences in Early Childhood Education*. New York: Holt, Rinehart & Winston, 1971.

Anderson, R. and Shane, H., (eds.), *Readings in Early Childhood Education*. Boston, Mass.: Houghton Mifflin, 1971.
12. Cicirelli, V., et al., *The Impact of Head Start; an Evaluation of the Effects of Head Start on Children's Cognitive and Affective Development*. Vols. I & II. Bladensburg, Md.: Westinghouse Learning Corporation, 1969.
13. Smith, J.S. and Bissell, J.S., "Report Analysis: The Impact of Head Start," *Harvard Educational Review*, 1970, 40, 51-104.
14. Coleman, James S., *Equality of Educational Opportunity*. U.S. Dept. of Health, Education and Welfare, Office of Education, 1966. A Publication of the National Center for Educational Statistics, OE-38001.

15. Ball, S. and Bogatz, G.A., *The First Year of Sesame Street: an Evaluation.* Princeton, N.J.: Educational Testing Service, 1970.

16. Tierney, Joan D., "The Miracle on Sesame Street," *Phi Delta Kappan*, v. 52, Jan., '71.

17. Handler, Ellen, "Organizational Factors and Educational Outcome: A Comparison of Two Types of Preschool Programs." Urbana, Ill.: University of Illinois, 1971. (mimeographed)

18. Fitzsimmons, Stephen J. and Rowe, Mary P., *A Study in Child Care, 1970-71. Vol. 1: Fundings.* Cambridge, Mass.: Abt Associates Inc., 1971.

19. Westinghouse Learning Corporation (Westat Research) OEO Contract 800-5160. *Day Care Survey 1970*, April 16, 1971.

An Analysis of Curriculum Policy-Making

Michael W. Kirst and Decker F. Walker

Introduction

Any organization or institution with purposes of its own develops policy ("a body of principles to guide action" (Lerner and Lasswell, 1951, p. ix) for dealing with recurring or crucial matters. Schools normally formulate policies on a variety of matters including promotion of students, grading, grouping of students for instruction, and dress for students. Schools also implement policies formulated by other bodies, most notably policies of the district administration, the state and local boards of education, and the U.S. Congress. The policies executed by schools include specifically educational policies as well as others which, while they may have educational aspects, are not unique to schools or even characteristic of them. Among the most important of the specifically educational policies of schools are those pertaining to what children study in school. Children in school are normally required to study some subjects, forbidden to study others, encouraged to pursue some topics and discouraged from pursuing others, provided with opportunities to study some phenomena but not provided with the means of studying others. When these requirements and pressures are uniformly and consistently operative they amount to policy whether we intend so or not. We shall call such explicit or implicit "guides to action" *curriculum policy* and the process or arriving at such policy we shall call *curriculum policy-making*.

Our purpose in this paper is to explore what is known about curriculum policy-making in the public schools of the United States, relying whenever possible on demonstrable conclusions of formal studies, the resorting when necessary to conventional wisdom, common sense, personal experience, and outright speculation. We do not intend to give an historical account of the development of either the policy-making process or the policies produced by it. Rather we are primarily interested in the present status of the policy-making process. For this reason we shall direct our attention exclusively to works published since 1950. Even though we are aware of many interesting and informative earlier treatments of parts of this topic (for example, Lippmann (1928), Counts (1928), Nelson and Roberts (1963), and Krug (1964)) limitations of time, space, and energy forbid a more historical approach. The reader should also keep in mind that treating such a broad topic in a paper of this size means that we shall have to deal in national-scale generalizations without mentioning the numerous exceptions that can be found in the country's diverse regions, states, and 19,300 school districts. We hope that the perspective for future research directions such an approach provides on the problems of curriculum policy-making will compensate for the exceptional cases that are virtually certain to appear in spite of our best efforts to eliminate them.

In this country, school policy, including curriculum policy, is determined at many levels. State legislatures require the study of some subjects. State and local boards of education commission and endorse courses of study which specify content to be included in these courses. The professional employees of the school districts from the superintendent to the teacher's aide have varying degrees of influence in the determination of courses of study, textbooks, supplies, allotments of time, and the like which embody curriculum policy. Given such a complex system of public policy-making, a naive observer might expect curriculum policy-making to be the scene of conflict and uneasy accommodation, as are most political issues in our democracy. And, indeed, we do find signs of powerful influences of political and social events on curriculum policy-making. For example, in a study of *professional* discourse in the field of curriculum—the periodic policy statements of the Educational Policies Commission, the yearbooks of the National Society for the Study of Education, the publications of professional scholars, and other influential publications in the curriculum field—Pilder (1968) found that this literature reflected most of the major national political tensions in the period he studied (1918-1967). When immigration was a national issue, Americanization was a curriculum issue. When totalitarianism posed a threat to democracy, education for democratic life was a concern in curricular discourse. When World War II created a shortage of trained workers, manpower training became an important theme in writings or curriculum. When Sputnik shocked the nation, softness of existing curricula was cited as a major contributing factor in our national decline. The school curriculum was entangled in these national political issues even though the federal government was formally and in theory not a party to educational questions, especially curriculum questions.

Such evidence as this indicates that the determination of the public school curriculum is not just *influenced* by political events; it *is* a political process in important ways. By "political" here and elsewhere in this article we refer not merely to the processes by which we are governed or govern ourselves. Throughout curriculum policy-making political conflict is generated by the existence of competing values concerning the proper basis for deciding what to teach. The local school system and the other public agencies responsible for these decisions *must* allocate these competing values in some way, even though this means that some factions or interests win and others lose on any given curriculum issue. The inevitability of conflicting demands, wants, and needs is responsible for the necessarily political character of curriculum policy-making which cannot be avoided even by the adoption of some mathematical decision-procedure. Some legitimate authority must decide (and perhaps bargain and compromise) among the conflicting policy viewpoints.

Yet when professional educators write about the curriculum or study it they rarely conceive their subject in political terms. The words "policy," "politics," and "political" do not even appear in the indices of any of the major textbooks in the field (Tyler (1949); Smith, Stanley and Shores (1950); Gwynn (1960); Taba (1962); and Saylor and Alexander (1966)). When these tests treat conflict it is always conflict among ideas, never conflict among individuals, interest groups, or factions within school system bureaucracies. In past issues of *The Review of Educational Research* one finds consistent acknowledgment of the existence of political influence on curriculum, but no mention of policy or policy-making, nor any attempts to compare or contrast curriculum policy-making with other types of public or private policy-making. Instead, both sources use such terms as "decision-making," "planning," "development," and "management." National, state, and local political figures, as well as parents, taxpayers, and other interested parties and the organization that represent their interests are then treated as "influences" on curriculum "decision-making." These terms and the ideas that accompany them embody an image of curriculum determination that plays down if it does not altogether ignore the conflict and accommodation characteristic of policy-making in all but the most monolithic institutions. Consistently followed, this image leads the investigator to search for some sort of mechanism for deciding "scientifically" what children should study in school. More importantly for present purposes, this ideal sidesteps the political questions of who should have a say in determining curriculum at what stages in what ways with what impact. Instead, it holds out the promise of resolving competing claims at the level of principle. Here is one clear statement of this position:

(I)f curriculum development is to be a rational and a scientific rather than a rule-of-thumb procedure, the decisions about these elements (of the curriculum) need to be made on the basis of some valid criteria. These criteria may come from various sources—from tradition, from social pressures, from established habits. The differences between a curriculum decision-making which follows a scientific method and develops a rational design and one which does not is that in the former the criteria for decisions are derived from a study of the factors constituting a reasonable basis for the curriculum. In our society, at least, these factors are the learner, the learning process, the cultural demands, and the content of the disciplines. Therefore, scientific curriculum development needs to draw upon analyses of society and culture, studies of the learner and the learning process, and analyses of the nature of knowledge in order to determine the purposes of the school and the nature of its curriculum.

(Taba, 1962, p. 10)

Once such an ideal has been adopted, it is difficult to avoid disapproving of political resolutions of curriculum questions. And, once political solutions to curriculum questions are seen as deficient or inferior, the tendency is to lump all the complex and varied means by which personal and group interests are defended and advanced in curriculum issues under the vague and somewhat sinister term "influences" and to treat them as aberrations rather than as normal and necessary, if not altogether desirable, aspects of public policy-making.

In this review we will treat the determination of the public school curriculum as a process of public policy-making which is necessarily political in character. We choose *not* to concentrate on the interaction of strictly political institutions (in the narrow sense of political) and educational institutions. Our concern is with the whole range of processes which eventuate in the curriculum of the local public schools. Since local districts have ultimate authority and responsibility for carrying out curriculum policy and much authority for determining it, we shall focus our attention on the curriculum decisions of local schools and the activities of individuals and groups in local school systems as they engage in these collective decisions. Inevitably this focus draws us into a consideration of the state, regional, and national factors—governmental and private—that condition and constrain local decision-makers. In light of these aims this paper is perhaps most accurately described as an exploratory review of the literature—exploratory not because the topic is *new* but because it has not been treated in this way before.

Value Bases

For most of their recorded history schools have regarded their curricula as fixed quantities, not variables to be adjusted in the interest of achieving some goal. The Latin root of the word "curriculum" means "race-course" and the virtue of a race-course is that it is fixed and standard. For centuries the European curriculum was fixed, bounded by the study of the *trivium* and the *quadrivium*. Moreover, for most of the last three hundred years the curriculum in Western schools has changed but slowly, consisting of literacy training in the vernacular and in arithmetic, supplemented with Bible study for most of those who got any education, and study of the "disciplines"—higher mathematics, history, the national literature, languages, philosophy, and, increasingly, the natural sciences—for the intellectual elite. So long as the curriculum changed only slowly there were few occasions for conflict and little use for political processes.

But the image of the race-course has not really been an accurate one for the curricula of the schools in Western civilization since the 17th century. The race itself would be a more accurate symbol of the increasingly agitated jockeying for position in the curriculum that has characterized the last 300 years. First the vernacular languages, then the physical sciences, then the biological sciences, applied sciences, and engineering, and, most recently, the social sciences, successively fought their way into the curriculum at the upper levels of the educational system, whence they have exerted pressure for entry into the curricula of the lower schools. In the lower schools other pressures to include more immediately useful material in the curriculum dating from at least the 1850s (Herbert Spencer's *Education: Intellectual, Moral and Physical* (1870) is an early landmark) eventually produced such curricular offerings as home economics, the agricultural and industrial arts, physical education, driver training, and sex education.

These developments have reached their logical (and absurd) conclusion in the present situation of the elementary schools where teachers may be expected to teach and children to learn reading, writing, several varieties of arithmetic, geography, spelling, science, economics, music, art, foreign languages, and history at the same time as the children are helped to develop physically, morally and intellectually, and are molded into good citizens. Furthermore, if the school is to take advantage of the millions of dollars invested in national curriculum development, each of these matters must be addressed independently with specially developed and packaged materials in the hands of specially trained teachers. Things are hardly less chaotic in secondary schools.

All this confusion has provoked continued conflict over the proper bases for deciding what to teach. Should schools teach those things that are likely to be immediately useful in life outside the school or should they teach those things that are most fundamental to an understanding or organized knowledge? Should they emphasize the development of individuality or the transmission of the cultural heritage? What are schools *for*, anyway? So long as there is disagreement on the proper bases for assessing the worth of the curriculum, there are bound to be conflicting views concerning its composition. The authoritative allocation of these value conflicts is the essence of what we mean by the political process in curriculum decision-making. We would identify as salient over the last several decades four broad bases for assigning value to curriculum elements—tradition, community, science, and individual judgment. These value bases are positions around which people's preferences tend to congregate. They are neither mutually exclusive nor exhaustive, but they do represent major streams of thought and feeling among individuals and groups concerned with the school curriculum.

The appeal to tradition, exemplified in recent times by the Great Books program and the Council for Basic Education, rests on the assumption that those subjects of study that have survived the test of time are in the long view most beneficial and therefore should receive the highest priority in the curriculum. The appeal to science, the newest and probably the fastest growing basis for curriculum decision-making, has received strong support from many influential groups, including the U.S. Office of Education. This appeal rests on the assumption that educational and psychological research will reveal those capabilities that are essential to the performance of those activities the cultivation of which is the school's responsibility. In this view the school curriculum should give first priority to the development of these basic capacities. The appeal to community presupposes that every school is part of a community of association and interest in which resides the ultimate criterion of usefulness, relevance, and beneficiality of any curriculum element. Therefore, those matters which deserve first priority in the curriculum are to be determined by the community, either directly or via its representatives or by studies of the community. The appeal to individual judgment amounts to a skeptical denial of any rational value basis for curriculum-making beyond the student's own values, needs and desires as these are manifested in his own considered judgments. Adherents of this position argue that any basis for curriculum that purports to provide general, *impersonal* answers to Spencer's question "What knowledge is of most worth?" is doomed to failure.

Each of these value bases has its supporters and detractors who use political techniques to bolster their position. There are schools that stand primarily and reasonably consistently on only one of these bases. The curriculum of St. Johns University in Annapolis is based largely on the appeal to tradition as are the curricula of a number of private "Latin" schools; several medical schools have reorganized their curricula along predominantly scientific lines (Henderson, 1969), and experimental programs with a scientific basis are widespread, most visibly in preschool and primary school programs (Pine, 1968 and Bereiter and Engelman, 1966); many so-called free schools and free universities across the country as well as "progressive" or "radical" schools base their programs on a particular community or on the free choices of individual students (Stretch, 1970). But by and large public school programs seem to be a heterogeneous mixture of these different bases reflecting political compromises among the heterogeneous values in any state or local district. A study of the value bases for various elements in the school curriculum and the groups who advance and defend each basis would add considerably to our understanding of curriculum policy-making.

The Use of Decision Tools: Disjointed Incrementalism

The acceptance of any definite value basis, when this is possible, simplifies the determination of the curriculum considerably by providing a limited and well-defined set of criteria for narrowing the bewildering array of curricular choices. But adopting a single clear and consistent basis of value does not entirely resolve the political conflict in curriculum policy-making. Those who agree that the truths honored in our tradition should be the primary curriculum elements may still disagree over whether certain classics should be taught in English translations, Latin translations, or the original Greek. They may argue whether to include Vergil together with Tacitus and Julius Caesar in a fixed time of study. They may differ over the amount of time to be allotted to the Bible and other more strictly oriental texts. The resolution of such problems requires a decision procedure in addition to a value basis.

The oldest and simplest solution to this problem is to endow an individual or small group with the authority to make these decisions by exercising profession- al and presumably expert judgment. This decision-making body can be related to the community that gives it power as a government is related to its constituency (traditional school boards), as the management of a firm is related to its customers (voucher systems), or in any of a number of other ways ranging from tight control of decision-makers by the community to virtual independence.

But this only pushes our search one step further. What sort of decision-pro- cedures do these groups follow? They adopt what Lindblom and Braybrooke (1963), call a strategy of disjointed incrementalism. Disjointed incrementalism is a name for a collection of "relatively simple, crude, almost wholly conscious, and public" strategies for decision-making which "taken together as a mutually reinforcing set . . . constitute a systematic and defensible strategy." (Lindblom and Braybrooke, 1963; p. 82). The major features of disjointed incrementalism are (1) acceptance of the broad outlines of the existing situation with only marginal changes comtemplated, (2) consideration of a restricted variety of policy alternatives excluding those entailing radical change, (3) consideration of a restricted number of consequences for any given policy, (4) adjustment of objectives to policies as well as vice versa, (5) willingness to reformulate the problem as data become available, and (6) serial analysis and piecemeal alterations rather than a single comprehensive attack. In short, curriculum decision-makers use informal methods of decision-making.

This is no surprise considering the history of the field, the state of the art of formal decision-making methods, the complexity of the school as a phenom- enon, and the paucity of reliable data about the events taking place within the classroom and their effects on children. This absence of formal decision-making procedures complicates the task of comprehending the political processes involved in decision-making since informal methods are more complex, diffuse, and irregular. There are indications that modern decision tools may begin to be used to decide what to teach, however, and before looking more carefully at the existing decision processes it might be interesting to glance at three of the most promising of the developing formal procedures.

The first sort of formal procedure to be employed still does not have a name, although several of the operations that make it up are named. For convenience let us call it behavioral analysis. This method, an educational application of techniques developed in the time-and-motion studies of the early 1900s (see Taylor (1911) and Gilbreth (1914)), begins with the activities students are being trained to engage in. It consists of analyzing these activities into a hierarchy of prerequisite capabilities, i.e. performances such that success at a higher-level performance implies the ability to succeed at all the lower-level performances which together constitute the prerequisites of the higher-level performance. After this "task analysis" has been completed, instructional sequences are designed which lead students step-by-step up the hierarchy to more and more complex performances. For examples of behavioral analysis see Gagne (1965), Lewis and Pask (1965) and Miller (1962).

Like behavioral analysis, which was developed by psychologists engaged in military and industrial training, the next cluster of related techniques have been taken from military and industrial contexts and applied to educational problems. These techniques go under various names—Program Planning and Budgeting Systems (PPBS), cost-effectiveness analysis, and systems analysis. We need not describe these widely known methods, but their educational applications may not be familiar and therefore merit a few words. The first step in all these methods is to specify either the complete set of achievements desired of students or a representative subset of these. Measures are then constructed of these educational outputs. Measures are also taken of the costs of the inputs used in teaching students to succeed in achieving these goals. Then the relative costs and benefits of different educational programs are compared quantitatively. For examples of these methods applied to education see Levin (1970), Ribich (1968), Kaufman (1967), and Joint Economic Committee (1969).

The third method of curriculum decision-making might be called empirically derived computer-based decision-making. It consists of identifying a large number of content units, each containing a large number of specific desired competencies. Students and teachers are asked to complete questionnaires and these, together with aptitude and achievement information on each student, are stored in a computer. The machine uses this information to make initial content decisions for each student. Achievement test information and student and teacher reactions are fed into the machine and it, in theory, at least, automatically changes its decision-rules to optimize achievement subject to constraints of interest and involvement. No such system is in full operation now, to our knowledge, but simpler versions are (for example see Harnack (1969)), and there is no reason to doubt that fully operational systems will be available presently.

These are tentative first steps toward more formal procedures for designing curricula. Whether further significant steps will follow quickly or at all is a moot question. The methods outlined above are relatively simple applications of rather simple ideas, almost certain to prove less than fully adequate. Curriculum decision-making presents a severe test of any formal decision tool. There is no clear and simple criterion of success such as profit or number of enemy dead. Each of the methods sketched above relies on behavioral objectives as criteria of value. That is, the users of each method assume they have been supplied with a complete list of the "behaviors" desired by the school and that all the school's real objectives can be expressed in the form of these behaviors. This point is vigorously disputed in the professional literature. For example, see Atkin (1963), Eisner (1967), Eisner (1969), Jackson and Belford (1965), and Moffet (1969). Some individuals and groups strongly oppose even the attempt to define such criteria on the grounds that they would necessarily leave out the more evanescent benefits of education. Indeed, we are hard pressed to specify the educational benefits of, for example, play for children even though most of us believe that play can and does have educational value.

Even if we could get wide agreement on operational goals, however, the most signficant goals are likely to take a long time to achieve and the assessment of the beneficial effects of a complex treatment on a distant objective is a presently insoluble technical problem. An even more elementary problem is to find satisfactory measures of the subtle effects we want, such as the ability to apply what is learned to unfamiliar situations, the ability to learn new things quickly and surely, and the ability to decide what knowledge is appropriate to a given problem. It will be interesting to see how far we are able to get toward a solution of these difficulties in the last third of the twentieth century.

And finally, these procedures leave open the political questions of who will determine the goals and the decision-rules and in whose interest. It seems reasonable to suppose that if the staff of the school—teachers and adminis-trators—make these determinations the results would reflect *their* value bases. Are their bases substantially different from those of the public at large? Even assuming they are not, is it not possible that they would become different in the future? And is it not virtually certain that the goals and decision-rules adapted will differ markedly from the preferences of some substantial groups or interests in the larger society? How will the conflicts generated in these situations be resolved?

In summary, curriculum decisions are not based on quantitative decision techniques or even on a great deal of objective data. This leaves a great deal of latitude for deliberation and for complicated political processes to resolve conflicts of values among various groups and individuals. As we will see, these value conflicts are resolved through low-profile politics, but, even so, there is a considerable amount of overt political interaction.

Major Influences on Curriculum Policy

At this point we would like to turn our attention to the structure and process of political influence in the making of local school district curriculum policy. By influence we mean the ability to get others to act, think, or feel as one intends (Banfield, 1961). A school superintendent who persuades his board to install the "new math" is exercising political influence on a curriculum issue. A related concept is what Gergen calls points of leverage—an individual or institution that has the capacity to effect a substantial influence on the curriculum output of a school system (Bauer and Gergen, 1968). An individual or group that has leverage is one that can make a big difference in the outcome of conflicts over curriculum policy. Our focus here is on the content of curriculum policy rather than the priority curriculum receives in budget allocations, etc. Our perspective is from the local school system and our focus is on the decisions of what to teach to children.

A mapping of the leverage points for curriculum policy-making in our local schools would be exceedingly complex. It would involve three levels of government, and numerous private organizations (including foundations, accrediting associations, national testing agencies, textbook-software companies), and interest groups, such as the John Birch Society. Moreover, there would be a configuration of leverage points within a particular local school system including teachers, department heads, the assistant superintendent for instruction, superintendent, and school board. Cutting across all levels of government would be the pervasive influence of various celebrities, commentators, interest groups, and journalists who use the mass media to disseminate their views on curriculum. It would be very useful if we were able to quantify the amount of influence of each of these groups or individuals and show input-output interactions for just one school system, much less a representative sample. Unfortunately, this is considerably beyond the state of the art, and we must settle for a less precise discussion. (For a critique of such concepts as political influence for constructing empirical political theory see James G. March, "The Power of Power," in Easton (1969).)

We can distinguish three ways in which national or regional agencies affect state and local curriculum policy-making—by establishing minimum standards, by generating curricular alternatives, and by demanding curriculum change. We shall treat these three types of effects on policy-making separately even though some groups effect policy-making in more than one of these ways.

Groups that Establish Minimum Curriculum Standards

From the vantage point of a local public school system, flexibility in determining curriculum content is constrained greatly by several outside groups. The political culture of this country has emphasized "local control" and played down the role of the national government. The curriculum area has been singled out as one where a uniform national standard and substance should be avoided. Federal aid to education was stalled for years in large part because of a fear that the federal dollar would lead to a uniform national curriculum (Sundquist, 1969). Visitors from abroad, however, are usually surprised by the coast-to-coast similarity of the curriculum in American public schools. In effect, we have granted political influence over curriculum to national *nongovernment* agencies that demand a minimum national curriculum standard below which few public schools dare to fall.

A good example of this is the leverage on curriculum that private accrediting associations display. State governments also accredit but it is the private regional accrediting organizations that really concern the local school officials. These accrediting agencies define specific curriculum standards and criteria required for their stamp of approval. The largest of the regionals, the North Central

Association, uses written reports for its judgments but others employ site visitors. The accrediting agencies' curriculum standards are highly detailed. For instance, a sample recommendation included in the *Visiting Committee Handbook* of the Western Association of Schools and Colleges (1965) provides "that written criteria be set up for the evaluation and selection of textbooks" (p. 20); "that continuing study be given to offering four years of language . . ." (p. 22); and "that broader use of the audio-lingual approach be explored" (p. 21).

The political influence of the accrediting agency is based on the faith *other* people have in the accreditation. Since loss of accreditation is dreaded by every schoolman, these accrediting agencies can bring almost irresistible pressure on the curriculum offerings of a local school. The accrediting agencies often are a force for supporting the traditional curriculum and resisting radical changes (Koerner, 1968). In effect, accrediting agencies make value judgments about what should be taught but their credo stresses professional judgments.

Testing agencies in the United States are also largely in private hands and exert a "standardizing" influence on curriculum. The Educational Testing Service, for instance, has an income of about $20,000,000 a year from its tests. Over a million students take the College Boards and seven hundred institutions require it. Consequently, local schools do not have a choice as to whether they shall offer the dozen subjects covered by the achievement exams of the College Boards. These tests do not entirely determine the detailed content of the curriculum but they do limit what teachers can spend their time doing. Moreover, national standardized reading or math tests given in the pre-high-school grades may determine a great deal of the specific content of the reading or math curriculum. Local schools want to look good on these nationally normed tests.

While the testing agency and its panels of expert advisers largely determine the content of the standardized tests used in elementary schools and junior high schools, in high schools the tests tend to be dictated largely by the colleges and universities. The tests follow guidelines laid down by colleges as part of their entrance requirements. For those students who take a college-preparatory course the high-school curriculum is determined almost entirely by college entrance requirements. And the prestige accorded to the subjects required for entrance by colleges undoubtedly influences nore non-college-bound students (probably via their parents) to take these courses. The tyranny of college entrance requirements over the secondary school curriculum has been a persistent complaint of high schools. In the late 1930s the Progressive Education Association sponsored a study, called the Eight Year Study (Aikin, 1942), of the secondary-school curriculum in which they asked for and received permission to waive entrance requirements for the students in the experimental schools. Students from these schools were not required to have so many units of English, history, and so on in order to be admitted to college, but only a recommendation from their principal. An evaluation of the performance of these students in college showed them to be equal to students in similar schools in most respects and superior in many (Chamberlin, 1942). The design of this study has been criticized, but no one has attempted to replicate it, and entrance requirements remain.

State departments of education and state boards of education have also had a traditional role in setting and enforcing minimum curriculum standards. This role has varied enormously depending on whether the political culture of the state supported what Daniel Elazar (1965) called a centrist or localist policy. In New England, the local schools enjoy an autonomy from state controls that goes back to the hatred of the English royal governor, while Southern states often mandate textbooks and courses of instruction. Most states do not mandate the school curriculum to any great extent. A 1966 survey (Conant, 1967) revealed the great majority mandate courses in the dangers of alcohol and narcotics, only half require work in U.S. history and physical education, and less than half (ranging from 46% to 2% of the states) require instruction in other specific subjects. Although California and Iowa have over 30 curriculum prescriptions, over half the states have fewer than ten. Enforcement of state board curriculum mandates is very spotty, and local districts with strong views can circumvent the weak enforcement machinery.

It is often the newer subject areas (vocational education, driver training) that have used state law to gain a secure place in the curriculum. These subjects were introduced into the curriculum amid great controversy after 1920, whereas mathematics and English never had to use political power to justify their existence in the school curriculum. Consequently, the "standard" subjects are less frequently mandated by state law.

Associations of teachers of special subjects can be very influential at the state level and use their power base for preserving state curriculum requirements. Vocational education, physical education, and home economics teachers use their NEA state affiliate to ensure that their specialities are stressed in the local schools. They are also supported by the manufacturers of sports equipment and home appliances. The driver-education teachers are a newer state lobby but so effective that almost all states mandate driver education.

Ironically, the teachers of academic subjects are usually poorly organized and not united at the state level. Nobody consults them and their minimal influence is indicated by the national trend to require less professional training for teaching licenses in physics, math, or history than for home economics or industrial arts (Conant, 1967). The impact on curriculum policy of these organizations that set minimum standards and tend to support the status quo is summarized by James Koerner:

Suppose a local board, aware of the obselescence and flaccidity of much that passes for vocational training . . . decides to reduce its program in these areas. In theory this is one of its sovereign rights. In practice several things occur to change its mind. First, the vocational education lobby goes to work on other members of local government and on the state legislature or state department of education to protect the extensive interests of vocational education teachers. Second, the regional accrediting association comes to the aid of the status quo and makes threatening noises, suggesting and then perhaps demanding, on pain of disaccreditation . . . that the board rescind its decision. Third, the NEA state affiliate "investigates" and through its considerable power 'persuades' the board to a different view (Koerner, 1968; pp. 126-127).

Alternative Generators

Operating in the political environment of the local school are several organizations and individuals who provide alternatives with respect to curriculum. The range and nature of the curriculum alternatives proposed by these organizations is restricted by the minimum standards and requirements discussed in the prior section.

Most curriculum decisions are made at the local level; outside agencies can only provide alternatives to choose from. School boards, superintendents, directors of curriculum, principals, department chairmen, and teachers must take the final steps in deciding what to teach. As we have seen, state officials and the state legislature usually prescribe certain rather broad limits. The power of local officials to select is also bounded, however, perhaps more severely than by state laws, by the decision-alternatives available to them. If, ten years ago, a school had wanted to teach a history of America that gave the black man a place in it, they would have had to write the textbook themselves. Some schools attempt such things, but most do not. Teachers do not feel able to do the job, and the board has little money for released time or research assistance. So, until recently, most schools could not opt for integrated history even if they were so inclined. It is only now becoming possible for schools to teach a reasonably balanced account of the wresting of this continent from its aboriginal inhabitants. Until 1960 it was not possible for a school to teach modern physics unless it was blessed with a truly outstanding teacher.

The bald fact is that most teaching in our schools is and must be from a textbook or other curriculum package. We do not trust teachers to write their own materials, we do not give them the time or money, and we insist on standardization. So long as this is true, the suppliers of these materials will have a potentially powerful effect on the curriculum.

Who supplies these decision-alternatives to local schools? Until ten years ago the unequivocal answer to this question would have been "textbook publishers." But a lot has happened in the interim. Textbook publishing has become part of an enlarged education industry which produces all sorts of printed, electronic, and mechanical devices for classroom use. Also, the federal government, private foundations, and various nonprofit organizations of scholars, teachers, and laymen have taken a more active role in producing curriculum materials. Nevertheless, the textbook is undoubtedly still the most widely used piece of educational technology and textbook publishers are still powerful influences on the curriculum. It has been estimated in Texas that 75% of a child's classroom time and 90% of his homework time has been spent using textbooks (Governor's Committee on Public Education, 1969). Thus the publisher's control of the content of the textbook is virtual control over the curriculum.

But the power of the textbook publisher is a brittle sort of power that cannot stand up against serious opposition from any large segment of the population. Some publishers still put the unit on evolution in the center of the biology textbook so that the books destined for Southern and Western schools can readily be bound without those pages. Sections on "Negro history" were once added in the same way. Publishers cannot (or will not, which amounts to the same thing) stand up against the demands of their customers. Nor can publishers spend millions of dollars developing materials for one course as the National Science Foundation has supported projects in the sciences and mathematics. Apparently, in spite of their potential power, publishers have *not* been able to operate as independent agents. Instead, they reflect the conflicting desires of their customers—the local schools and in some areas the state authorities. Black (1967) offers an account of this process, but more careful and systematic studies of the influences (in this context the term is useful and accurate) on textbook content are needed.

Research is also needed on the relative efficacy of textbooks and various other factors such as teacher's guides, courses of study, and the teachers' own views in determining what is actually taught in classrooms. Most studies of the curriculum assume that what appears in the textbook or course of study is what is taught. But a few observational studies of science teaching—Gallagher (1967), Smith (1970), Kaiser (1970)—seem to show that teachers do not simply reflect the views of the curriculum writers. The teachers in these studies projected a conception of their subject and of teaching different in important ways from the conception embedded in the phalanx of curriculum materials they were using. We should exercise extreme caution in interpreting the results of studies of curriculum policy-making which assume that policies formulated outside the classroom make their way undistorted to the pupil. Studies which describe the kinds of changes policies tend to undergo in filtering through the school staff to pupils would be extremely valuable.

Where there is state adoption, the State Department of Education seems to exercise considerable leverage. In Texas the State Commissioner nominates members to serve on the State Textbook Committee and must approve books recommended by the Committee. Texas State Department specialists draw up the detailed criteria for the publishers' bids including the topics to be covered. The selected books are distributed at state expense to every schoolroom but the same textbook must stay in service for six years. Districts who want to "stay on top of things" must do so at their own expense (Governor's Committee, 1969).

The U.S. government has become a very powerful influence on the curriculum in the past ten years. Because of the fragmented federal budgeting of monies for curriculum development it is not possible to determine exactly how much the government, mainly through the National Science Foundation and the Office of Education, has spent on curriculum development over the past 10 years. This figure is very large, however, and dwarfs all previous curriculum development efforts by states, regions, localities, and private enterprise. As an index of the impact of government-sponsored courses, one estimate has it that over 50% of our schools use the new physics and chemistry while 65% use the new biology (Koerner, 1968).

Federal agencies have not sponsored the development of controversial curricula. The National Science Foundation, in particular, perceives its role as one of "course improvement," not the creation of new courses (Campbell and Bunnell, 1963). Therefore, almost all of the money allocated to curriculum development by the federal government has gone to update and improve the existing curriculum. Thus we have new math, new physics, new biology, new social studies and new English but not psychology, sociology, economics, philosophy, problems of modern living, interpersonal relationships, sex education of film-making and -viewing. But federal agencies have decided which proposed "improvements" to finance and they have exerted certain pressures on the staffs of projects they finance, including pressure to state objectives and to conduct evaluations using these objectives. See Grobman (1969) and Marsh (1964) for accounts of the interactions between project staffs and federal agencies. Will these federal agencies continue this pattern, will they expand their efforts to genuinely new courses, or, on the other hand, will they cut back on their funds for curriculum development in disillusionment over the failure of test results to show definite superiority of the new curricula?

No one can foresee the path federal policy on curriculum will take in even the next few years. Agencies of the federal government jumped from virtually no influence to a place of preeminence at one stroke of the pen, when the National Defense Education Act became law. President Nixon has proposed the creation of a National Institute of Education. He has also inaugurated a "right-to-read" campaign to encourage emphasis on reading in elementary and junior high schools. Sesame Street, a nationally televised preschool program, has been produced under the auspices of the U.S. Office of Education. Until now, the federal government's influence has been a conservative one, educationally speaking, but it has an important role and when the right circumstances arise we have every reason to believe that federal agencies will seize the initiative in curriculum matters.

Another set of powerful agents in curriculum-making are the foundations. Over the past 10 years they have generally seen their role as one of supplementing and balancing the efforts of the federal government. When the federal government was financing only projects in mathematics, science, and foreign languages, the foundations were financing projects in the arts and social sciences.

The foundations have also been bolder to fund efforts in nonstandard courses, including psychology, economics, and photography among many others. All that is known of the policies of the foundations that have supported curriculum development over the past decade—chiefly the Ford, Rockefeller, Carnegie and Kettering—are their declarations. We have not been able to locate a single study or evaluation of the foundations' effects on curriculum. We can understand the difficulty of studying this problem, but in view of its importance one might expect at least a case study. The foundations, too, are relatively new to curriculum development and foundations, too, must rely on local or state education authorities to accept the new materials or on interest groups to present political demands for change to such authorities.

Although the two major sources of funds for curriculum planning in this country are relatively new and therefore not fully dependable, there are steadier, if less copious, sources. Professional associations of scientists, engineers, and business and professional men have supported curriculum development efforts related to their professional interest. They will no doubt continue to do so as long as they can be convinced of the need for new curricula in their special field. Local school districts provide a modest amount of money for updating their schools' curriculum. We have no dependable estimates of the amount of money spent by individual school districts on curriculum but the figure must surely be quite small for individual districts. Occasionally regional or statewide curriculum development projects have been funded well enough and long enough to permit thorough substantial efforts. The state of New York through its Board of Regents has been outstanding in this respect. And, of course, private businesses, chiefly textbook publishers in the past, but increasingly amalgams of publishing and electronic firms spend (nobody knows how much) for curriculum development. Curriculum development will likely be forced to rely chiefly on these traditional sources of money in the next decade, since the pressing problems of foreign involvement and noneducational domestic issues such as race relations, the environment, and poverty will leave at best a moderate priority for educational concerns unrelated to such issues.

But sources of money are not the only factors influencing the alternatives placed before the local decision-maker. Sources of ideas and expertise are also crucial. The major source of ideas for curriculum change has always been the college or university. The last twenty years have seen an intensified reliance on college and university professors in the form of national curriculum commissions and university-based projects. In most cases the participation of professors has been as subject-matter experts—scientists, mathematicians, historians, etc. But a few psychologists have been employed to advise projects on methods. Education faculty have not been heavily involved in projects.

University professors do not, of course, constitute anything like a unitary block of opinion on curriculum questions. In fact, they have been a major source of much-needed diversity in the once seemingly stagnant curriculum of the

American school. Nevertheless, university professors tend to regard education as an entirely intellectual affair, whereas long tradition in this country and, indeed, the Western world, emphasizes moral, physical and aesthetic concerns. Many of the scholars who become involved in the public school curriculum through the federally supported national curriculum projects shared MIT physicist Jerrold Zacharais' view that "our real problem as a nation was creeping antiintellectualism from which came many of our educational deficiencies." (Koerner, 1968; p. 62). This value orientation differs significantly from that of the general public which, if it chose, could reassert the claims of less intellectual matters for attention in the curriculum.

If university faculty do not represent any organized body of opinion, their professional associations sometimes do and when they do they can be extremely influential. The role of the American Association for the Advancement of Science and the American Institute for Biological Sciences in getting evolution into biology books over the strong objections of fundamentalist Christians as reported by Grobman (1969) and Black (1967) shows that these associations can be influential when they are united and determined. The American Mathematical Society sponsored the School Mathematics Study Group until the Sputnik-induced National Defense Education Act authorized the National Science Foundation to finance it as an independent enterprise. As Turner (1964) describes its activities, the American Council of Learned Societies was extremely influential in recent revisions of social-studies curricula. This organization urged its constituent societies to see what they could do about revising the curriculum in their disciplines; it commissioned nine scholars in various social sciences to investigate the relations between the social sciences and the social studies (eventuating in the widely read report *The Social Studies and the Social Sciences* (1962)); it conducted a survey to determine what the constituent societies were doing about curriculum questions; it sponsored a conference of scholars and educators to formulate a K-12 design in the humanities and social sciences; and, finally, it commissioned a study of the present state of the social studies curriculum. How effective were these actions? We cannot say without further research.

In addition to universities and professional associations, private firms harbor vital curriculum expertise. Publishers use their sales organizations to ferret out the likes and dislikes of the schoolmen who buy their books and they "edit" the book with one eye on this information (Black, 1967). Strangely enough, this network of salesmen is the only reasonably dependable comprehensive mechanism for compiling the preferences and prejudices of local schools on curriculum matters. This part of the curriculum policy-making process badly needs careful study.

Twenty years ago we could have stopped our treatment of the contributions of private firms to curriculum decisions with textbooks. But not anymore. IBM has bought SRA, Xerox has bought American Educational Publications, GE and

Time have formed General Learning, RCA has bought Random House, and CBS has bought Holt, Rinehart and Winston. These firms can produce curriculum alternatives in the form of text materials, programmed sequences, films, software and hardware for use in computer-assisted instruction, and similar devices which have potentially powerful effects on the school curriculum, and which few other agencies have the resources or expertise to produce. The new notions of performance contracts and vouchers are supported by both federal agencies and private firms, but the corporations will formulate the specific curriculum packages and contract with local districts who have federal money.

Finally, we cannot conclude this discussion of groups that generate curricular alternatives without considering professional educators themselves. Teachers, former teachers, supervisors, and administrators write textbooks and devise curriculum materials. Their ideas, published in professional journals and school-district publications, constitute a constantly renewing pool of alternatives from which they and their colleagues can draw in making curriculum decisions. Frequently, however, teachers' contributions are specific practices rather than general *principles*. But teachers often produce the teachers' guides and courses of study that embody the details of district curriculum policy. Furthermore, teachers served on the staffs of the major curriculum development projects which have powerfully affected the public school curriculum in recent years. The published accounts of these projects—Marsh (1963), Merrill and Ridgway (1969), Wooton (1965), and Grobman (1969) raise some doubts about the importance of teachers in the decision-making that took place in these projects. For the most part it seems that teachers were assigned the role of commenting on the "teachability" of the ideas generated by university scholars. It is a measure of the depth of our ignorance that we cannot cite any reasonably hard evidence pertaining to the kind and degree of power teachers have in curriculum policy-making at any level.

Groups Demanding Curriculum Change

Most of the groups generating curricular alternatives are also important sources of demands for curriculum change. Foundations are concerned mainly with inducing certain kinds of changes in schools. They supply money to finance individuals willing to generate alternatives that show promise of encouraging these changes. The U.S. Office of Education has in recent years taken a more active stance in dispensing funds for research, development, demonstration, and dissemination. They state that "the goal of these efforts is to generate alternatives to current educational practices that schools may adopt in whole or part as they see fit." *(U.S.O.E. Bureau of Research, 1969, p. i)*. But they seem more and more to see their role as one of *producing change*, rather than simply making change possible. Some organizations demand curriculum changes but do not concern themselves with creating additional options. Rather, such groups support one of a number of existing competing alternatives. An example of this sort of organization is the Council for Basic Education. The CBE has lobbied consistently for greater emphasis on the fundamental intellectual disciplines. CBE's credo is the following:

That school administrators are encouraged and supported in resisting pressures to divert school time to activities of minor educational significance, to curricula overemphasizing social adjustment at the expense of intellectual discipline, and to programs that call upon the school to assume responsibilities properly belonging to the home, to the religious bodies, and to other agencies.

CBE attempts to influence curriculum policy-makers through publication, conferences, and other uses of the media. It does not produce curriculum materials but it lobbies for existing materials consistent with its views. The organization does not have local chapters. It is an example of an interest group operating entirely through journalism and popular writing to influence board members, PTAs, and voters to demand curriculum change in their locality.

Most large national organizations (the Chamber of Commerce, the National Association of Manufacturers, the John Birch Society, or the AFL-CIO) have attempted at one time or another to influence curriculum policy on particular nationwide issues. In fact, such a variety of powerful national interest groups can enter the arena on any given disputed question that it is probably desirable to think of two separate policy-making processes—*normal policy-making* and *crisis policy-making*. These not specifically educational interest groups would probably be relatively weak forces in normal policy-making, but extremely powerful in crisis policy-making. The relevant literature on crisis policy-making is much too large to review here. It includes many, if not most, of the references cited already. Crises occur at such short intervals in the history of American education—immigration, the great Red scare, war, depression, war again, Sputnik, racial violence, war again—that crisis policy-making is normal and normal policy-making exceptional. What seems to be needed in this area is theory which would distill some useful generalizations from the details presented in the numerous case studies and historical and journalistic accounts.

In summary, when a school district faces the problem of putting together a course it has only three basic choices. The whole problem can be left to individual teachers; groups of teachers can make the plans and teaching materials for the whole school; or materials can be purchased. American public schools increasingly favor the last approach. Therefore the sources of these materials are, and will probably remain, important determinants of the curriculum. The sources we have identified are the projects financed by the federal government and private foundations, college and university faculties, professional associations, private business, and organizations of laymen. But the fact of the matter is that any group with sufficient talent and resources can prepare curriculum materials and possibly start a trend that will sweep these other sources either aside or along.

The Local Community and Curriculum Policy

Roland Pellegrin surveyed the whole field of innovation in education and concluded:

... the greatest stimili to changes in education originate in sources external to the field. What I have shown is that the sources of innovation lie largely outside the local community, and in most instances outside the education profession. (Pellegrin, 1966; p. 15).

This statement would appear to apply to curriculum and to refer to the organizations and individuals discussed in the previous sections which provide most of the ideas, alternatives, and value orientations adopted by school officials. Today we see a good example of this in the teamwork of corporations and the federal government to implement performance contracts. The role of the local lay community in curriculum change, however, appears minimal. In the local community, it is primarily actors within the school system who decide whether a break is to be made with the traditional curriculum. The mayor and city council have no influence.

The minimal political leverage of the community is evidenced by a nation-wide Gallup poll (Gallup, 1969) showing the public knows almost nothing about the substance of education and is not involved with broad curriculum issues. Gallup reported that most of the information that the public receives about schools concerns "happenings"—the hard news—reported in the newspapers or other media. Gallup concluded: "knowledge about education is very limited, at least the kind of knowledge that has to do with curriculum and goals of education." When asked to tell how they would judge a good school, the public replied, first, qualified teachers (vaguely defined by most respondents), second, discipline, and third, physical equipment. The "biggest" problem of the public schools is discipline (26%) while only 4% see curriculum as the biggest problem. Gallup observed that this lack of information does not stem from a lack of public interest:

When asked specifically what kind of information they (the public) would like to have, the answers deal to a large extent with the courses taught—the curriculum—innovations being introduced and why—college-requirements—and the like. Significantly, there is great interest in the very areas that most school publicity presently neglects—the content of courses and the educational process versus school operations. (Gallup, 1969; p. 9).

This limited public role undoubtedly stems in large part from the point made at the outset of this paper—curriculum is considered an issue to be properly settled by professional educators trained in these matters. Of course, the community does get involved in curriculum issues on occasion. Roscoe Martin (1961) surveyed a large sample of suburban citizens, mayors, presidents of Leagues of Women Voters, and officials of local Chambers of Commerce and concluded:

These areas (curriculum, textbooks, subversive activities, personalities, athletics, race relations) provide a reservoir for what we have called episodic issues—issues which emerge under unusual or special conditions and shortly subside. Thus, it is not textbooks which cause concern, but a particular textbook under a special set of circumstances. (Martin, 1961; p. 55).

Martin and other writers have concluded that community influence seems most often to be a *negative action* such as the defeat of a bond issue, tax increase, school board member, or the termination of controversial curriculum offerings like sex education. On the other hand, Gittell et al., in a study of six cities concluded:

. . . innovation can only be achieved as a result of strong community participation with power to compel both new programs and expenditure increases necessary to finance them. The brief experience in Philadelphia under Dilworth suggests that substantial community involvement provides both the pressure for change and a community atmosphere favorable for obtaining the necessary financing. (Gittel, 1967).

Gittell was referring to innovations of all types and it is not clear to what extent her findings are relevant to curriculum. All the studies demonstrate, however, that the historic separation between education and general government has left minimal influence to the mayor and the city council in curriculum (Salisbury, 1967; Gittell, 1967; Martin, 1961; Rosenthal, 1969; and Saxe, 1969). Saxe (1969) in his survey of 50 mayors noted a traditional "separation of functions" between schoolmen and city officials epitomized in one mayor's comment that "I do not intend, however, to become involved in school issues such as curricula, bussing of students, and matters of that type, since this is clearly the responsibility of another agency." (p. 249) but he notes that "a majority of the mayors cooperating in this survey (20 out of 32) . . . [are] reconsider[ing] their "hands off" attitude." (p. 250).

At the local level, then, curriculum decisions have been very much an internal issue to be decided by school professionals. Indeed we have some evidence that decisions on curriculum in middle-sized and large systems are often made within the school bureaucracy beneath the superintendent. The formal institutional description of powers and perogatives would lead one to believe that the school board plays a more decisive role in curriculum policy-making than it seems to play. Indeed, research has shattered the myth of lay control of schools, at least over curriculum.

The School Board

The limited influence of the school board deserves further examination. Curriculum decisions require an analysis of the philosophy and substance of education. Lay school boards usually have no expert or even part-time staff independent of the school bureaucracy. Board members are also part-time officials who meet at night once or twice a week after a full day in a responsible position. These busy laymen are usually not presented with performance criteria or test data with which to question the curriculum judgments of the superintendent and his staff. Curriculum proposals are rarely related to measurable objectives nor do they undergo systematic analysis as we saw in the first section. The use of disjointed incrementalism for curriculum decisions does not assist a lay board in playing a crucial decision-making role.

The method of school board elections also limits the board's perspective on curriculum matters. The Gallup poll indicates that curriculum issues are usually not presented to the voters as election mandates. Moreover, as Robert Salisbury (1967) points out, traditionally the board has the same viewpoint as the superintendent as far as representation of wards or ethnic groups is concerned: "Regardless of ethnic, racial, religious, economic, or political differences in other areas of urban life, education should not legitimize those differences. Education is a process that must not be differentiated according to section or class, and the city is a *unity* for purposes of the school program." (Salisbury, 1967; pp. 408-424). Consequently, school boards and superintendents have historically resisted a differentiated curriculum for Italians, Irish, black, Chicanos and other ethnic, racial, or religious groups.

The Superintendent

To date, very few studies have differentiated political influence and leverage within the school bureaucracy. There has been a tendency to treat the superintendent and his bureaucracy as one actor and compare their role to school boards, city officials, community interest groups, etc. Those studies of large school systems that have researched the bureaucracy find it wields substantial influence.

Superintendents have guarded curriculum decisions as an area of their professional competence, and they have been viewed by many researchers as the key figure in the innovation process. (Carlson (1965) and Makenzie (1969)). As Martin (1961) concluded that he (the superintendent) is as much a policy maker as he is a manager in the narrow sense; for he enjoys an expertise, a professional reputation, and a community position which combine to give him an almost irresistible voice in school affairs. (p. 61).

In his study of Allegheny County, Pennsylvania and the state of West Virginia, Carlson (1965) found that superintendents were the "agricultural extension agent" as well as the "experimental station" for the new math. The superintendents who adopted new curricula interacted frequently with a peer group of other superintendents who were also innovators. In short, a group of professional friends spread the new math to each of the members of the group. There were certain key superintendents in these counties who were viewed by other superintendents as good advisors and opinion leaders on curriculum. In West Virginia, however, the State Department's advice was often sought. Looking at Carlson's data from another vantage point, superintendents who did *not* adopt curriculum reform programs 1) had less formal education, 2) received fewer friendship choices among local superintendents, 3) knew well fewer of their peers, 4) participated in fewer professional meetings, 5) held less prestigious superintendencies, 6) perceived less support from their school boards, and 7) relied more on local sources for advice and information (Carlson, 1965; p. 64). It is worth noting that the innovations Carlson explored were developed by the federal government and foundations. In effect, the superintendent mediates between outside demands for change and the local population.

Since Carlson's study, a new group of federally supported regional education laboratories have sprung up and very little is yet known about their role. But a recent study in the San Francisco Bay area (Hamrin, 1970) found that ideas for curriculum change were derived generally from the literature and from awareness of changes occurring in other schools.

The School Bureaucracy

While a superintendent can, if he chooses, block most internal demands for changes in official district wide curriculum policy (other than "episodic issues" like sex education) it is not clear, especially in large cities, whether he is closely involved in many important curriculum decisions. The key bureaucratic officers appear to be Assistant Superintendents for Instruction and Department Chairmen (Hamrin, 1970; Carlson, 1965) who work in committees with groups of teachers. In effect, many curriculum policies are made on a piecemeal basis—academic department by department and they may not be changed for many years through any formal decision. We know very little about this bureaucratic bargaining and conflict. We are more certain that the influence of the principal seems small because as Pellegrin (1966) notes, "he is burdened with such a multitude of managerial activities that it is extremely difficult for him to devote the time and effort required for innovation on a substantial scale." In effect, the principal is too bogged down in day-to-day management to be more than a middleman between the teacher and the central office for the implementation of curriculum. This is despite the stress the formal job description of the principal puts on curriculum leadership.

Teachers

It may seem somewhat odd to leave detailed consideration of the teacher until so near the end of a paper on curriculum policy-making, but we have been concerned with curriculum policy that affects several teachers (e.g. the entire English department). Teachers have autonomy with regard to the mode of presentation of material within their own classroom. The teacher regulates her own schedule and methods of instruction. But studies dealing with curriculum innovation at the classroom level find "teachers seldom suggest distinctly new types of working patterns for themselves." (Brichell, 1964). Another study put it this way:

It is a unique school indeed in which teachers discuss their classroom problems, techniques, and progress with one another and with their principal. In most schools teachers practice their own methods—rarely hearing, or even caring, if one of their colleagues is experimenting with some new teaching device or technique. (Chesler, et. al., 1963).

Teachers are increasing their control of salary, promotions, and working conditions through collective bargaining. But surveys reveal that the political energies of teachers at this time are focused on "bread and butter" issues, such as pay, class size, and relief from noninstructional duties. To date, their influence or bargaining rarely extends to *curriculum*. James (1966) found that demands from teacher organizations in 14 cities related to staff benefits and not to curriculum. It is quite possible, however, that curriculum will become a concern of future teacher negotiations. Curriculum issues are beginning to appear among the contract demands of teacher organizations but as yet these have not been central issues, issues over which a strike might occur. Perhaps as differentiated staffing arrangements bring teachers together over curriculum concerns, curriculum issues will receive more attention from teacher organizations. The accountability movement may result in curriculum performance standards in teacher contracts.

Students

Students have no influence in any formal sense over what they learn. This is so obvious a fact that research to establish it would be superfluous. Of course, decision-makers sometimes take students' views into account, but not usually. Even surveys to assess student opinion are rare. But students, to the distress of parents and school officials, vote with their feet on major curriculum questions. Enrollments in high-school physics are declining at a greater rate since the new physics began to be taught. It is only speculation, but perhaps the increased interest among students in "free schools" is a reaction to a curriculum over which they have little control and which they see as overly rigid and intellectualized. This is a matter that needs further study.

In sum, what we have described as the actors and organizations that influence curriculum policy making could be presented on the simplified grid below.

Table 9-1
Influences on Curriculum Policy-making

	National	State	Local
General legislative	Congress	State legislature	(City Councils have no influence)
Educational legislative	House Committee on Education and Labor	State school board	Local school board
Executive	President	Governor	(Mayor has no influence)
Administrative	HEW-USOE	State Department	School superintendent
Bureaucratic	OE (Bureau of Research), National Science Foundation (Division of Curriculum Improvement)	State Department (Division of Vocational Education)	Department chairmen, Teachers
Professional association	National testing agencies	Accrediting associations, NEA State Subject Matter Affiliates	County Association of Superintendents
Other private interests	Foundations and business corporations	Council for Basic Education	John Birch Society NAACP

Distinctive Features Of Curriculum Policy-Making

It might be useful as a summarizing device to compare curriculum policy-making with other types of policy-making. For several reasons economic policy provides a fairly close analogy to educational policy. In our economic system everyone's decisions to buy and sell ultimately shape the economy. In our educational system the decisions of thousands of local boards shape educational policy. Economic questions are usually considered too complex to permit direct voting. For this reason some economic decision-makers are insulated from the electorate and those who are not so insulated usually confine their economic campaign positions to being against inflation and recession, although they will take stands on particular hot issues such as the oil-depletion allowance, or wage-price controls. Similarly, although to a lesser degree, parents are not expected to understand or to vote on the new math or the new social studies. Nor do candidates for election to local school boards normally take campaign stands on curriculum issues, except on particular hot issues such as sensitivity training and sex education.

But the analogy between economic policy and curriculum policy cannot be carried very far. Curriculum policy is primarily and traditionally the concern of the states and localities, even though the federal government's role is rapidly expanding. And when curriculum policy is determined it is a long way from implementation. Supposing that a policy decision survives emasculation by the administrative hierarchies of federal agencies and state and local officials, it still faces a pocket veto by 2,000,000 classroom teachers. So long as teachers consider themselves professional agents with some autonomy in curriculum questions by virtue of their professional expertise, policy implementation will be a matter of persuasion rather than direction. Of course it is possible that teachers will be replaced by meachanical and electronic devices or at least be so cowed as to make them dependable agents of policy. But the increasing unionization of teachers indicates that they will at least have a say in the determination of the policies they are asked to carry out.

Not only classroom teachers stand between policy makers and their goals, however. Numerous other agencies such as the College Entrance Examination Board, the national accreditation committees, scholarly, scientific and professional organizations as well as specifically educational pressure groups vie for a voice in curriculum policy-making. It seems highly unlikely that any one agency, even the federal government, could wrest policy-making autonomy from so many hands. But the example of Sputnik has shown that if a national emergency is frightening enough, centuries-old traditions can be swept aside in one session of the Congress, so one should not rule out the possibility of national educational planning for the U.S.

Even assuming that curriculum policy could be successfully formulated and consistently carried out, several barriers to the attainment of policy objectives remain that are inherent in the educational enterprise. One of these is the necessarily long-range nature of educational goals. A significant and stable change in the reading level of junior-high-school students cannot be obtained in less than a year and will probably take three or four years to appear *assuming we know how to get it.* Learning anything important takes time and therefore results are delayed. When results appear it is difficult to counter the argument that other forces than the policy change account for the results. For example, Tuddenham (1948) found evidence of a striking increase (a full standard deviation) in the mean absolute score on the Army Alpha intelligence test between World Wars I and II. Schaie and Strother (1968) reported a similar finding in a study comparing the differences in the tested mental ability among cohorts (generations) with the changes in score due to aging. He concluded that "a major proportion of the variance attributed to age difference (i.e., to aging) [on tests of basic mental abilities] must properly be assigned to differences in abilities between successive generations." (p. 679). Both investigators speculated that improved education of later generations was largely responsible for the apparent increase of scores on tests of mental ability. No propensity to assign this effect to the efforts of the public schools has yet appeared in or out of educational circles, but might they not be responsible? But then, the result could be due to TV or to the training programs of industry or to the armed forces' efforts. The question seems academic in any event. How could one determine the extent to which this increase in scores was due to the continually shifting practices of public schools over a quarter century?

Another difficulty of making, executing, and evaluating curriculum policy is the necessary ambiguity and generality of educational goals. Some educational goals are unnecessarily ambiguous. Such blatant examples as "appreciation" and "understanding" are notorious among students of education. But when these gratuitous sources of ambiguity have been eliminated considerable additional ambiguity remains. This is necessarily so for at least two reasons. First, because of the necessarily long interval between teaching and the adult use of the thing taught, together with the rapid rate of change in society generally, we must prepare students for a world whose outlines can be seen dimly at best. The age group with the largest responsibility for running the world today is, let us say, about 50 years old. They began school in 1926 and graduated from high school in 1938. Could we reasonably expect the educational planners of that period to have anticipated the specific knowledge, skill, and attitudes that would have begun to prepare these people for their lives today—for urban decay, television, atomic power, cold war, guerilla war, computers, pollution, future shock, and the knowledge explosion? If we make curriculum policy we must either make it concretely and in detail, with virtual certainty that much of the plans will be rendered useless by unexpected change, or make it somewhat general and loose in the expectation that in this way our students will be prepared for a greater variety of possible futures. It is somewhat like the difference between training an athlete for the decathlon and training him for a single event. If you don't know what events will appear in the games you can either train for one event and hope it appears or train for the decathlon and hope your athletes can bone up on their best event when they find out which events are scheduled.

A second barrier to precise, detailed curriculum policy-making is our meager knowledge of the phenomena of schooling. An elaborate argument to substantiate our ignorance is out of place here. Suffice it to say that trying to construct a complete school curriculum according to the currently accepted principles of behavioral science would appear to be roughly equivalent to trying to create a living plant using 17th-century alchemy.

In spite of the difficulties of systematic curriculum policy-making, efforts in this direction are virtually certain to increase. The steadily increasing role of federal and state governments, the increasing willingness of elected officials to speak out on educational questions, the increasing willingness of mass media to publish achievement test scores of local schools, National Assessment, which will provide detailed information on the educational attainment of American youth, and demands for community control, are portents of an increasingly political approach to curriculum questions on the part of the general public. As one observer has noted: "It seems to be that, at least in the giant cities, it is academic to debate closer educational-political cooperation. Whether we like it or not, the events of the day will not permit a fragmented approach to education in the city." (Saxe, 1969; p. 251). This development, whether one anticipates it with eagerness or dread, merits careful attention from educational scholars and researchers.

Bibliography

Aikin, Wilford. *The Story of the Eight-Year Study*. New York: Harper and Brothers, 1942.

Atkin, J. Myron. "Some Evaluation Problems in a Course Treatment Project," *Journal of Research in Science Teaching* 1:1, 1963.

Banfield, Edward. *Political Influence*. New York: Free Press, 1961.

Bauer, Raymond and Gergen, Kenneth. *The Study of Policy Formation*. New York: Free Press, 1968.

Bereiter, Carl and Engelmann, Siegfried. *Teaching Disadvantaged Children in the Preschool*. Englewood Cliffs, New Jersey: Prentice-Hall, 1966.

Black, Hillel. *The American Schoolbook*. New York: Morrow, 1967.

Brichell, Henry M., "State Organization for Educational Change". In Miles (ed.), *Innovation in Education*. New York: Teachers College Press, 1964, pp. 493-531.

Campbell, Roald F. and Bunnell, Robert A., *Nationalizing Influences on Secondary Education*. Chicago: Midwest Administration Center, 1963.

Carlson, Richard O. *Adoption of Educational Innovations*. Eugene: University of Oregon, 1965.

Chamberlin, Charles D. *Did They Succeed in College?* New York: Harper and Brothers, 1942.

Chesler, Mark, et al., "The Principal's Role in Facilitating Innovation", *Theory Into Practice* 1:2, 1963.

Conant, James B. *The Comprehensive High School: A Second Report to Interested Citizens*. New York: McGraw-Hill, 1967.

Counts, George. *School and Society in Chicago*. New York: Harcourt, Brace, 1928.

Easton, David (ed.). *Varieties of Political Theory*. Englewood Cliffs, New Jersey: Prentice-Hall, 1969.

Eisner, E.W., "Educational Objectives: Help or Hindrance?", *School Review* 75:3, 1967.

Eisner, E. W., "Instructional and Expressive Educational Objectives: Their Formulation and Use in Curriculum", in American Educational Research Association *Instructional Objectives*. Chicago: Rand McNally and Company, 1969.

Elazar, Daniel. *American Federalism*. New York: Crowell, 1965.

Gagne, R. M., "The Analysis of Instructional Objectives for the Design of Instruction", In Glaser (ed.). *Teaching Machines and Programmed Learning II: Data and Directions*. Washington, D. C.: National Education Association, 1965, pp. 21-65.

Gallagher, James J. "Teacher Variation in Concept Presentation in BSCS Curriculum Program." *BSCS Newsletter,* No. 30, January, 1967.

Gallup, George. *How the Nation Views The Public Schools.* Princeton: Gallup International, 1969.

Gilbreth, Frank B. *Primer of Scientific Management.* New York: D. Van Nostrand, 1914.

Gittell, Marilyn, et al., "Investigation of Fiscally Independent and Dependent School Districts". Washington, D. C.: Office of Education, Cooperative Research Project No. 3237, 1967.

Governor's Committee on Public Education. *Public Education in Texas.* Austin: Texas Education Agency, 1969.

Grobman, Arnold. *The Changing Classroom.* BSCS Bulletin No. 4. Garden City: Doubleday and Company, 1969.

Gwynn, O. Minor. *Curriculum Principles & Social Trends.* 3rd Edition New York: The Macmillan Company, 1960.

Hamrin, Gerald. "An Analysis of Factors Influencing Educational Change". Unpublished doctoral dissertation, Stanford University, 1970.

Harnack, Robert S., et. al. *Computer-Based Resource Units in School Situations.* Buffalo: State University of New York, 1969.

Henderson, Algo D. "Innovations in Medical Education". *Journal of Higher Education* 40:7, 1969.

Jackson, Phillip and Belford, Elizabeth, "Educational Objectives and the Joys of Teaching," *School Review* 73:3, 1965.

James, H. Thomas, et al. *Determinants of Educational Expenditures in Large Cities in the United States.* Stanford: School of Education, 1966.

Joint Economic Committee. *The Analysis and Evaluation of Public Expenditures: The PPB System.* U. S. Congress, 91st Congress, 1969.

Kaiser, Bruce. "Development of a Teacher Observation Instrument Consistent With the Chemical Education Material Study." Unpublished doctoral dissertation, Stanford University, 1969.

Kaufman, Jacob. "An Analysis of the Comparative Costs and Benefits of Vocational Versus Academic Education in Secondary School." Contract OEG-1-6-00512-0817. U.S. Office of Education, 1967.

Koerner, James. *Who Controls American Education.* Boston: Beacon Press, 1968.

Krug, Edward. *The Shaping of the American High School.* New York: Harper and Row, 1964.

Lerner, Daniel and Lasswell, Harold D. (ed.) *The Policy Sciences: Recent Developments in Scope and Method.* Stanford: Stanford University Press, 1951.

Levin, Henry M., "A Cost Effectiveness Analysis of Teacher Selection", *Journal of Human Resources* 5:1, 1970.

Lewis, Brian N. and Pask, Gordon, "The Theory and Practice of Adaptive Teaching Systems". In Glaser (ed.). Teaching Machines and Programmed Learning II: Data and Directions. Washington, D. C.: *National Education Association,* 1965, pp. 213-266.

Lindblom, Charles and Braybrooke, David. *A Strategy of Decision.* New York: Free Press, 1963.

Lippman, Walter.*American Inquisitors.* New York: Macmillan, 1928.

Mackenzie, Gordon N., "Curricular Change: Participants, Power, and Process". In Miles (ed.). *Innovation in Education.* New York: Teachers College Press, 1964, pp. 399-424.

Marsh, Paul. "The Physical Science Study Committee: A Case History of Nationwide Curriculum Development." Unpublished doctoral thesis. Graduate School of Education, Harvard University, 1963.

Martin, Roscoe. *Government and the Suburban School.* Syracuse: Syracuse University Press, 1962.

Merrill, Richard J. and Ridgway, David W. *The CHEM Study Story: A Successful Curriculum Improvement Project.* San Francisco: W. H. Freeman, 1969.

Miller, Robert B., "Analysis and Specification of Behavior for Training". In Glaser (ed.). *Training Research and Education.* Pittsburgh: University of Pittsburgh Press, 1962, pp. 31-62.

Moffett, James, "Misbehaviorist English: A Position Paper". In Maxwell and Tovatt (eds.). *On Writing Behavorial Objectives For English.* Champaign, Illinois: National Council of Teachers of English, 1970, pp. 111-116.

National Council for the Social Studies. The Social Studies and the Social Sciences. New York: Harcourt, Brace, and World, 1962.

Nelson, Jack and Roberts, Gene. *The Censors and the Schools.* Boston: Little, Brown, 1963.

Pellegrin, Roland J., "An Analysis of Sources and Processes of Innovation in Education". Eugene: Center for the Advanced Study of Educational Administration, 1966.

Pine, Patricia. "Where Education Begins". American Education 4:14, 1968.

Ribich, Thomas I. *Education and Poverty.* Washington: Brookings Institution, 1968.

Rosenthal, Alan. *Pedagogues and Power.* Syracuse: Syracuse University Press, 1969.

Salisbury, Robert H., "Schools and Politics in the Big City", *Harvard Educational Review* 37:3, 1967.

Saxe, Richard W., "Mayors and Schools", *Urban Education* 4:3, 1969.

Saylor, J. Galen and Alexander, William M. *Curriculum Planning For Modern Schools.* New York: Holt, Rinehart and Winston, Inc., 1966.

Schaie, K. Warner and Strother, Charles R., "A Cross-Sequential Study of Age Changes in Cognitive Behavior", *Psychological Bulletin* 70:6, 1969.

Smith, B. Othaniel, Stanley, William O., and Shores, J. Harlem. *Fundamentals of Curriculum Development.* New York: World Book Company, 1950.

Smith, John. "The Development of a Classroom Observation Instrument Relevant to the Earth Science Curriculum Project." Unpublished doctoral dissertation. Stanford University, 1969.

Spencer, Herbert. *Education: Intellectual, Moral, and Physical.* New York: D. Appleton and Company, 1870..

Stretch, Bonnie Barret, "The Rise of the 'Free School,' " *Saturday Review,* June 20, 1970.

Sundquist, James. *Politics and Power.* Washington, D.C.: Brookings Institution, 1969.

Taba, Hilda, *Curriculum Development: Theory and Practice.* New York: Harcourt, Brace and World, Inc., 1962.

Taylor, Frederick W. *Principles of Scientific Management.* New York: Harper and Brothers, 1911.

Tuddenham, Reed D., "Soldier Intelligence in World Wars I and II" *American Psychologist* 3:2, 1948.

Turner, Gordon B., "The American Council of Learned Societies and Curriculum Revision." In Heath (ed.). *New Curricula.* New York: Harper and Row, 1964, pp. 136-160.

Tyler, Ralph. *Basic Principles of Curriculum and Instruction.* Chicago: The University of Chicago Press, 1949.

United States Office of Education. Bureau of Research. *Support for Research and Related Activities.* April, 1969.

Werle, H. D., "Lay Participation in Curriculum Improvement Programs", Dissertation Abstracts 25:5081. 1964.

Wooten, William. *SMSG: The Making of a Curriculum.* New Haven: Yale University Press, 1965.

10 Teacher Characteristics and Their Influence on Pupil Performance

Alexander M. Mood

The purpose of this chapter is to summarize the present state of our knowledge of how teacher characteristics influence pupil performance. It would be more accurate to say, though, that the chapter will mainly be concerned with explaining why it is that we know so little, in fact, essentially nothing of a quantitative nature about how teacher characteristics influence pupil performance. Over the past several decades an enormous amount of data have been collected by educational administrators and research workers, hordes of analysts have poured over the data, libraries full of reports have been written; yet we stand today very much as if none of this effort had taken place—very much as if we had nothing but plain common sense as a basis for understanding how teacher characteristics may be related to learning. Would you like to appraise the extent to which a teacher's personal enthusiasm enhances learning? Just use your own judgment. That's as reliable as anything you will find in the reports. The same goes for teacher's experience, teacher's age, teacher's scholastic aptitude, sex, ethnicity, tolerance, beauty, charisma, amount of education, any characteristic you want to name.

To understand these statements we must first consider the best collection of data available these days. It was collected by the U.S. Office of Education in the fall of 1965 in response to a directive of Congress that the Office examine the equality of educational opportunity in the U.S. public schools. Many distinguished analysts have chosen to use it in their recent efforts to fathom with some kind of precision what is going on in the process of education. Researchers such as Coleman, Mayeske, Levin, Bowles, Hanushek, and Michelson, have used this data and some of their published reports are listed in the bibliography.

We had high hopes for it when we were collecting it. We were careful to get a great deal of relevant information that had never before been collected. We were determined to relate students' learning to all the important factors that might affect it. Thus, besides giving students tests of their knowledge of certain subjects, we gave their teachers a test to find out something about how much they knew; we obtained some data on teacher attitudes to find how well motivated they were, how pleased they were with their choice of a profession, how they liked their students and their schools and their supervisors and the communities in which they lived. We obtained information about the children's parents, their standard of living, their education, their participation in the child's

195

education, their ambitions and plans for their children. We gathered information about the school in great detail and about the administration of the school. We got information about the community and its attitudes toward education and financial support of education. All these matters are presumed to have some effect on a child's education and it was our intent that the data gathered by this survey (which will be called the EEO survey for Equal Educational Opportunity) would for the first time enable us to assess the magnitude of their effects. A detailed description of the data and of models used to analyze the data may be found in a report entitled Equality of Educational Opportunity and published by the U.S. Government Printing Office; it is often referred to as the Coleman report after its principal author but we shall call it the EEO report in deference to Professor Coleman's desire that the contributions of others not be slighted.

A fundamental lesson learned from the EEO survey is this: *the factors affecting a child's learning are thoroughly entangled and we have not yet discovered how to disentangle them.* It is worth spending a little time to make it absolutely clear what is meant by this statement. Let us consider just two factors which surely must, as a matter of common sense, influence children's learning: parent's education and teachers' verbal ability; let us consider a highly over-simplified example so that we can carry through the arithmetic in our heads and see directly the basic import of entanglement. I am using purely arbitrary data here—not data from the EEO survey.

Table 10-1
Adjusting Pupil Scores for Parents Education and Teacher Verbal Ability

Type of Neighborhood	Ghetto	Blue Collar	Upper Income
Average pupil reading scores	52	68	92
Average years of parents' education	8	12	16
Pupil scores adjusted for parents' education	52	48	52
Average teacher verbal ability	42	52	82
Pupil scores adjusted for teacher verbal ability	52	58	52
Pupil scores adjusted for both parents' education and teacher verbal ability	52	52	52

Let us suppose that a reading test was given to a number of fifth grade classes in ghetto schools, in schools in predominently working class neighborhoods, and in schools in very well-to-do neighborhoods and suppose that the average scores of the children were as shown in the first line of Table 10-1. Suppose also the average number of years of education of the children's parents were as shown in the second line of the table. The pupil average scores are very different in the three kinds of neighborhoods and we can think of a number of reasons why that might be expected. For example, the average amount of education of parents is different. The simplest possible model would adjust the scores to take account of these parent differences, then we would put them on a more comparable basis for examining other factors that might influence them—such as teacher experience, quality of school, class size, for example. We can adjust the children's reading scores to take account of parents' education in various ways; the results of a very satisfactory adjustment are given in the third line of the table. This adjustment happens to consist of (for reasons we need not go into) subtracting from the two higher pupil scores five times the additional years of education of the parents; thus the number 48 in the third line of the table is obtained by subtracting five times four from 68.

Now let us turn to a second factor which might influence pupil achievement, teacher verbal ability, and suppose that the average marks of the teachers in the respective neighborhoods were 42, 52, and 82 as shown in the fourth line of Table 10-1. If the original pupil scores are adjusted effectively by these numbers the results are found to be 52, 58, 52 as given in the fifth line of the table. (The adjustment consists of simply subtracting from the two larger scores the amount of verbal ability increase; thus $58 = 68 - (52 - 42)$ and the 52 in the third column is obtained by reducing 92 by the difference between 82 and 42.) Finally if the original average pupil scores are jointly adjusted by both average years of parents' education and average teacher verbal ability, they become identical as shown in the last line of the table.

Now we construct Table 10-2 from the first, third, fifth and sixth lines of Table 10-1 by subtracting the smallest number in each line from the largest in order to record the largest difference between the scores in each of those lines.

Table 10-2
Adjusting Differences in Pupil Scores

	Largest Difference between Scores	Reduction Achieved by Adjust- ment	Percent Reduction
Average pupil score	40		
Scores adjusted for parents' educa- tion	4	36	90%
Scores adjusted for teacher verbal ability	6	34	85%
Scores adjusted for both	0	40	100%

The second column shows the amounts that the three adjustments reduced the largest difference; the third column shows the percent of reduction. Finally we construct Table 10-3 to bring out what is meant by entanglement of the effects of parents' education with effect of teacher verbal ability. The three percentages in this table are derived from those in Table 10-2 as follows. We note in Table

Table 10-3
Percent Reduction in Differences in Pupil Scores

Percent reduction in largest difference that can be:	
Uniquely associated with parents' education	15%
Uniquely associated with teacher verbal ability	10%
Associated with either parents' education or teacher verbal ability	75%

10-2 that the adjustment for teacher verbal ability alone reduces the maximum difference between scores by 85%; when the adjustment for parents' education is applied in addition to the teacher adjustment then there is an additional 15% reduction (the reduction goes from 85% to 100%). This 15% is something the teacher adjustment could not achieve so it is said to be uniquely associated with parents' education. Similarly the teacher adjustment, when applied over and above the parent adjustment, increases the reduction by 10% (from 90% to 100%), so that 10% is said to be uniquely associated with teacher verbal ability. The remaining 75% can be associated with either the effect of parents' education or the effect of teacher verbal ability. The total reduction associated with parents' education is that 75% plus the 15% which is uniquely associated with parents' education. The total reduction associated with teacher verbal ability is that 75% plus the 10% uniquely associated with teacher verbal ability.

The 75% measures the degree of entanglement between the effects of these two factors. If we were asked on the basis of the (purely hypothetical) data in the first table whether parents' education or teachers' verbal ability was more important to children's education, we could only answer that the effects overlap so much that it is impossible to say. In some of the research papers, particularly those of Mayeske (*A Study of Our Nation's Schools*, and *Teacher Attributes and School Achievement*), the percentage overlap between effects of two or more factors is called the commonality of the effects; it is defined a little differently (in terms of the mean square differences between scores instead of the maximum difference) but the basic concept is the same. If we should add a third factor, say average class size, then it would have a small unique percentage associated with it and the two unique percentages of 15% and 10% associated with the two factors already considered would become smaller; there would be overlaps or commonalities between each pair and there would be a commonality that could be associated with any of the three factors. An example is given below of a calculation of this kind made by Mayeske.

One of the major findings of the EEO study was that a student's learning seemed to be quite dependent on his fellow students (or peers). If his peers are good students and well motivated toward learning, then his learning is likely to be enhanced. The following table, which is taken from the volume by Mayeske et al. (1970), gives percentages of achievement associated with two factors:

quality of peers and quality of schools. Both of these factors are represented by index numbers which combine a number of characteristics. The quality of a school is determined by its teacher's qualifications as well as various characteristics of the facilities, equipment, curriculum, administration, accreditation, finance, organization, and so on. The percentages in Table 10-4 may be interpreted as entirely analogous to those we computed for Table 10-3. We see here in real data how large the overlap is between these two factors.

Table 10-4
Relationship of Peer and School Quality to Student Achievement

Percentage of student achievement associated with peer quality and school quality.			
	3rd Grade	6th Grade	9th Grade	12th Grade
Uniquely associated with peer quality	7.4	9.7	10.6	7.5
Uniquely associated with school quality	3.9	4.1	4.6	4.0
May be associated with either peer or school quality	45.1	69.1	71.5	74.7

In Table 10-5 below, which is also taken from Mayeske, the school quality index deals with three factors: peer quality, teacher quality, and other school quality aside from teacher quality which is simply denoted in the table by OS to stand for *other school*. The fact that most of the overlap occurring in the third line of Table 10-4 moves up to the fourth line of Table 10-5 leads one to believe that teachers definitely dominate other school factors in influencing learning.

Table 10-5
Grade Level and Factors Influencing Pupil Performance

	3rd Grade	6th Grade	9th Grade	12th Grade
Uniquely associated with peers	7.4	9.7	10.6	7.5
Uniquely associated with teachers	3.1	2.7	1.7	1.7
Uniquely associated with OS	0.8	1.0	2.1	2.2
May be associated with peers or teachers	34.6	54.7	48.9	45.1
May be associated with peers or OS	0.7	0.6	1.9	2.1
May be associated with teachers or OS	0.0	0.4	0.8	0.1
May be associated with peers or teachers or OS	9.7	13.9	20.6	27.5

Professor Henry Levin notes that not only the Coleman studies but a number of others find teachers to be the most prominent school factor and that this finding is quite in accord with common sense. Teachers certainly dominate the whole process and provide essentially the whole point of contact with schools so far as the children are concerned. Professor Herbert Kiesling is not so sure. Some of his own studies indicate that good administration is very likely to be found when school projects are successful and he can point to examples of successful projects which used rather mediocre teachers. He makes the further point that analyses which focus too much on teachers would not enable one to detect good management; its good effects would simply appear to emanate from teachers.

Now let us turn to another matter that is well illustrated by the foregoing calculations. It is that *the order in which one makes adjustments for two different factors makes a great deal of difference*; to be a little clearer about what is happening it is wise to use both orders. A similar consideration applies when more than two factors are being included in the analysis. The point is simply this (referring to Table 10-2): if we adjust scores for parents' education to get a 90% reduction in the maximum difference between scores and then adjust the differences for teacher verbal ability to get an additional 10% reduction, we might be inclined to suppose that parents' education was far more important to learning than teacher verbal ability. Of course, using this false reasoning, we would conclude that teacher verbal ability was much more important if the order of the two factors were reversed in making the adjustments.

We have been charged with making this error in the EEO report and we did in the sense that we were not nearly careful enough to point out that we were concerned with the relative sizes rather than the absolute sizes of the effects of school factors. In the analysis of the EEO survey data we first adjusted pupil scores for family socio-economic status and then we looked at various school factors such as teacher ability, class size, quality of library and science laboratory facilities, type of curriculum, and so on. Naturally the first adjustment for socio-economic effect reduced the size of these various school effects. The purpose of the analysis was to rank the school factors in order of importance so that school administrators would be given some indication of where it might be most profitable to put additional resources. It seemed reasonable to us and still seems reasonable to me to do this ranking with that part of the learning effect that is uniquely associated with schools. However, so much has been made of the smallness of the school effects that I wish, in retrospect, that we had done the ranking both ways—with the total school effect as well as with the unique school effect. The two rankings would have come out much the same way with the effect of teachers well ahead of the effect of any other school factor. This is the one positive quantitative thing we can say about the role of teachers in education; we cannot say how big their effect is but it certainly appears to be distinctly larger than any other component of the school system.

The primary point that we have been making in all the foregoing illustrations and arguments is this: we cannot say much about the size of the teacher effect on children's learning because that effect overlaps and is thoroughly entangled with other effects in a way that we are thus far unable to unravel.

The question naturally arises as to whether it will ever be possible for researchers to unravel the various influences affecting learning and say something quantitative about them. I have no definite answer; my guess is that it may be impossible to separate them completely but that, in time, competent research can go a considerable way in that direction. It seems to me that there is some cause for optimism despite conspicuous failure to date because the failures have given us useful clues as to how research efforts should proceed. We need to develop a fairly comprehensive set of factors which do not overlap. The set must be comprehensive so that every educational influence that we can think of can be associated with some factor or can be divided up among several factors. If the set is not complete then there will be no chance to investigate the overlap between elements included and those not included and there will be the difficulty noted earlier by Professor Kiesling in connection with good management that effects which really belong to one factor will be erroneously attributed to another. The individual components must overlap as little as possible—preferably not at all. It will not be possible to define such a set of factors heuristically; we shall have to gather data in large quantities many times over and engage in a sort of sequential successive approximation to such a desirable set.

One secret of success in this kind of research program will be to create variables (or proxies for variables) that are highly specific to a given factor—that is, are little correlated with other factors. Another secret of success will be in devising structural relations (described below) which will enable us to declare that an apparent overlap is in reality the result of a second relation. Thus achievement may appear to be related to both peer quality and teacher quality in a single equation; but perhaps a system of two simultaneous equations is the correct representation with achievement being related to teacher quality in one equation and peer quality related to teacher quality in the other.

One reason that we have made so little headway is that we have tried to deal with a very complicated phenomenon in a relatively simple way. A teacher alone is terribly complicated, a child is equally complicated and the interaction between them multiplies one large set of complications by another large set. Our investigations have not begun to comprehend the interaction between the child and the teacher. Most investigations typically settle for a few bits of barely relevant data about a teacher—mostly items that are easy to come by such as age, sex, certification, salary, years of experience, amount of graduate education, etc., the kinds of things that can be picked off of the personnel records. Of course it is utterly impossible to look at such fragmentary crumbs of information and form any impression at all of the teacher behind them. As noted above, we tried to get a fuller specification of the teachers in the EEO survey. The most successful element of that attempt was a little verbal test which scored the competence of teachers to discriminate between certain usages of words. By successful I mean that many investigators (Coleman, Levin, Bowles, Hanushek, Michelson) found that it was a more faithful indicator of children's learning than any of those things that are found on the personnel record. That should surprise no one. The verbal score, in some small way, gives a clue to the teacher's intellectual competence. Those things on the personnel record (years of experience, amount of graduate work) give virtually no clue at all as to the teacher's competence.

We have here, then, one dimension of a teacher, verbal competence, that seems to be well related to children's achievement. It is instructive to think briefly of the tremendous variety of teachers that might have the same verbal score ranging from warm, concerned, dedicated, conscientious, imaginative, talented individuals to unconcerned nobodies who are there strictly for the paycheck. From another point of view we can think of how many other dimensions of teacher competence there are. I recently spent a little time trying to assemble a complete set of teacher characteristics that might be as significant to learning as verbal competence. The list turned out to contain about fifty such characteristics. (It can be found in the U.S. Office of Education publication entitled *Do Teachers Make a Difference?*). I have no idea how complete it is or how comparable the items on it are but it gives us at least a hint that in the EEO survey we were very far indeed from obtaining any substantial characterization of a teacher. That is some kind of lesson. We thought we were going much farther than others had gone but in reality we went just about one step.

In conclusion we are in a very primitive state of the technology of specifying or statistically describing a teacher—not as a person, which would be much harder, but simply as a teacher. The same goes for students. The same goes for interactions between them.

Another aspect of our failure to grapple with the learning process in a quantitative way has to do with our use of proxies for factors when we do not know how to measure the factors directly. In some lines of investigation there is a history of development and fairly thorough understanding of the extent to which proxies are suitable substitutes for the real thing. In education there has been no such history of development in some very important areas. We have uncritically continued to use proxies that have a long history of use but which have not a shred of evidence of validity. Years of *graduate education* is a proxy for educational know-how; the presumption is that teachers are learning how to teach better when they take graduate courses. Analyses of the EEO survey data convince me that that presumption is wrong. Specifically, the fact that the *verbal score* seems to be so much better related to children's learning than *years of graduate education* convinces me that the latter is no proxy at all for educational know-how; educational know-how consists of far more than verbal facility yet here we see a measure of that one skill dominating a measure that is expected to represent the whole complex of skills. It also overwhelmingly dominates *years of experience*, another favorite proxy for educational know-how. This outcome of recent studies is most unsettling because it undermines the basic rationale of educational administration. It seems to be altogether possible that our whole incentive structure for teachers rests on sand.

Professor Henry Levin mentioned another myth of educational administration, desirability of small class size, that persists despite endless studies which show that class size has little or no connection with achievement. Still when administrators get more money, they frequently start hiring more teachers and reducing class size. Levin believes that this strategy accomplishes nothing because it has no noticeable effect on teacher behavior; she conducts a class of 30 pupils almost exactly like she conducts a class of 40 pupils. Some investigators definitely find a positive correlation between achievement and class size; the finding is explained by the tendency of principals to put their better teachers in charge of the larger classes in their schools.

There is one other serious limitation to our understanding of teacher effects and any other effect. It is the simplicity of our models which tend to be simple linear regression models connecting dependent to independent variables. This limitation is mostly a consequence of the simplicity of our data. It is clear though that any real analysis of learning will require more elaborate structure in our models. We cannot assume, for example, that peer quality is an independent influence; it must arise in part at least from parent quality or from teacher quality or both. Levin and Michelson have begun to build somewhat more realistic structure into models.

Professor Levin discussed one such structural relation developed in his own analyses of the EEO data. It dealt with a variable called *efficacy* which represents a student's belief in his own capacity to do things and to have a measure of control over his life. If one looks at achievement as a function of efficacy he finds, as expected, that they are positively related. One also finds that efficacy is negatively related to family size. If one examined the statistical relationship between achievement and family size he would conclude that large family size inhibits achievement. But, according to Levin's work, it would not make sense to put family size into an equation determining achievement; one needs at least two simultaneous equations: one relating efficacy to family size (among other things) and another relating achievement to efficacy (among other things). With this kind of structure one avoids putting himself in the doubtful position of claiming that large families per se inhibit learning. He also gives educators a little better clue about what is going on with children from large families and what might be done about it instead of simply reconciling themselves to an inevitable educational outcome of family size educators can consider the intermediate variable, efficacy, and perhaps find ways to improve that despite family size; that is, they can regard the difficulty as possibly not entirely confined to a domain over which they have no control.

Since we know so little about the relation of teacher characteristics to learning, does it follow that nothing can be done now with respect to teachers to improve education? Not at all. From the point of view of educational administration, much can be done by observing the results of the educational process. Of course more could be done if the process were thoroughly understood. Meanwhile administrators can simply observe which teachers do a good job of raising their pupils one grade level during the year and which don't. They can reward those that do and penalize or weed out the others. In using this type of management administrators must not let their attention be monopolized by grade levels in academic achievement only. Personal development is just as important as academic development. Teachers must be evaluated not only on the basis of how well children perform on tests of reading, writing and arithmetic but also on tests of self-confidence, social competence, responsibility, ethics, ambition and creativeness.

I should make clear that I am not suggesting that, say, fourth grade teachers should be expected to raise all their pupils to the fifth grade level by the end of the year. Some of their charges may have been far behind in certain skills—perhaps at only the second grade level. In that case the teacher's goal is to raise them at least one level—to the third grade level. This kind of evaluation of teachers would go far to eliminating poor teachers from schools despite tenure laws. When a teacher observed that she was regularly accomplishing significantly less with children than other teachers had accomplished in the past with the same children, she would be very much impelled to look about for a different line of work.

Bibliography

Bowles, S.S., and Levin, H.M., "Determinants of scholastic achievement," *Journal of Human Resources*, Vol. 3, No. 1, 1968.

Coleman, J.S., et al., *Equality of Educational Opportunity*, U.S. Government Printing Office, Washington, D.C., 1966.

Hanushek, E., *The Education of Negroes and Whites*, unpublished Ph.D. dissertation, Mass. Inst. of Technology, 1968.

Hanushek, E., "The production of education, teacher quality, and efficiency," *Do Teachers Make a Difference?* U.S. Government Printing Office, Washington, D.C., 1970.

Levin, H.M., "The failure of public schools and the free market remedy," *Urban Review*, Vol. 2, No. 7, 1968.

Levin, H.M., "A new model of school effectiveness," *Do Teachers Make a Difference?* U.S. Government Printing Office, Washington, D.C., 1970.

Mayeske, G.W., et al., *A Study of Our Nation's Schools.* U.S. Office of Education, Washington, D.C., 1970.

Mayeske, G.W., "Teacher Attributes and School Achievement," *Do Teachers Make a Difference?* U.S. Government Printing Office, Washington, D.C., 1970.

Michelson, S., "The association of teacher resourceness with children's characteristics," *Do Teachers Make a Difference?* U.S. Government Printing Office, Washington, D.C., 1970.

Mood, A.M., "Macro-analysis of the American educational system," *Operations Research*, Vol. 17, pp. 770-784, 1969.

Mood, A.M., "Do Teachers Make a Difference?," *Do Teachers Make a Difference?* U.S. Government Printing Office, Washington, D.C., 1970.

Mosteller, F., and Moynihan, D.P. (eds.) *On Equality of Educational Opportunity*, Random House, N.Y., 1970.

Ribich, T.I., *Education and Poverty*, Brookings Institution, Washington, D.C., 1968.

11

Technology and Learning: An Analysis of Current Issues

C.R. Carpenter

Search for a Frame of Reference

Four considerations are proposed as background for designing instructional technology strategies and their relationship to the education processes: (1) Education is more of a demand-generating than a demand-satisfying operation; problems are usually transformed into other problems rather than solved. (2) The expanding work and increasing responsibility of education can be accomplished only by using the results of this century's many revolutions in communication technologies. The scope of the required effort greatly exceeds the limits of traditional educational operations of established institutions. (3) Educational efforts on a national scale are increasing the demands for improved quality and relevance of instruction. (4) Educational efforts are being evaluated within a socioeconomic framework where performance criteria and accountability are key concepts. The profound issues confronted are public academic freedom, academic seclusion, and rational analysis of educational work.

The National Commission on Instructional Technology completed its reviews, arguments and publication in 1970, therefore, in this chapter the work of the Commission on Instructional Technology will be emphasized because of its possible eventual significance for local school district policies and because of the significance and promise of the Commission's recommendations for educational development of the United States.

In general, an attempt will be made to present four different developments in instructional technology which have relevance to policy formulation and strategy planning for education. A summarization of the main proposals of the Carnegie Commission report, which proposed the Commission on Instructional Technology (Carnegie Commission on Educational Television 1967) will be presented first, then the recommendations of the National Commission on Instructional Technology, which relate to policy formulation operations in the areas of instructional technology (Tickton 1970) will be discussed. Finally, a discussion of the highlights of a conference on "Telecommunications: Toward National Policies for Education," (Meaney and Carpenter 1970) will be presented.

Some Contingencies of the Broader Educational Task

Let us consider the roles and functions for designing educational strategies using instructional technology (Center for Educational Research and Innovation 1970). Within the boundaries of these considerations or factors lie intriguing and difficult problems for educators and policy makers in our schools, colleges, and universities. The first factor is the general scientific model of defining a problem, selecting or developing methods and procedures for solving the problem, and then actually solving a problem. Using the similar industrial model, we define the need for a product, assess the market potentials for the product, produce the product, sell it, make a profit, and satisfy a social need.

These are *not* models for action that are appropriate because education is a different type of enterprise. Education seems to create more and more demands on the system the better it performs its task of educating, training, inspiring, and developing people. In essence, *education is a work-generating process.* Hence, we never really *solve* educational problems clearly and completely; we merely create other kinds of problems, and frequently these transformed problems require different dimensions and kinds of work. These self-generating, open, creative kinds of need-generating functions of education are important since they indicate that the problem solving models of the scientific laboratory, or the model of industrial enterprise products are not analogous to models of education and learning activities.

A second factor or assumption is that we can accomplish the increasing job of education only by using improved traditional methodologies complemented by new, advanced, and effective instructional methodologies. One set of available resources that can be used for restructuring traditional methodologies is that of communication technologies. The developed systems can be made to map the scope and range of the requirements and conditions that confront contemporary education. The full development and use of appropriate instructional technology is therefore imperative for modern education.

A third set of factors is that this society is in a phase of extremely rapid change, that these changes are both regressive and developmental, and that there are increasingly *varied* demands for educational results.

Charles Frankel stated some of these new demands in his keynote address at the Georgia Conference on Instructional Telecommunications: "What are the prevailing expectancies that are expanding or contracting, and which should importantly affect modifications in educational operations? What are the people's realistic hopes and disillusions about education that have to be considered? (Meany and Carpenter 1970, p. 20)." These considerations relate closely to the scale of the educational job which confronts us as do the population growth and training requirements for a society in which *service needs* are growing rapidly in amount and complexity.

A fourth factor is that we can no longer evade the imperative need for responding to both the public and professional demands for educational accountability defined by economic and performance terms. Perhaps we have evaded for too long dealing rationally and responsibly with the issues of *real world policies and economics.* Perhaps, also, our idealistic conceptions of what education is and how it operates have given us escapist delusions from the rigors of performance accountability relative to costs and the returns on investments of human talents (Bolvin 1969 and Bord 1969).

The issues of public education, public communications, and new responsibil-ities clearly are contingent upon the unsolved factors of *public academic freedoms.* The need for public academic freedom to explore crucial social issues with vigor and precision constitutes a new challenge for adaptive educational developments. How do we manage to be freely academic within the restraints of traditional institutions and at the same time meet the professional requirements for direct, analytical, rational confrontation of real world conditions? How can we avoid the inhibiting effects of public condemnation and the paralyzing effects of adverse public opinion?

These are a few of the contingencies that define the educational tasks of broadening and changing the demands made on education and for effectively applying instructional technology as important components of instructional systems.

Search for the Roles of Instructional Technology

Educators and researchers need to evaluate systematically the expectations and possibilities that instructional technology will increase instructional effective-ness, decrease educational deficiencies, provide better conditions for learning, and maintain or reduce costs (Carpenter 1970). Clearly understanding instruc-tional communication technologies, their scope and potentials relative to the broad fields of science and technology as they operate within the general social context is equally as important as gains in efficiency and in cost/benefit advantages. Furthermore, rational analysis of the results of the modern com-munication revolution and of how these results can be transferred and applied advantageously in the field of educational and instructional communications requires a public and professional understanding that is not presently clearly in evidence. This understanding we can and must develop (Bushnell 1969, Davis 1969, Marx 1969).

The International Federation for Information Processing Conference on Computer Education 1970 formulated as one of its principal recommendations the proposal that training, public education, and broad information dissemina-tion are required on the theme of "computer appreciation." It was proposed that schools and universities create courses of study for computers like those for art appreciation (International Federation for Information Processing 1970). Perhaps we need to broaden this proposal to include a wide spectrum of communication technologies and instructional systems which need to be thoroughly understood by both professional educators and the public. Surely we need to correct the prevailing negative attitude of many influential professional educators toward technology and its use and effects. We need to transform hostility and aggression toward a *neutral* technology so that it can be optimally applied in education. These negative reactions of professional educators toward technology may be an aggression displacement mechanism that can be channeled into constructive behavior by well designed broadcast appreciation courses explicating the essential roles of computers, tape recorders, and distribution-display systems as useful educational instruments.

A recent study of the history of Title VII of the National Defense Education Act of 1958 (legislation which supported "new media" research and development programs that have essentially disappeared from the U.S. Office of Education) suggests that researchers frequently first create a technology and then we look for a problem to solve with that technology (Filep and Schramm 1970).

Some interesting questions for researchers are these (Parkus 1969): What do we do with a developed instructional technology which justifies the cost and will earn a profit for its manufacturer? How do we use the full potential of communication technologies correctly for valid educative purposes? How do we specify the important educative functions to be served by technology and then insure that these deserving functions be served?

Concerning the last question, Charles Frankel's concept of increasing intellectual mobility is one broad function that needs to be served by a mature communication technology (Meaney and Carpenter 1970).

The search for and the organization and assimilation of information are examples of operations that urgently need to be served by advanced technologies. Another challenge is the reduction of the barriers to information flow to people separated by geographic spaces, such as is the plight of the rural people of this country. It is apparent that we can move information easier than moving people. As populations increase and intolerable urban congestion mounts, the problem of moving stimulus material for learning to people rather than moving people to stimulus material might become a desirable and essential strategy for providing many kinds of educational opportunities to all people who need and want to learn. These problems can be resolved by modern instructional technologies when properly engineered.

Technology and Humanistic Considerations

Of the many issues debated during the extended early discussions of the Commission on Instructional Technology, one of the most frequent was that of humanism and technology. At first impression, the discussion of humanism and technology seems to be a diversionary tactic of people resistant to adaptive change. But the more exposure to serious debate, and the more reading on the issues of human values and the communication media, the more real and critical the issues become for those involved in instructional technology.

The issues are real, at least in the sense that people thinking them so make issues real, and therefore we must confront them intellectually. The issues are real, also, in the sense that the negative belief systems of educational decision-makers toward instructional technologies often have prevented the systematic and otherwise justified applications of technological developments to the urgent and growing requirements of education that cannot be resolved by other available and conventional means.

In making these applications there are several points which directly relate to the formulation of educational plans and policies. *The application of instructional technology on a significant scale does importantly change whole educational systems* (Bolvin 1969 and Dempsey 1969). There is a kind of "plus value" that is not the simple clean-cut solving of a problem as would be the case in a scientific laboratory or in an industry. There are many "side effects" to innovations which need to be anticipated and regulated by planners. However, in the formulation of plans and policies, in the projection of technological innovations into a society or educational system, we frequently ignore both the "plus values" and "side effects."

Some interesting problems to be solved are: What are the comparable side effects and plus values in our field connected with introducing communication technologies? What are the effects of presenting more and more people with more and more *flat* representational worlds in books, and on cathode tube faces? What is the response and effect on developing children of the vast amounts of broadcast stimuli that represent flat abstract worlds? For the world of print, of film and tape, even with depth perception, is flat; even with sound and color it is still representational and sign symbolic, not iconic, authentic, or realistic. It is not the three dimensional touchable, feelable world of plants, of bark and leaves, and of animals furry, or slimy, in a wet forest pond. The world of print, picture, and sounds isn't a world that children can reach out and touch; they can't surround it, or be surrounded by it.

Incidentally, the flat reflected world is very confusing to wild chimpanzees. Jane Goodall, who studies them in the Gombe Stream Reserve of Tanzania, reports that when she presented a mirror to them, they explored and tried to perceive the mystery of the flat reflections of themselves. They looked and reached behind the mirror and tried to touch the reflected image.

One wonders how much intellectual maladaptation is being created by broadcasting so many representational worlds in the intellectual communication stream to so many millions of people, and what compensatory educational developments are needed. These questions are posed only as examples to stimulate thinking about these and other possible side effects of extensively introducing instructional technology into the worlds of children without providing other balancing of modes of stimulation for learning, personal growth, and development. We are obligated, in any assessment of the implications of instructional technology upon school district policy, to consider both the losses and the gains, the transformations and the permutations, the positive and negative factors that occur when in the design strategies of educational systems we optimize *teaching-learning ecologies* by using many kinds of instructional technologies.

There are side effects that should be considered in relation to the application to education of the results of the twentieth century communications revolution. The effect of communications overload on people's social and individual adjustments is one such effect. Perhaps we have a communications overload rather than an "information explosion." In any event, the phenomenon should be analyzed. What is the real and truly *new* information, and what is reiteration or duplication? Since we may be making merely more and more copies of the same thing, these are curical questions that need answers. Policy formulations should include precautions against communications overload, the constant bombardment of people by information that is lacking in utility and meaning for them and that is selected only by the protective buffering of personal perceptual-cognitive processes. Policy formulation may need to take cognizance, also, of the contamination in information channels. There may be the need to provide varied and new processes of selection or regulation of our communication channels in order to provide the *essential information that has adaptive values* and that deserves to be emphasized in our organized information systems. The distribution channels of television, radio, newspapers, and other print may need to be decontaminated of nonadaptive or disruptive content because these media have almost continuous positive and negative interactions with more formal educational and cultural efforts. If these issues are valid, do we have acceptable procedures for implementing corrective measures?

One regulative procedure is that of increasing the standards and quality of public telecommunications, both educational and commercial, public and private. The nonuse, as well as misuse, of these vast learning resources deserves the attention of professional educators and responsible citizens.

The adaptive use and the transformations that can be made from one medium to another need to be developed so that resources for learning are available when and where needed for the optimal interactions with appropriate kinds of people in the diverse learning publics.

Robert Hudson, speaking informally during the Georgia Conference on Telecommunications, made the point that very soon we shall have available satellite relay systems for greatly speeding up and extending distribution of programs. Hudson asked, "What is education doing (now) to prepare for satellites?" He states this challenging proposition: "What programs have we now, or are developing, for satellites when they are available and in what quantities? We should be planning for the use of satellites rather than worrying about installing closed-circuit television in certain school systems." Dr. Hudson cites only the satellite relay example of the great disparity between communications technological potential and long-range planning to use effectively these future developments. Radio and motion pictures, community cable systems and computers, teaching devices and a superb publication technology are other examples. To review, we are neglecting using communication technology as we should for *instructional* purposes, and also we are misusing vast available communication resources which could be made to serve educational and cultural purposes.

In Munich, Germany, educators are busily engaged in designing a modern Instructional Communications Institute that will cost the equivalent of several million dollars. West Germany has three television channels used principally for training and education with strong emphasis on *adult* and *technical education.* No channels are exclusively available for commercial uses in West Germany. Advertising functions are served in the evening by limited blocks of advertising time. The three channels are used principally for the transmission of useful public information and for instruction. The Soviet Bloc countries have a similar pattern of use for television broadcasts.

Operations in England, Japan, Germany, Sweden and the Netherlands suggest that we need to examine models of very different *patterns of use* of public communications resources, their allotments and priorities, and to assess them critically with the view of adopting them in the United States. As one approach to improve planning and policy formulations, we need to study continuously the management and application of educational communication systems in Japan, India, Russia, Yugoslavia, Italy, France, the British Isles, and Canada as one means of arriving at a frame of reference for judging the merits and weakness of our system.

The Commission on Instructional Technology

The most important product of this National Commission was planned to be a report to President Nixon and to the Secretary of Health, Education, and Welfare. About two hundred documents were contributed or contracted for and used as documentation for this report. Many of these documents have been published by the Academy for Educational Development (Davies 1969 and Tickton 1970).

The Carnegie Commission defined initially, in 1967, the functions of the Commission on Instructional Technology by stating that it should study intensively and in depth, over adequate time, the place of modern technology in the educational systems of the nation. In particular, it was suggested that the commission be concerned with the role of the Federal government in the responsible relationship of sponsoring *instructional* broadcast media, with emphasis on radio and television.

A redefinition of the assignment as outlined by the Carnegie Commission Corporation was indicated and this definition became the first task of the commission itself. Instructions from U.S. Commissioner of Education Harold Howe, II, sketched a very broad charge to the commission: namely, to assess the potentials of *all kinds of instructional technology* for all areas and levels of education including continuing education, and with special reference to the most critical educational problems of the nation.

Definition of Technology

The broad inclusive definition of technology can be made more concrete by describing a site visit by the commission on instructional technology to the U.S. Air Force Academy, Colorado Springs, Colorado.

This visit and the context of the academy demonstrated vividly that technology does not consist merely of television, teaching machines, radios, and computers. It became clear that this whole institution is a product of industrial technology, and functions as a complex of modern communications technologies; the buildings and their shapes, the acoustical properties of classrooms and other interior designs and lighting, the traffic and information flow systems, and even the composition and colors of building materials: all of these components are part of the instructional technological system of the academy.

Harold B. Gores, the president of Educational Facilities Laboratories, New York, argued that no sharp lines can be drawn between instructional technology and other components of the academy's learning and living environment. It was agreed, furthermore, that modern technology also includes human factors; people are essential parts of a complete and operable technological system. For a needed focus, however, the commission elected to limit its explorations, studies, and deliberations to informational or communication technologies and their applications to the context of learning and teaching for the improvement of learning.

The commission made site visits to selected educational situations, for example, to the Palo Alto school system and Stanford University to study computer assisted instruction. Visits were made by commission and staff members to various kinds of schools, school systems, and institutions of higher education that were believed to be leaders in applying technology to instructional problems.

Recommendations

After more than a year's work of study, observations, and discussions, the commission made the following recommendations. The first two recommendations proposed changes in the organization of Federal agencies. Recommendation one proposed the establishment of a National Institutes of Education (NIE), and recommendation two proposed a National Institute for Instructional Technology (NIIT). The model selected was the National Institutes of Health. Regardless of the controversies that sometimes rage about the work of the National Institutes of Health, they are probably the most conspicuous and constructive development that the Federal government has accomplished in the area of health. The educational programs of the Department of Agriculture exemplify other great achievements and possible models. In scope and complexity the nationwide problems of education are equally as critical and massive as the conditions of health and disease, agriculture and rural life, and population increase and ecology. However, it is agreed that at the Federal level we do not have entirely adequate national instruments for dealing with these educational conditions, let alone importantly improving them.

In a sense, to recommend the National Institutes of Education was not part of the mission of the Commission on Instructional Technology (Krathwohl 1969). We were charged to deal with instructional technology, but it became evident to the commission that instructional technology without a *substantive context* cannot be properly conceived or applied. Therefore, the commission was compelled to say what, in a national setting at the Federal level, would be required for instructional technology to have a proper base or operational context. Therefore, we proposed first that National Institutes of Education be established, and then that one of a number of these institutes should be a National Institute for Instructional Technology. There could be other institutes, for example, on human learning, the assessment of human variabilities and capacities, and the training of the handicapped, disadvantaged, and exceptionally talented.

The National Institute for Instructional Technology would administer, it was proposed, a number of action programs: the Regional Educational Laboratories (RELS) and the Research and Development (R&D) Centers that already are working would be extended and strengthened. These laboratories and centers, after evaluation by the commission, were judged to be organizations with very great possibilities and potentials for research and for applying the results from many relevant sciences and technologies to serve the critical educational needs of different regions of the nation.

The commission was concerned about strengthening research programs that apply directly to the field of education. Accordingly, the commission recommended early concentration on programs of educational research and development, and it added to research and development a phase of application. The research, development, and dissemination sequence of NDEA, Title VII, that was so splendidly conducted until abandoned by the U.S. Office of Education, does not complete the cycle from theory through development to practical results. *Research and development* must be followed by effective *application* (RD&A), and not merely by *dissemination* or *diffusion*. The application stage is frequently most complex and requires its own special strategies. Eventually, after intense debate, the thinking and expressions of the commission included RD&A as the genetic code for creative research-based innovations in education. RD&A symbolize, also, the essential sequential steps that include end products and consequences. The payoff from research is found in effective application or at least transformation, or integration and differentiation, of targeted problems and peoples. The great efforts of the U.S. Office of Education for dissemination of Title VII results often fell short of effective application with viable innovation and results, and the programs generally lacked cybernetic feedback regulators for subsequent cycles of research and development.

Recommendation three is for a program under the NIIT that would encourage and yield production of high quality instructional material. A very successful component of modern instructional technology is printing and publishing (Locke and Engler 1969). Some electronically fixated broadcast professions forget that printing and publishing are also very advanced contemporary technologies. For example, the reproduction of color photographs is a recent technical development that rapidly has become a fine and applied art. High speed printing is an equally impressive technical development. In the area of publishing, we have no concern about this being a very successful and profitable, even though a wasteful and environmentally contaminating, private enterprise. However, in other areas of instructional technology, especially the production of programs for electronic hardware, there is great disparity between the facilities that are available and operational, and the programs or software for them that have been produced, tested, and are ready for use (Parkus 1969 and Smith 1969). The commission was very sensitive to the lack of adequate amounts and quality of instructional program materials for many kinds of broadcast, electronic display, and computer media. Therefore, it was proposed to encourage the procurement and/or production of high quality instructional material on a scale to match the available capabilities for the distribution and display of programs by equipment that we already have available. This recommendation proposed no less than a radical revision of priorities for the nation's educational communication capabilities. Can "software" for the electronic media be produced as successfully as print is produced, marketed and made available for educational uses?

All of the Regional Educational Laboratories, it was observed, have "software" production capabilities for instructional programs. However, they, too, are not adequate to present requirements, nor are they in balance in terms of the total range and scope of educational requirements that they are attempting to meet. For example, very little is being done to produce instructional programs for community and junior colleges or for higher education. Nevertheless, the RELS have great possibilities for creatively producing and testing instructional programs that are needed for all regional uses. The efforts of our RELS are principally focused on programs for young children. Perhaps this is currently justified, but the R&D Centers and RELS surely can be expected, with proper

Federal, state, and local support, to respond more broadly than at present to educational needs at all levels of educational and instructional program requirements (Bushnell 1969).

Recommendation three also asks for action by NIIT to make available the vast amount of instructional, nonprint material that exists in the world which could be used for instruction. When such material is not actually available at points of use for instructional processes, it really does not exist for the learner or the teacher. A film, no matter how excellent, if it is in Germany, Russia, Japan, or California, instead of in the classroom when it is needed, does not have any possible effects on teaching or learning. It was proposed, therefore, that the NIIT design and build a new kind of procurement library; this library would *search, find, procure, transform*, and *prepare for use* a wide variety of selected high quality instructional materials for many media from worldwide sources.

Distribution of these materials could be delegated to private enterprise (Centre for Educational Research and Innovation 1970). The Encyclopaedia Cinematographica of West Germany, to cite an example of what can be done, has available about 2000 short, documented, and authentic silent films with printed commentaries prepared by authorities in a wide range of subjects: engineering, science, anthropology, biology, behavioral science, and ecology. These unique documentary teaching films are available from the Pennsylvania State University which distributes them in the Western Hemisphere. The central operation as visualized is to collect, transform, and distribute instructional materials and to make them instructionally useful and available at a reasonable cost. Some kinds of instructional productions may be needed to anticipate future requirements. Others may record transitory events which will disappear, and need urgently to be captured in appropriate recordings. A transformation is often required, for example, from one medium to another, such as from film to videotape or vice versa. Also, transformation or transfer of information among models of communication may be needed to make the materials most useful and available.

The major libraries of our nation lack policies, plans, and operations for including a great many kinds of educational media materials. Generally our libraries are book fixated, and they neglect film and tape recordings. Either we must create separate institutions for the storage, retrieval, and distribution of many kinds of photographic and electronic media; or we must modify the plans, developments, and operations of our libraries. Determining how to manage, store, retrieve, and distribute multimedia learning materials may become a major problem for the proposed National Institute of Instructional Technology (Meaney 1969).

Recommendation four is particularly relevant to densely populated urban areas. It proposes the development of holistic, viable models of what can be done by educational technology applied on an optimum scale. There is nothing that we need more in programs for developing and using instructional technology than full scale operational models that are dramatically successful and highly visible to the American public, to other nations, and to legislators.

Findings of "no statistically significant differences" resulting from controlled research in the areas of film and television learning are numerous and most researchers are discouraged with the effects of this research. When practical people can see no significant differences in patterns of uses and results, and when they see little practical significance to single variable research, then the results have limited value for strategy planners and policy formulators. Researchers must develop and construct full scale community models that are integrated into operational educational systems, or which include these systems, where the results can be observed clearly.

The commission suggested that the District of Columbia be selected as the site for this nation to develop fully the potential of instructional resources and technologies and to display a viable, successful, visible application of the full scale use of communication technology in education at all levels including continuing adult instruction. The commission proposed that technology be appropriately included as a major component of the model educational system, and not merely as a demonstration, of whatever size, that would be temporary or transitional. Enough temporary and limited projects have been started which faded when funds cease to flow from sources outside the system. What is needed are soundly planned, enduring operations that can be constantly modified and adapted to the changing conditions and requirements of such an urban complex as our nation's capital, or great cities like Los Angeles, San Francisco, Chicago, and Atlanta.

The commission was disturbed by what it perceived as a serious lack of training in the area of instructional technology, and also in educational administration and management. Recommendation five contains a proposal, therefore, that does not flatter those of us who are identified with educational professions. The commission held that we are not getting from schools of education and graduate schools the required training for people who take top-level management positions in our educational systems. Consequently, the commission proposed that schools of law, of business, and of engineering be enjoined to cooperate in training educational administrators. The commission began to believe that maybe the "gatekeepers" of change, the critical decision makers, who are most directly responsible for crucial decisions in education, are those who are also responsible for retarding the application of technology in education. They are the policymakers and planners at various levels of administration, not the teachers and faculty members as is so often alleged to be the case.

Recommendation six refers to the very interesting but frustrating problems of relationships among the educational-industrial-governmental complex (ERIC Clearinghouse on Educational Media and Technology 1970). General Learning, the Radio Corporation of America, Raytheon, and even the Rand Corporation and System Development Corporation are industries and agencies that are of necessity converting from the Department of Defense market to a hoped-for educational-information market. And a considerable amount of trial and error exploration, along with some failures and successes, has occurred and is still in prospect. Perhaps guidance, understanding, and joint planning with shared information can help industries find their true places in the educational *nonbook* marketplace, thus making it possible for industries to provide due and essential contributions to national educational developments.

Educationally oriented industries, such as General Electric and RCA, seem inhibited and confused because they cannot talk with comprehension to each other, to Federal agencies, or even to educators. Meaningful dialogues must be staged, intensified, extended, and made realistic in terms of contractual relations for all parties (Locke and Engler 1969 and Parkus 1969).

Therefore, the commission proposes the establishment of a National Council of Instructional Technology with representatives from different levels of the educational systems, the Federal government, and industry. In particular, the council should have high level administrative representation from industry, education, and cognate government agencies. A weak model for a National Council exists in the Educational Media Council with headquarters in the office of the National Association of Educational Broadcasters in Washington, D.C. It has rather comprehensive representation of media people, but the critical educational and industrial decision-makers are not on this council. The proposed National Council of Instructional Technology, administered by the NIIT, should provide a meeting place for industrial decision-makers, and for Federal, state, and local educational members concerned with policy formulation and planning tasks. In summary, a central problem which needs attention is that of transferring and redirecting industrial and business resources into the service of education in a manner that is practical for business and also acceptable and most useful for education.

Appropriations Required

Finally, the commission for most of its short working life avoided building a budget unit by unit, step by step, and as systematically as could have been desired. Education lacks a firm tradition of cost-effective budget building, especially in the area of instructional technology (Bord 1969 and Kiesling 1969). Generally, educators test the tolerance limits of demand or the asking-giving thresholds rather than build a systematic and defensible budget for instructional technologies.

The commission did make some general estimates of the financial requirements for putting its recommendations into effect. The first general round of estimates added up to about $250 million for launching and establishing the recommended institutes and programs. However, when the commissioners who were working on the problem were asked to make estimates of the funding that each would require were he to be actually responsible for each operation, the resulting final estimates rose to $565 million.

Summary of Recommendations

In summary, there are certain general propositions and themes on which the commission had complete concensus. The members had no reservations about the need for using the *systems approach* in education, and especially in planning the applications of instructional technology. The commission members fully approved, also, the multimedia concept of instructional technology and urged coordination of strategies for selecting and using appropriate media for clearly specified teaching-learning functions.

The commission strongly agreed that today's society should master the available instructional technology before the technology masters our society. Finally, the commission recognized the need for clear, publicly conspicuous, and successful models of developments of instructional technology. To provide a national challenge, the commission proposed the building of a holistic system of educational technology in the District of Columbia. This challenging large scale, integral development should be engineered and built at the earliest possible date. Also, it was unanimously agreed that a National Council on Instructional Technology should be established promptly for mobilizing industrial resources for national instructional uses.

The National Conference on Telecommunications Policy in Education

The Joint Council on Educational Telecommunications of Washington, which has close relevance to planning and policy formulation in the area of educational technology, organized and conducted another activity, the National Conference on Telecommunications Policy in Education. The conference was held at the Georgia Center of the University of Georgia in Athens in December 1968, and 115 leaders in the area of educational media were invited to participate. The title of the report of this conference is *Telecommunications: Toward National Policies for Education* (Meaney and Carpenter 1970).

Those at the conference were from such agencies as COMSAT, the President's Task Force on Communications Policy, RCA, the FCC, the USOE, the Ford Foundation, and the National Cable Television Association. The conference, by bringing together people who had exceptional competence and experience, was planned to make general contributions to policy formulation, strategies, and plans for the use of *telecommunications* in education on a national level.

Among other proposals, the conference recommended that channels in the relay satellites be reserved and ensured for educational and public service purposes. Such reserved channels will be needed, also, in future international affairs and, eventually, in world government.

The second important general proposal was to encourage the development of two-way communication for education and training, and especially for home study centers. The conference recommended using developed and appropriate telecommunications systems to reach and train dispersed rural populations, many of whom are disadvantaged. This is an obviously appropriate but neglected use of telecommunications. Various patterns of communication media systems were described for instructing individuals from dispersed populations in home study centers and for providing education for persons who need training but who cannot be a part of the formal education system. There was debate on what definable educational functions can and cannot be mediated by the "educational establishment" and, therefore, what kinds of educational needs must be otherwise served. For example, should some educational services be provided by private industry on specifications-performance-cost bases? However, it was asked whether, where schools, colleges, and universities fail, private industry could be expected to succeed. Evidence on this point remains to be provided.

The conference discussed how to formulate national policies and develop plans to exploit fully the possibilities of communications technology and particularly of those media that might be related to critical and growing social problems. The need for sustained research, development, and application was once again recognized and affirmed. The conference urged government and private industries to establish policy frameworks for encouraging continuous professional training and development in education and for providing, wherever needed, facilities for professional technical training in the use of new telecommunication and educational and instructional systems. Policies are also required, it was noted, to safeguard the copyrights of authors, and such policies should protect both private and public interests.

References

Bolvin, J.O. 1969. *The New Technology and Its Implications for Organizational and Administrative Changes.* Notebook no. 149, paper requested by the Commission on Instructional Technology: Academy for Educational Development, Inc., Washington, D.C.

Bord, N.A. 1969. *Application of Cost Analyses to Instructional Technology.* Notebook no. 147, paper submitted to the Commission on Instructional Technology for Information: Academy for Educational Development, Inc., Washington, D.C.

Bushnell, D.D. 1969. *Introducing the Docile Technology in Memoriam of CAI.* Notebook no. 153, paper requested by the Commission on Instructional Technology: Academy for Educational Development, Inc., Washington, D.C.

Carnegie Commission on Educational Television 1967. *Public Television: A Program for Action.* Harper & Row, New York.

Carpenter, C.R. 1970. Improving the Quality of Instructional Materials. *Educational Broadcasting Review* 4:34-46.

Centre for Educational Research and Innovation 1970. *Educational Technology: The Design and Implementation of Learning Systems.* A Report with Recommendations to Member Countries, 2nd Draft, Organisation for Economic Cooperation and Development, Paris, France.

Davies, D. 1969. *Training Personnel for Roles in Instructional Technology.* Notebook no. 157, paper requested by the Commission on Instructional Technology: Academy for Educational Development, Inc., Washington, D.C.

Dempsey, M.J. 1969. *Some Reflections Upon the Relationships Between the Restructuring of Schools and Communications Technology.* Notebook no. 159, paper requested by the Commission on Instructional Technology: Academy for Educational Development, Inc., Washington, D.C.

ERIC Clearinghouse on Educational Media and Technology, 1970. *Trends in Instructional Technology.* The Eric at Stanford 1970 Planning Project, Stanford University, Stanford, California.

Filep, R. and Schramm, W. 1970. *A Study of the Impact of Research on Utilization of Media for Educational Purposes Sponsored by NDEA Title VII 1958-1968.* U.S. Office of Education, Washington, D.C., and Institute for Educational Development, New York.

International Federation for Information Processing, 1970. *World Conference on Computer Education*, 1970, *Recommendations.* Cito Offset en Boekdrukkerij, Amsterdam, Netherlands.

Kiesling, H.J. 1969. *On the Economic Analysis of Educational Technology.* Notebook no. 175, paper requested by the Commission on Instructional Technology, Academy for Educational Development, Inc., Washington, D.C.

Krathwohl, D.R. 1969. *Proposal for Development of National Institutes of*

Education in the Department of Health, Education, and Welfare. Notebook no. 141, paper submitted to the Commission on Instructional Technology for Information, Academy for Educational Development, Inc., Washington, D.C.

Locke, R.W., and Engler, D. 1969. *Instructional Technology: The Capabilities of Industry to Help Solve Educational Problems.* Notebook no. 43, paper requested by the Commission on Instructional Technology, Academy for Educational Development, Inc., Washington, D.C.

Marx, L. 1969. *Notes for a Humanist Critique of Technological Innovation in Teaching.* Notebook no. 64, paper requested by the Commission on Instructional Technology, Academy for Educational Development, Inc., Washington, D.C.

Meaney, J.W. 1969. *The Multimedia Age.* Notebook no. 79, paper requested by the Commission on Instructional Technology, Academy for Educational Development, Inc., Washington, D.C.

Meaney, J.W., and Carpenter, C.R., eds. 1970. *Telecommunications: Toward National Policies for Education.* Report of the National Conference on Telecommunications Policy in Education, the Georgia Center for Continuing Educations, Athens, Georgia, 4-6 December 1968, Joint Council on Educational Telecommunications, Washington, D.C.

Parkus, L. 1969. *Computer Assisted Instruction in Elementary/Secondary Education: The State of the Art.* Notebook no. 186, paper requested by the Commission on Instructional Technology, Academy for Educational Development, Inc., Washington, D.C.

Smith, M.H. 1969. *Cooperative Planning and Production: Problems, Pitfalls, and Privileges.* Notebook no. 203, paper requested by the Commission on Instructional Technology, Academy for Educational Development, Inc., Washington, D.C.

Tickton, S.G., ed. 1970. *To Improve Learning: An Evaluation of Instructional Technology.* 2 vol., R.R. Bowker Company, New York and London.

Bibliography

Brown, B. Frank, *Instructional Technology and the Student: The State of the Art*, Notebook no. 150, paper requested by the Commission on Instructional Technology, Academy for Educational Development, Inc., Washington, D.C., 1969.

Carpenter, C.R., "The Commission on Instructional Technology and Its Report," *Educational Broadcasting Review*, (1970).

Carpenter, C.R., *Statement Before Subcommittee on Economic Progress of the Joint Committee of Congress of the United States: Automation and Technology in Education: A Report*, U.S. Government Printing Office, Washington, D.C., 1966.

Carpenter, Lane and Richard Speagle, *Commission on Instructional Technology Staff Report: Statistical Abstract on Instructional Technology*, Vol. 2, Notebook no. 199, paper submitted to the Commission on Instructional Technology for Information, Academy for Educational Development, Inc., Washington, D.C., 1969.

Commission on Instructional Technology, *To Improve Learning*, A Report to the President and the Congress of the United States by the Commission on Instructional Technology, U.S. Government Printing Office, Washington, D.C., March 1970.

Final Report of the President's Task Force on Communications Policy, U.S. Government Printing Office, Washington, D.C., 1967.

Morgan, Robert M., *Instructional Technology in Vocational Training*, Notebook no. 184, paper requested by the Commission on Instructional Technology, Academy for Educational Development, Inc., Washington, D.C., 1969.

Rand Seminar Series in Education, *Emerging Issues in Education: Policy Implications for the Schools*, The Rand Corporation, Santa Monica, California, 1970.

Smith, Karl U., *Recommendations Regarding Further Emphasis in Educational Technology as Based on Behavioral Cybernetic Projections*, Notebook no. 206, paper requested by the Commission on Instructional Technology, Academy for Educational Development, Inc., Washington, D.C., 1969.

Stanford Center for Research and Development in Teaching, *Third Annual Report*, Stanford University, Stanford, California, 1968.

Wentworth, John W., *Cable Television and Education*, Notebook no. 209, paper requested by the Commission on Instructional Technology, Academy for Educational Development, Inc., Washington, D.C., 1969.

Part IV:
Issues and Directions for Promoting Educational Change

12

Issues and Insights into Accountability in Education

Leon M. Lessinger

There is an accountability movement in education. Its rate of diffusion throughout the vast educational enterprise, at all levels, matches that of the scientific management phenomenon of the second decade of this century. In somewhat the same manner that relevance, innovation and behavioral objectives were the "in" words in the 1960s, it would appear that accountability is the key educational concept for the 1970s. Indeed, if presidential initiatives, state legislation, school board policy development and professional interest are reliable indicators, education may be said to have entered a new "age of accountability." What is this phenomenon? Where did it come from? Why is it spreading so rapidly? What are its pitfalls and promises? How can our educational enterprises become accountable?

Actually the concept of accountability is not new. Evidence of analogous efforts in education are available through study of practices at the University of Bologna in the 15th century. In England and parts of Africa during the last third of the 19th century, a form of present-day accountability prevailed. The 1642 and 1647 laws of the Massachusetts Bay Colony show the nature of accountability perhaps better than any other historical examples.

In colonial America educational accountability was linked with religious and social accountability. The Puritan Colonists saw the need for some form of mandatory education to assure themselves that young people could read the Bible. Whereas the 1642 Act had omitted the establishment of schools, the 1647 "Old Deluder Satan" Act held each town of fifty householders accountable for providing a school for instruction in basic skills. The selectmen made it clear that schools are necessary, not on the grounds that schools are a particular good in themselves but because education is important in achieving desirable ends.

Kinds of Accountability Distinguished

A supermarket is accountable for the produce it sells—if the produce is spoiled, the consumer may bring it back for a refund. A corporation is accountable for its earning record—if the record is poor, the shareholders may replace the management. A politician is accountable for his performance in office—if he has neglected his constituents' interests his rival may be elected. Our public schools have lost the accountability expressed in the Satan Deluder Act and similar laws passed by states in the 18th and the 19th century.

Schools are presently accountable to the public in several ways. They are accountable financially—they must demonstrate that funds have not been embezzled or squandered and that in fact the published budget has been followed. To accomplish this accountability each state requires an independent fiscal audit and a public report. Schools are accountable custodially—they must show that the children are in safe, healthful, orderly surroundings and that they know the whereabouts of each child during the entire time he is in school.

Schools are accountable to the college admission's offices and to the accrediting associations. They must show that they offer a specified college preparatory program for a defined number of hours (Carnegie Units), mark on an A,B,C,D,F basis to determine a grade point average rank, employ teachers with required degrees, maintain working conditions and materials approved as professional standards by their accrediting association and produce students who can pass standardized college entrance examinations at defined levels. They are strictly accountable to the colleges for the foregoing for the penalties are clear—withdrawal of accreditation and failure to place students in colleges.

But schools are not accountable for designated learning outcomes. They are not required to show the extent to which the tax monies and resources used are translated into intended student accomplishment.

Accountability: Theory and Definition

Accountability in education is best viewed as both a movement and a theory. As a movement it began with the administration of Title VII and VIII of the 1965 Elementary and Secondary Education Act—the Bilingual and Drop-out Prevention programs respectively. In that administration, guidelines were developed and enforced in 1969 to control the granting of the discretionary funds that: (a) provided for the allocation of small amounts of money to enable school systems showing creative solutions to a definite need as stipulated in the act to obtain technical assistance in the form of management support services; (b) required objectives to be written in performance terms; (c) mandated an independent audit of the accomplishment of the performance objectives stipulated by the proposer, and (d) allowed sub-contracting to the private sector in the form of performance contracts.

The Texarkana, Arkansas, school system project (a consortium of several districts) made use of the entire accountability "package." The remaining eighty-five bilingual and drop-out prevention projects which were funded utilized all but the allowance for performance contracting with private enterprise. Interest in the Texarkana project became so great that by mid-1970 an accountability movement had begun with over fifty school systems participating in performance contracts with private enterprise. The Office of Economic Opportunity launched a five million dollar project to test the potential of performance contracting, and Rand Corporation was employed by H.E.W. to monitor performance contracting around the nation and to develop a Performance Contracting Handbook for school officials.

By 1971, it was clear that an accountability theory had emerged in the literature, and the concept was being widely discussed by school boards, legislatures, the executive branch of state and federal governments, and local school systems.

The basic theory of accountability is that school personnel have an inescapable responsibility to account for the accomplishment of the students entrusted to them in terms of the specific performance objectives they—the educators—have publicly established as a condition for the receipt of resources. Put simply, school teachers, administrators, and board members must answer to the public for the progress of students in terms of the resources allotted for that accomplishment. A comparison with an earlier theory—scientific management— may illustrate the notion of accountability more clearly.

In scientific management, efficiency in the input-output sense is the end and aim. To accomplish greater efficiency, leaders of enterprises remove the planning function from the implementing function by: (a) defining the tasks the workers are to perform; (b) selecting the proper or best workers to perform the defined tasks; and (c) using motivation (generally in the form of monetary incentives) to ensure a high level of performance.

Accountability on the other hand stresses *effectiveness*. It scrutinizes and tries to optimize the achievement of objectives stipulated by the entity receiving resources to carry out the objectives. Whereas an efficiency theory concentrates on optimizing the process of achieving objectives, an effectiveness theory stresses product or outcome as agreed upon and allows process to go relatively free.

Implicit in accountability theory is the assumption that a product feedback program will operate much as a thermostatic control to alert decision makers and operators to the quality of their processes in terms of the product and therefore to make adjustments in favor of increased effectiveness. (It is obvious that this will effect efficiency also.)

"Accountability means many things to many people . . . this umbrella aspect makes a neat definition impossible."[1] Technically it is a policy in which an agent, public or private, entering into a contractual agreement to perform a service, will be held answerable for performing according to agreed upon terms, within an established time period and with a stipulated use of resources and performance standards. In practical terms it is a policy declaration formally adopted by a legal body such as a board or legislature, stipulating that for which one is accountable and to whom, and requiring independent and public reports of dollars spent and resources used to achieve results. The concept rests on four fundamental bases: stipulated responsibility, actual accomplishment, independent review and a public report.

Accountability can be formally defined. It means the continuing assessment of the educational achievement of students in an educational system; the relating of levels of achievement attained to the state and community's goals and expectations to the resources allocated, and to the techniques professionally employed for facilitating learning; and the full dissemination of the findings and analyses to the parents, teachers, taxpayers and citizens.

Educational accountability in policy form demands a student-centered approach. It specifies the formulation of educational goals and objectives which serve both as guides for action and guidelines for measuring progress toward satisfactory implementation of the goals and objectives. It insists upon the responsibility of schools and colleges for providing educational benefits for every student accepted for enrollment and for preventing failure. It provides for objective reports on the performance of students and of units of faculty and on progress of the school or college toward fulfilling its institutional purposes. And it also provides for experimentation with new techniques for systematic improvement and discarding of ineffective and inefficient processes.

Under the accountability aegis, learning is kept in primary focus. While courses and other "inputs" are needed, they are seen as sub-systems, groupings of components thought to effectively and efficiently achieve desired and clearly communicated objectives consistent with and derived from institutional purposes.

Accountability as public policy reflects three basic rights for public expenditures for educational purposes. First, each learner has a right to be taught what he needs to know in order to take a rewarding and productive part in our society. Second, taxpayers and elected representatives have a right to know what educational results are achieved by a given expenditure for education, and third, the schools have a right to be able to draw on the talent, enterprise and technology from all sectors of society, instead of being restricted or limited to their own talent, enterprise and technology.

Some sample policy statements which clearly move in the accountability direction are now presented. From the Florida Department of Education:

By the end of 1972, techniques for improving educational management will be available and readily accessible to all school districts in Florida. . . . These will include techniques for (a) obtaining criterion-referenced measures of pupil achievement in grades K-6 in basic skill areas taught in those grades, (b) obtaining detailed analyses of educational costs, and (c) obtaining analyses of the effectiveness of resource utilization, with recommendations for improvement.

By the end of 1974, competencies expected of teaching personnel in elementary and secondary schools will be clearly identified. Evidence will be available showing relationships between teacher competencies and pupil learning. Teacher training techniques will be available for use in preservice and inservice teacher education programs which are aimed at the specified competencies. Evidence will be available to state policy makers which shows the extent to which teacher efforts on pupil learning support various credentialing requirements.

By the end of 1976, techniques will be available and accessible to each school district which will make it possible for every child who is not severely handicapped to master the basic skills of communication and computation during the elementary grades of schooling at an average per pupil cost which is within the range of the normal operating budget of any school district in Florida.[2]

From the Oregon State Board of Education: The State Board will:

Require school districts to identify their instructional objectives in the primary grades and to carry on a continuous process of evaluation in reducing the pool of non-readers or poor readers.

Require, as part of the evaluation process, that districts be accountable for data on their effectiveness in teaching the basic skills. . . .[3]

Other examples from around the nation from local levels as well as the state levels could be cited. Clearly this is a trend away from the detailed specification of personnel or program requirements and toward a system for making educators accountable for results which their programs achieve. From this standpoint, accountability as policy represents a new strategy: to provide greater flexibility to those who operate or lead educational programs and, at the same time, make them accountable for results.

Why Accountability Now?

It appears that three major recent developments have influenced the rediscovery and widespread demand for application of accountability to education:

1. the near exponential increases in educational costs since World War II without a compensating increase in discernible productivity.
2. the dissatisfaction of elements of the public with disclosures (primarily from federal programs) that a large portion of our youth do not meet minimal standards of literacy or vocational accomplishment.
3. the modern management developments in the military and industry that have taken us to the moon and have increased the productivity of certain enterprises—all in the public spotlight.

The optimism about the value of education is still there and continues to be strong, but serious doubts have arisen about the school's capability actually to deliver on its promises. As Chase points out, "It is somewhat paradoxical that faith in education is at an all time high; . . . while confidence in the schools may be at an all time low."[4]

Americans, by the start of the 1970s, had begun to question the effectiveness of their schools. During the 1960s (following Sputnik) concern over the schools largely had centered on responsiveness or relevance of curricular offerings to life in a changing society, to certain groups' needs, or bias in the professional middle-class outlook of teachers. Now the concern had qualitatively changed. What was being asked related to competency. It was being charged that the schools were unable to teach effectively—if the criterion of that teaching effectiveness was learning.

Accountability is *not* a response of educators. It did not arise in the schools, and it is not widely embraced by school personnel. The press comes from outside, from parents, students, school boards, legislators, governors, the President, and most importantly, the taxpayers. It has an "or else" quality. Vouchers, the use of performance contracts with private enterprise, and an increasing withdrawal of funds necessary to operate the schools are part of the reply to "or else what?"

By all counts America has the most extensive and expensive school system in the world. Its students stay longer, are offered the most variety of programs, have the best paid teachers, and are housed in comparatively adequate facilities. It sends more students on to college than any nation in the world, and has an enviable supply of textbooks and other materials for use by its staff and clients. But what of its productivity? What are the American people receiving in terms of student accomplishment for all this expense? Surprisingly, perhaps, it is not possible to answer.

In a nation that lists among its best selling books each year almanacs and compendiums of statistics it is not surprising that we do know a lot about our schools. We know how many teachers there are, how old they are, and even how tall they are. We know the same about school buildings. We know the number of library volumes per child, the language laboratories, the space per child, and even the amount of money to service the debt incurred in each of the more than 17,000 school systems. What we don't know is what is produced by all these teachers, books, space, and debt. If learning is the criterion, we cannot unearth the progress (or lack of it) in a single school or school system. Up to the present, quality was (and is in most cases) thought to inhere in the nature of inputs. Standards relate almost solely to inputs, and accreditation, the limited form of quality assurance available, revolves around such considerations.

The shape of the age of accountability in the decade of the seventies already has a firm outline. Throughout 1970 and 1971, after leaving the U.S. Office of Education, the author lectured and served as a resource person to school boards, administrative groups, teacher associations, and a variety of governmental agencies and bodies in over thirty states. In virtually every one, there were school board members, state legislators, governors or their key staff men, chief state school officers, and concerned citizens considering some form of action to: (a) reorganize their state's educational systems; (b) effect broad changes in financing education at every level; and (c) improve educational practice, management, and results. By early 1972, at least five states—California, Colorado, Florida, Ohio and Wisconsin—had produced statutes that reflect this concern. Twelve more have such legislation pending.

The President's special education message of 1970 had begun with the sentence "American Education is in urgent need of reform." It was apparent that some awareness of this need was widely shared. People were becoming aware that with few exceptions no single body gives its full attention to all phases of education in a state—even though education, in terms of budget alone, is the biggest business a state has. Further, as other needs become more pressing—pollution, transportation, welfare, crime prevention, to name a few—education came more and more to have to justify its yearly claim for increases in competition with these highly visible and dramatic claimants. At the appropriations table, under sharp scrutiny, it was becoming clear to everyone that in education, planning is poor, priority-setting is largely avoided, the goals of economic efficiency and educational effectiveness are scarcely formulated—let alone being achieved—and that there is great dissatisfaction in not knowing what is being achieved by the schools for the increased monies demanded.

Accountability as policy was being aimed at two critical goals: increased productivity and self-renewal. States and communities were using a variety of tools to implement their accountability thinking including: the setting aside of development capital for bid to schools and/or private enterprise; the use of performance contracts for disbursing development capital (mostly federal funds); the employment of independent educational accomplishment auditors for both feedback on policy demands and inspection; the mandated use of behavioral objectives in instructional programs; statewide testing plans; the forcing of program, planning, budgeting approaches; the extensive employment of system analysis techniques for need assessment and program planning; the development of management information systems; the use of internal performance contracting to obtain *quid pro quo* in salary negotiations; and the turning down of tax and bond referenda that didn't stipulate clearly the relationship of needed money to actual results which would be forthcoming through the use of such funds.

The implications for the schools are not difficult to describe, and they have been foreshadowed in the earlier discussion. In the 1970s schools would be required to:

1. State instructional objectives in performance terms
2. Supply data on student accomplishment
3. Employ outside reviewers of student accomplishment
4. Justify requests for new money by stipulating its relationship with desired objectives
5. Strengthen management capabilities
6. Use outside resources—both community and private enterprise
7. Be accountable for results to the public through public reports

The post World War II trend of education as a closed system was clearly being terminated.

How Can Schools and Colleges Be Accountable for Performance?

To meet the demands of accountability—to relate resources to learning and accomplishment—schools and colleges must reform: (a) the manner in which they deliver educational benefits; (b) the traditions which undergird their purposes; (c) the leadership styles and competencies of those who manage; and (d) the manner in which they are evaluated and subsequently improved.

And they must accomplish this reform in an enterprise which:

1. Spends less than 1/3 of 1 percent of its budgets for research and development
2. Does not use the research and development it has
3. Lacks a technology of instruction
4. Lacks an orderly means of cooperation in behalf of its clients
5. Has few effective mechanisms for productive discussion and negotiation with its personnel

Elsewhere I have discussed in some detail some strategies to accomplish this reform.[5] In general it will take the adoption of clear accountability policies, the setting aside of developmental capital to be administered through grants-management, the use of limited and pin-pointed performance contracting with staff and/or outside agencies, the use of professionally sound independent reviewers of accomplishment, and the employment of know-how from the rapidly growing field of educational systems technology.

The reform needed is possible only through a faculty and administrative agreement to change from group-paced, time-contingent learning to a personalized performance or results-contingent learning. This means: (a) learning material organized in units that can be made available in alternate versions to meet individual needs or learning styles and that can be easily updated to incorporate innovations in teaching technique and new knowledge; (b) individual contact by each student with teachers and peers as well as small group encounters; (c) a supportive educational logistics; and (d) a faculty with demonstrated competence to perform teaching activities having substantial promise to optimize learning in students.

Considering that the central aim of a school or college is to facilitate learning in students, everything else that an institution does in the name of education which is not directly supportive of this goal needs close scrutiny and justification.

Teachers are professionally accountable for:

1. The provision of a rewarding experience for a student who asks questions and discovers answers
2. The stimulation of each student to determine and solve learning problems with increasing independence
3. The provision of an environment that facilitates the process of learning
4. The prescription of learning activities best suited to each student's entering repertoire
5. The provision of instruction leading to accomplishment of objectives, using media and modes suited to individual and preferred learning styles
6. The use of positive motivation through scheduling of desirable events that are contingent upon satisfactory completion of objectives
7. The use of evaluation and feedback at frequent performance-based intervals permitting direct guidance to student and teacher
8. The provision of special supplementary and/or remedial activities to strengthen the learning process

Superintendents, school board members, college presidents, deans, teachers, regents, and others interested in furthering increased accountability in education might consider the following seven-point action program:

1. Adopt and implement specific accountability policies, i.e., policies that stress unit and system results that can be independently reviewed and reported.
2. Manage a systematic educational process to get good practice into prevailing practice in the classrooms and learning centers.
3. Set aside money as development capital to serve as educational R & D money.
4. Provide rewards for high priority results.
5. Institute a quality control procedure for all programs.
6. Use performance-type contracting with staff and/or outside agencies as part of the R & D program on a turnkey basis.
7. Involve the staff and students, in the design and implementation of the accountability program.[6]

The accountability movement is not without its detractors and critics. A growing literature raises some substantive issues. What are some of these issues?

Tyler in his article "Accountability in Perspective" reviews what he considers to be the six major issues. He lists:

1. The propriety or even the right of the lay public to ask for evidence of the effectiveness of professional work

2. The use of accountability procedures
3. The goals for which the schools are accountable
4. Whose responsibility it is to set the goals for which a school or system will be held accountable
5. The means by which the attainment of goals is to be measured
6. The range of persons who should be held accountable for the educational results of the school[7]

Dr. James E. Conner, Senior Education Associate of the U.S. Chamber of Commerce and the author compiled a list of common objections to educational accountability and have suggested some possible grounds for meeting those objections. The list and discussion follows:

Accountability for results in education is not possible because many objectives in education cannot be defined.

Even allowing that objectives for some aspects of education are difficult to list in specific terms, critical curriculum areas such as mathematics, reading, and career development are quite amenable to a listing of specific performance objectives and the means for measuring their attainment.

Progress is being made in specifying learning objectives in "difficult" areas such as social studies.

Accountability for results will not be possible until the classroom teacher has a greater role in decision-making.

One of the benefits of well designed accountability policy is to provide appropriate authority and resources to allow teachers and administrators to work toward agreed-upon objectives. Once educational needs have been determined and objectives set, professionals must be free to exercise judgment and skill.

Accountability is performance contracting with private enterprise, and as such, represents an attempt of business to reap profits from schools.

Accountability is a commitment to public disclosure of educational results and the assumption of appropriate responsibility for the outcomes of the educational effort. Performance contracting is only one mechanism used to bring about greater accountability for results. Its use, however, is not solely with private enterprise. As in the case of Mesa, Arizona, performance contracting may be used with a group of teachers. Performance contracting may also be arranged with non-profit groups. Accountability may spur the privatization of some educational services. At any rate, competition between the public and private sector for the delivery of educational and related services can serve as a stimulus to improvement in the schools.

Accountability dehumanizes the learning process.

There are few things more inhumane than having adults and youth with insufficient learning and skills which denies them a productive role in society. Having over 24 million functional illiterates in the adult population is hardly humane. Hundreds of thousands of our young coming out of our colleges and secondary schools with no salable skill is certainly not humane.

Educational Accountability is a humane concept because it addresses directly what must be done to help all who go through the educational system to become all they may become. It is a humane concept because it confronts the responsibility for providing teachers and administrators the resources and conditions to achieve determined objectives.

Accountability will lead us to programmed instruction.

Accountability does not embrace a particular approach to a philosophy of education. Because it leads to a more open discussion of alternatives, many different approaches will be considered, among them programmed learning. What accountability policy encourages is a thorough exploration of problems and needs before deciding upon solutions.

Accountability is a conservative—even a reactionary philosophy. In fact, it is a form of facism because it encompasses the centralized management of the economic, political, social and technological aspects of society and suppresses individuality.

Accountability as a concept is apolitical. It's true that in the hands of a conservative, it may take on a conservative hue, and vice versa in the case of liberal. However, because stress is on accountability for results, all partners in the education process are far more likely to feel a stronger sense of responsibility for their part in the decision-making process.

It is difficult to see how a concept which emphasizes a mutual determination of what people want of education can be reactionary. Indeed, it is those who resist a clear consensus who are the reactionaries.

Because an enlightened accountability policy must stress mutual accountability, decision-making becomes *decentralized*. Greater autonomy is given to those most directly involved in carrying out the goals of the educational enterprise. In fact, accountability should ultimately bring about far greater autonomy (not less) for individual teachers and school units.

Accountability develops the climate whereby individual initiative and creativity can flourish. Rather than stifling individuality, accountability fosters it.

Accountability is oriented toward the perfection and validation of "what is" rather than "what ought to be."

Much of the success of an accountability commitment is dependent upon involvement of all community partners in education in deciding upon what is wanted of education. The process whereby the "wants" of education are evolved is called needs assessment. Before it is possible to determine "what ought to be" it is necessary to find out "what is." Therefore, we can say, "Yes, accountability is concerned with "what is" but only as one step in determining where the educational enterprise is going and the extent of resources required to reach determined goals."

Accountability is a threat to professional status and collective bargaining.

There is nothing in the accountability concept which would threaten or lower the status of the educator. Quite the opposite may be true. Because accountability focuses on what is relevant in terms of what is required of teachers and administrators to "get the job done," many arbitrary requirements and standards for teaching may be eliminated. The state of Florida, for example, is moving to eliminate many extraneous professional requirements. This action resulted from accountability policies and legislation which revealed clearly that some professional requirements were irrelevant when measured against specific educational objectives.

As to collective bargaining, accountability may well change the nature of negotiations and contracts. If all accept the *quid pro quo* principle of negotiation, accountability could marshall in a new era of professional negotiations.

Accountability is a vehicle to punish teachers by fixing blame on them for performance inadequacies.

It is possible accountability may be used punitively. Everyone must be on guard to assure that educational needs and problems are approached objectively. This means that learning gaps are identified with an eye to removing barriers to educational effectiveness. An objective exploration will reveal many conditions obstructing the best intentions of good teachers. However, the community must guard against exhortations of more money as being the automatic answer to deficiencies in the educational delivery system. Use of adequate performance criteria can go a long way toward identifying barriers which obstruct both teachers and administrators.

Accountability is not just accountability for someone else. All partners share in accountability but all partners must be involved in deciding upon what the educational investment should produce.

Accountability may encourage the teaching of the readily quantifiable and discouraged attempts in areas where measurement is difficult.

It may be that the only goals chosen are those which can be most easily measured. But given the needs, priorities and goals of a community, it should be possible to devise measurable objectives in all curriculum areas. It is recognized that the task will not be easy, but the challenge must be accepted. The fact that school systems such as San Mateo, California and state education agencies such as Florida, Colorado, California, and Oregon are making progressive moves provide encouragement and support.

Educators cannot be held accountable for results because of many factors beyond their control: intelligence of children, family background, nutritional factors, health, societal influences, etc.

It is true there are factors which influence learning and growth, many of which are beyond the control of teachers or the school. Research supports the contention that a child who does not have an adequate breakfast before coming to school, or has stayed up late watching television makes a poor candidate for learning. This points up the importance of mutual accountability.

Once needs or learning gaps have been determined, what is the accountability of the teacher? He should know what the specific learning gaps are and be prepared to develop learning strategies founded on the best research. Barriers to effectiveness should be documented. Teachers cannot be held accountable for teaching a child with inadequate visual acuity how to read, but to have visual and other defects continue undetected is a failure in professional responsibility.

Accountability is not a concept to fix blame but to determine causes for learning breakdown. Mutual accountability must be emphasized to involve the resource provider, the resource users, and learners.

After we have provided adequately for education, we can begin to explore accountability. Accountability will not work so long as schools are without adequate funds.

Adequate funds for what? Americans have been very generous in support of their schools. But it is time communities explored "what" they want of education and the order of their priorities. Then, and only then, can the community, acting through its school board, or state legislature decide how much support it is willing to give to its cited educational goals. Clearly, educators cannot be held accountable for educational results where support is manifestly inadequate.

It is never too early to begin considering more effective and efficient ways to deliver educational services. Indeed, accountability can result in more economical practices which could provide additional support for schools. But it is quite conceivable the implementation of accountability policies will bring about increased costs, but such costs would be based upon a determination of clearly defined goals and objectives and consideration of alternative solutions.

Education lacks the technological and managerial sophistication to become accountable for results.

The technology and managerial know-how is currently available to enable educational services to be delivered much more effectively. Schools have been slow to respond to these developments. Colleges of education have prepared teachers as though there were no alternative to "one teacher for 30 children." Courses in educational administration have too often dealt with the "caretaker" aspect of educational programs rather than management based on clear, measurable objectives, and application of resources to meet those objectives.

Business has joined educators in upgrading the delivery system of education as in the case of Dallas, Newark, New Jersey, and at the state level in and Michigan and Massachusetts to name a few.

The American Association of School Administration through its Academy has pioneered in offering programs to school superintendents in the application of management science to education.

Because many school systems are underdeveloped in the area of management and the application of technology, resources may be required to meet the demands of accountability.

The effort to make schools more humane runs counter to the philosophy of accountability.

Accountability Requirements:	*Humaneness Requirements:*
precise objectives	*informality*
planning	*spontaneity*
validated practices	*flexibility*
measurement of outcomes	*individual differences & affective domain*
science	*art, openness, and joy*

Accountability in no way negates the objective to make the educative process more human. In fact, accountability can readily meet the requirements for more humane schools. The price of the humaneness requirements is a well trained staff held accountable for professional competence.

The accountability movement as we know it today, grew out of a concern for the poor performance of schools. What is new about accountability as currently advocated is "the impulse to relate *output* in some way to *input* . . . and the search for appropriate methods and systems of accomplishing this."[8]

Americans are a performance-minded and results-oriented people. Whether the matter be sports, transportation, plumbing, or dental care, Americans are dissatisfied with poor performance. Until the most recent past, educational performance was thought to reside almost solely in educational input—in teachers, facilities, student aptitude, and the like. Now it is turning to include student accomplishment provided by that input. Presently students are accountable (as are taxpayers and patrons), but schools and colleges as systems are largely independent of both quality control and accounting for performance. The price of maintaining this status-quo is continuing loss of support and accountability on the part of the clients and the financial supporters.

Burke's warning that "a nation without means of reform is without means of survival" is applicable virtually intact to the situation in education. Only the substitution of the word institution for nation is required.

Notes

1. Lennon, Roger T. "To Perform and to Account." *The Journal of Research & Development in Education*, Fall, 1971, p. 5.

2. Department of Education, Tallahassee, Florida. *The Florida Educational Research and Development Program 2nd Annual Report*. February 23, 1971, pp. 18-19.

3. Oregon Board of Education. *Oregon Education 1971: Biennial Report*. March 1, 1971, pp. 16-17.

4. Chase, Francis S. "Research and Development in the Remodeling of Education." *Phi Delta Kappan*, February, 1970, p. 299.

5. Lessinger, Leon M. *Every Kid a Winner: Accountability in Education*. Palo Alto, California: Science Research Associates, Inc., 1970.

6. Lessinger, Leon M., Dale Parnell & Roger Kaufman. *Accountability: Policies and Procedures* Vol. 1: Learning; Vol. 2: Students; Vol. 3: Personnel; Vol. 4: Management. New London, Conn: Croft Educational Services, Inc. 1972.

7. Lessinger, Leon M., and Tyler, Ralph W. (eds.). *Accountability in Education*. Worthington, Ohio: Charles A. Jones Publishing Company, 1971.

8. Lennon, Roger, T. "To Perform and to Account." *The Journal of Research & Development in Education*, Fall, 1971, p. 5.

Bibliography

Books

Burt, Samuel H. and Leon M. Lessinger. *Volunteer Industry in Public Education.* Lexington, Mass.: Heath and Company, 1971).

Committee for Economic Development. *Education for the Urban Disadvantaged: from Preschool to Employment.* Committee for Economic Development, New York, 1971.

Lessinger, Leon M. *Every Kid a Winner: Accountability in Education.* Palo Alto, California, Science Research Association Inc., 1970.

Machlup, Fritz. *The Production and Distribution of Knowledge in the United States.* Princeton University Press, Princeton, N.J., 1962.

Periodicals

Allen, James E. "Education and the Renaissance of State Government," *School and Society*, 97: 148-151, March, 1969.

Bain, H. "Self-governance Must Come First, Then Accountability." *Phi Delta Kappan*, 51:413, April, 1970.

Bair, Medill. "Developing Accountability in Urban Schools: A Call for State Leadership," *Educational Technology*, 11: 38-40, January, 1971.

Barb, B. "Why our Schools are Failing," *Parent's Magazine*, 44: 53-55, October, 1969.

Barro, Stephen M. "An Approach to Developing Accountability Measures for the Public Schools," *Phi Delta Kappan*, 52:196-205, December, 1970.

Bevans, K. "Accountability Octopus Gaines New Territory." *The Times*: (London), *Educational Supplement*. 2871:11, May, 1970.

Bhaerman, Robert D. "Accountability: The Great Day of Judgment," *Educational Technology*, 11: 62-63, January, 1971.

Blaschke, Charles L., Briggs, Peter and Martin, Reed, "The Performance Contract—Turnkey Approach to Urban School System Reform," *Educational Technology*, 10: 45-48, September, 1970.

Bratten, D. "Performance Contracting: How it works in Texarkana," *School Management*, 14: 8-10, August, 1970.

Briner, D. "Administrators and Accountability," *Theory into Practice*, 8: 203-206, October, 1969.

Buelke, J. "Educators and Accountability," *Michigan Education Journal*, 44: 25-26, February, 1967.

Bumstead, Richard A. "Lessinger's Logic," *Educate* 4:25-30, March, 1971.

Campbell, R.F. and D.H. Layton. "Growing Expectations for American Education," *Education Digest*, 35: 1-4, January, 1970.

Cass, J. "Crisis of Confidence, and Beyond," *Saturday Review*, 53: 61-62, September 19, 1970.

———. "Profit and Loss in Education: Texarkana and Gary, Indiana, *Saturday Review* 53: 39-40, August 15, 1970.

Cunningham, L.L. "Our Accountability Problems," *Theory into Practice*, 8: 283-292, October, 1969.

Daniel, K. Fred. "Moving Toward Educational Accountability: Florida's Program," Educational Technology, 11: 41-42, January, 1971.

Davies, D. "Relevance of Accountability," *Journal of Teacher Education*, 21: 127-133, Spring, 1970.

Deck, L. Linton Jr. "Accountability and the Organizational Properties of Schools," *Educational Technology*, 11: 36-37, January, 1971.

Deterline, William A. "Applied Accountability," *Educational Technology*, 11: 15-20, January, 1971.

Dillon, R.H. "Fine Art of Abdicating Responsibility," *Library Journal*, 92: 2885-2887, September 1, 1967.

Drummond, T.D. "To Make a Difference in the Lives of Children," *National Elementary Principal*, 49: 31-36, February, 1970.

Duncan, Merlin G. "An Assessment of Accountability: The State of the Art," *Educational Technology*, 11: 27-30, January, 1971.

Durstine, Richard M. "An Accountability Information System," *Phi Delta Kappan*, 52: 236-239, December, 1970.

Dyer, Henry S. "Toward Objective Criteria of Professional Accountability in the Schools of New York City," *Phi Delta Kappan*, 52: 206-211, December, 1970.

Education Commission of the States, *Compact* 4: 4-27 Covering the First and Second General Session of the Annual Meeting—Topics Include: "Accountability through National Assessment," "Accountability in Elementary and Secondary Education," "Accountability in Higher Education," October, 1970.

Ehrle, R.A. "National Priorities and Performance Contracting," Educational Technology, 10: 27-28, July, 1970.

Elam, Stanley. "Age of Accountability Dawns in Texarkana: Rapid Learning Centers," *Phi Delta Kappan*, 51: 509, June, 1970.

Filogamo, M.J. "New Angle on Accountability: Rapid Learning Centers," *Today's Education*, 59: 53, May, 1970.

Fox, E.J. and W. B. Levenson. "In Defense of the Harmful Monopoly; Merits and Limitations of the Voucher Plan," *Phi Delta Kappan*, 51: 131-135, November, 1969.

Gardner, James and Harold Howe. "What are Americans Receiving in Return for their Heavy Investment in Education?" *American Education*, 2: 24-26, November, 1966.

Garvue, Robert J. "Accountability: Comments and Questions," *Educational Technology*, 11: 34-35, January, 1971.

Geller, E. "Accountability: Right to Read Program and Integration vs Compensatory Education," *Library Journal*, 95: 1881, May 15, 1970.

Grayboff, Marilyn N. "Tool for Building Accountability: The Performance Contract," *Journal of Secondary Education*, 45: 355-368, Dec., 1970.

Grieder, C. "Educators Should Welcome Pressure for Accountability," *Nation's Schools*, 85: 14, May 14, 1970.

Harlacher, Ervin L., and Roberts, Eleanor. "Accountability for Student Learning," *Junior College Journal*, 41: 27-30, March, 1971.

Harmes, H.M. "Specifying Objectives for Performance Contracts," *Educational Technology*, 11: 52-56, January, 1971.

Harris, D. "Responsibility is Relevant," *PTA Magazine*, 64: 24-26, February, 1970.

Jencks, C. "Education Vouchers," *New Republic*, 163: 19-21, July 4, 1970.

Johnson, W. Frank. "Performance Contracting with Existing Staff," *Educational Technology*, 11: 59-61, January, 1971.

Jordan, Bennett. "Educational Accountability: A Crucial Question," *Junior College Journal*, 41: 23-25, March, 1971.

Kaufman, Roger A. "Accountability, A System Approach and the Quantitative Improvement of Education—An Attempted Integration." *Educational Technology* 11: 21-26, January, 1971.

Kennedy, John D. "Planning for Accountability Via Management by Objectives," *Journal of Secondary Education*, 45: 348-354, December, 1970.

Kirk, Russell. "Free Choice: A Voucher Plan; Giving All Students the Choice of Attending Either a Public or Private School," *National Review*, 21: 598, June, 1969.

Kruger, W.S. "Program Auditor: New Breed on the Education Scene," *American Education*, 6: 36, March, 1970.

Krull, R.P., Jr. "Accountability," *Instructor*, 79: 16, February, 1970.

Lessinger, Leon M. "A 'Zero-Reject' Program in a Comprehensive School District," *Journal of Educational Administration*, 7: 2, October, 1969.

―――. "Accountability and Curriculum Reform," *Education Technology*, 10: 56-57, May, 1970.

―――. "Accountability for Results," *American Education*, 5: 2-4.

―――. "Accountability in Education," *Education Change Through State Leadership*. Publication of papers presented at three meetings of ESEA Title III personnel from State Departments of Education, New York State Department of Education, Albany, New York, 1970.

―――. "Accountability in Public Education," *Today's Education* 59: 52-53, May, 1970.

―――. "Engineering Accountability for Results in Public Education," *Phi Delta Kappan*, 52: 217-225, December, 1970.

―――. "Focus on the Learner: Central Concern of Accountability in Education," *Audiovisual Instructor*, 15: 42-44, June, 1970.

―――. "Four Key Ideas to Strengthen Public Education," *Journal of Secondary Education*, 45: 147-151, April, 1970.

Lessinger, Leon M. and D.H. Allen. "Performance Proposals for Educational Funding: A New Approach to Federal Resource Allocation," *Phi Delta Kappan*, 51: 136-137, November, 1969.

_____. "Quality Assurance in Schools: The Nation's Most Important Business," *MASCD Journal*, 15-34, Spring, 1970.

_____. "Robbing Dr. Peter to 'Pay Paul': Accounting for Our Stewardship of Public Education," *Educational Technology*, 11: 11-14, January, 1971.

_____. "The Powerful Notion of Accountability in Education," *Journal of Secondary Education*, 45: 339-347, December, 1970.

Levin, H.M. "Making Public Schools Competitive: The Free Market Remedy," *Current*, 100: 25-32, October, 1968.Current

Lieberman, Myron. "An Overview of Accountability," *Phi Delta Kappan*, 52: 195-195, December, 1970.

Lopez, Felix M. "Accountability in Education, " *Phi Delta Kappan*, 52: 231-235, December, 1970.

Martin, Reed and Blaschke, Charles. "Contracting for Educational Reform," *Phi Delta Kappan*, 52: 403-406, March, 1971.

Mayrhofer, Albert V. "Factors to Consider in Preparing Performance Contracts for Instruction," *Educational Technology*, 11: 48-51, January, 1971.

McComas, J.D. "Accountability: How Do We Measure Up," *Educational Technology*, 11: 31, January, 1971.

Meade, E.J. "Accountability and Governance in Public Education," *Education Canada*, 9: 48-51. March, 1969.

Mecklenburger, James A., and Wilson, John A. "The Performance Contract in Gary," *Phi Delta Kappan* 52: 406-410, March, 1971.

Nordh, Deborah M. "Emphasis: Accountability and the Community College," *Junior College Journal*, 41: 3, March, 1971.

Packer, M.A. "Why Teachers Fail," *Journal of Teacher Education*, 19: 331-337, Fall, 1968.

Pell, C. and A.H. Quie. "Two Congressmen Look at American Education," *Childhood Education*, 46: 17-21, September, 1969.

Phillips, Harry L. "Accountability and the Emerging Leadership Role of State Education Agencies," *Journal of Secondary Education,* 45: 377-380, December, 1970.

Phillips, R.E. "Whose Children Shall We Teach?" *Education Leadership*, 27: 471-474, February, 1970.

Prattle, R. "Public School Movement: Phoenix or Dodo Bird?" *Education Digest*, 35: 1-4, December, 1969.

Roueche, John E. "Accountability for Student Learning in the Community College," *Educational Technology* 11: 46-47, January, 1971.

Scheid, P.N. "Charter of Accountability for Executives," *Harvard Business Review*, 88-98, July-August, 1965.

Stocker, Joseph and Wilson, Donald F. "Accountability and the Classroom Teacher," *Today's Education*, 60: 41-56, March, 1971.

Straubel, James. "Accountability in Vocational-Technical Instruction," *Educational Technology*, 11: 43-45, January, 1971.

Swanker, Esther M. and Bernard E. Donovan. "Voucher Demonstration Project: Problems and Promise," *Phi Delta Kappan*, 52: 255, December, 1970.

Swartz, R. "Performance Contracts Catch On," *Nation's Schools*, 86: 31-33, August, 1970.

Underwood, K.W. "Before You Decide to Be Accountable, Make Sure You Know for What," *American School Board Journal*, 158: 32-33, Sept., 1970.

Voegel, George H. "A Suggested Schema for Faculty Commission Pay in Performance Contracting," *Educational Technology*, 11: 57-59, Jan., 1971.

Weber, Robert E. "The Early Warning System and the Zero Failure School: Professional Response to Accountability," *Journal of Secondary Education*, 45: 369-376., December, 1970.

Wildavsky, Aaron. "A Program of Accountability for Elementary Schools," *Phi Delta Kappan*, 52: 212-216, December, 1970.

Yongo, Carmine A. "John Dewey and the Cult of Efficiency," *Harvard Educational Review*, Winter, 1964, pp. 33-53.

"Accountability for Whom? For What?" *Phi Delta Kappan*, 52: 193, Dec., 1970.

"Accountability Method Makes Failure the Teacher's Fault," *College and University Business*, 49: 45, July, 1970.

"After Texarkana, What?" *Nation's Schools*, 84: 37-40, December, 1969.

"Demand for Accountability," *Saturday Review*, 52: 64, December 20, 1969.

"Jencks Tuition Voucher Plan," *America* 122: 517, May 4, 1970.

"No Magic in Vouchers," *Nation*, 210: 773, June 29, 1970.

"Satisfaction Guaranteed or Money Back," *Saturday Review*, 53: 54-55, August 15, 1970.

"The Low Productivity of the 'Educational Industry,' "*Fortune*, October, 1958, pp. 135-136.

13

Performance Contracting in Education: An Introductory Overview

George R. Hall and James P. Stucker

Performance contracting was first applied to the education of public school students late in 1969. The publicity associated with the initial programs and the current dissatisfactions with the state of American education have resulted in widespread interest in and experimentation with this method of contracting. In typical applications, a local educational agency contracts with a learning systems contractor to educate a selected group of students, with the contract payment determined by the measured achievement of the students. Payment for services on the basis of student achievement and the involvement of private, profit-oriented firms in classroom activities have made performance contracting one of the most hotly debated innovations in American education.

This paper reviews the origins of the performance contracting movement in education, the current programs, and some constraints hindering the wider application of performance contracting. As the title indicates, this paper gives only an introductory overview. At this time few results of performance contracting projects are available. Therefore, the discussion must deal with applications and aspirations rather than attainments.

Performance contracting experience to date, however, does permit three generalizations. First, performance contracting achieved overnight publicity because it addresses several deeply felt and widespread dissatisfactions with the current state of education. Second, performance contracting is not a single structured program; rather it is a contracting technique that can be, and has been, applied in a number of different fashions. Third, performance contracting has been applied to only a limited number of academic subjects and this practice

This paper was prepared for the Rand symposia on *Emerging Issue in Education: Policy Implications for the School.* It is adapted and condensed from J.P. Stucker and G.R. Hall, *The Performance Contracting Concept in Education*, The Rand Corporation, R-699/1-HEW, May 1971, and from G.R. Hall and J.P. Stucker, "The Rand/HEW Study of Performance Contracting in Education," P-4558, The Rand Corporation, January 1971, and published in *Compact*, February 1971, pp. 6-9.

Any views expressed in this paper are those of the authors. They should not be interpreted as reflecting the views of The Rand Corporation or the official opinion or policy of any of its governmental or private research sponsors.

The work reported herein was performed pursuant to Contract No. HEW-OS-70-156 with the Department of Health, Education and Welfare.

This paper was prepared in the Spring of 1971. An addendum was prepared in the Spring of 1972 to reflect some of the results of the programs described. The Selected Bibliography was updated to February 1972.

is likely to persist until there are major advances in the state-of-the-art of educational measurement. We shall consider each of these points in turn.

The Origins of the Performance Contracting Movement

During the 1969-70 school year, two school districts entered into performance contracts with educational firms; in 1970-71 probably around eighty school districts have such contracts. The exact number cannot be ascertained, since new programs were started throughout the year and many have received little publicity. It is clear, however, that many local educational agencies (LEAs) have seized upon performance contracting with eagerness. This eagerness, we suggest, becomes understandable when we examine the origins of the movement.

One clear source of support for performance contracting is public concern over the failure of the schools to provide training—particularly in reading—that will convert students into effective and productive citizens. One-fourth of all students in the nation have major reading deficiencies, and more than three million adults are illiterate. This is a national problem, but it is especially severe for culturally and economically disadvantaged student populations.

Poor student achievement is nothing new; what is new is public awareness of its consequences and the realization that neither increasing the Gross National Product nor spending more money on education is an automatic cure. At the same time, the public is demanding far more than first-rate teaching of the three Rs from the schools. Burkhart (1970) ably describes the schools' predicament:

The schools, to their own astonishment, now are confronted with trying to save, through education, the poor, the physically and emotionally handicapped, and the culturally, socially and economically disenfranchised of the nation. Those in a position of responsibility know that we are doing less than a creditable job of facing these difficulties in our schools, because our teachers and schools are not geared for dealing with the realities of our national problems. However, these problems are the schools' problems. . . .

The fact that schools are now blamed when their students fail has important implications for performance contracting. In earlier days, learning was up to the student. If he failed to digest what the school offered, it was assumed that the fault lay in his laziness, lack of intelligence, or unwillingness to learn. Today the situation is reversed; many groups are demanding that schools somehow infuse all students with the skills necessary for the world of the 1970s. A landmark in this trend was the proclamation by James E. Allen (1969), then U.S. Commissioner of Education, of a "National Right to Read." Every student, Allen said, should leave school with the skill and desire to read to the full limits of his capacity, and public policy and action at both Federal and local levels should be directed to this goal. School systems have responded by searching for new methods to show their commitment to increasing student attainments, particularly for minority and disadvantaged students. This new school climate has led to a search for educational innovations and performance contracting has been seized upon as a promising candidate.

Another impetus toward performance contracting has been exasperation with the slow pace of technological change in American public school education. Rapid evolution of institutions and procedures has become a way of life in America, but education is a notable exception. The classroom of today may or may not be architecturally different from the classroom of thirty years ago; however, the usual classroom organization, materials, and techniques are remarkably similar.

Educational research and development, despite a paucity of funds, has produced many prototypes of new equipment, techniques, and procedures. Typically, an innovation is developed, tested, and demonstrated under "field test" conditions. Then a report is written and quietly relegated to library shelves while public education goes on unaffected.

Everyone involved with educational R&D, technology, or policy has been frustrated by this resistance to change—most of all, the suppliers of educational equipment, materials, and services. Many of them have entered the educational market since 1960, believing that their products and services would benefit students and yield a profit to the firms. The major market for new educational technology has not developed, however, and many firms have been rethinking their marketing strategies and have given much attention to guarantees to buyers as a way to market new technology to school systems.

A third strand in the pattern is the educational accountability movement. Taxpayers are loath to meet the requests of school officials for resources; estimates of the failure rate for voter approval of school bonds and tax increases run as high as 75 percent. A typical attitude of public officials was expressed by Minnesota Governor Harold LeVander when he complained that, "We've doubled the expenditures for education in Minnesota but we haven't doubled the quality" (Harrison, 1970).

One response by many education leaders, including executives for the U.S. Office of Education, has been to try to develop programs to promote educational accountability (Lessinger, 1970). The basic idea is that schools will be held responsible for educational outcomes—that is, what the students learn. Performance contracting has appeared to many educators to be an easy way to experiment with accountability (Sigel, 1971). Indeed, the notions of performance contracting and accountability have been so linked in the last few years that it is important to emphasize that they are separate but related concepts.

The final trend in the performance contracting movement has affected all governmental activities. This trend has been a dissatisfaction with traditional methods for obtaining goods and services for the public sector. There has been a search for new and more system-oriented and output-oriented procurement procedures. The new techniques, the developers hope, will lead to better analyses of the costs and benefits of governmental expenditures and provide private contractors with more incentives for efficiency and innovation. This development has occurred in such diverse sectors as water resources development, hospital insurance, and particularly, defense procurement. These experiments with new Government-business relationships in other public sectors have led to interest in similar experimentation in education.

In 1969 all these trends came together to produce the first performance contracts for educational services (Boomstead, 1970; Education Turnkey Systems, 1970; Lessinger, 1970).

The Diversity of Performance Contracting Programs

The variety of performance contracting programs is probably best perceived by examining some features of past and current programs. The programs are classified into four groups and presented in Tables 13-1 to 13-4. The first group contains completed 1969-70 programs. The second contains 1970-71 programs for student achievement. The third group comprises the programs in the structured experiment being conducted by the U.S. Office of Economic Opportunity. The final group contains programs that differ from the others in that they are concerned with the education of teachers rather than the direct education of students.

A major feature common to all the programs is that each involves a reading program, usually a remedial program. Many of the contracts also provide for the teaching of mathematics, but only three cover other subjects. Behavioral Research Laboratories is providing the entire curriculum for one elementary school in Gary, Indiana. The payments to BRL, however, are based on the students' achievements only in reading and mathematics. Jacksonville, Florida, has let a contract for the basic curriculum for a first grade class. In Dallas, Texas, some vocational skills are being taught under contract.

Two obvious differences among the programs concern contract prices and the range of the contractor's authority. Prices differ widely among contracts, depending mostly on how much of the educational program is contracted out. The last column in each of the tables is labeled "Target Payment," since no one knows what the actual contract payment will be until the achievement gains are measured. The figures were determined by computing the maximum amount the LEA might have to pay the LSC; however, no comparisons among the various figures should be made, since what is included in the LSC's price differs from one program to another. For example, in some programs the contractors are simply furnishing books or materials, while in others they are responsible for the entire range of classroom resources. In some programs the teachers remain on the district payroll, while in others the contractors are responsible for teachers' salaries.

Table 13-1
Completed Performance Contracting Programs

Educational Agency	Learning Systems Contractor	Subjects	Number	Grades	Maximum Payment[a]
Texarkana, U.S.A. (11/69)[b] (1969-70 phase)	Dorsett Educational Systems	Reading & Math	300	7-12	$135,000
Portland, Oregon (1/70)	Audio-Visual Supply Co. (E.D.L.)	Reading	130	7-8	1,200
Portland, Oregon (1/70)	Five reading teachers	Reading	140	7-8	1,500[c]
Portland, Oregon (6/70)	Six reading teachers subcontract with Open Court Publishing Co.	Reading	80	4-8	5,500
Portland, Oregon (6/70)	One reading teacher	Reading	55	5-6	1,500
Portland, Oregon (6/70)	Larrabee and Associates	Reading	200	4-8	500

[a]All dollar amounts are approximate.

[b]This program was conducted jointly in Arkansas School District No. 7 and the Texas Liberty-Eylau School District. Some of the techniques of the 1969-70 phase have been turnkeyed for the 1970-71 school year.

[c]This payment is in addition to regular salaries.

Table 13-2
Operational Programs, Fall 1970/Student Achievement

Educational Agency	Learning System Contractor	Program	Students		Target Payment
			Number	Grades	
Boston (Roxbury), Mass.	Educational Solutions	Reading	400	K-6	80,000
Colorado, State of	Dorsett Educational Systems	Reading	300	6-8	50,000
Cherry Creek	Dorsett Educational Systems	Reading	100	6-8	—
Denver	Dorsett Educational Systems	Reading	100	6-8	—
Englewood	Dorsett Educational Systems	Reading	100	6-8	—
Dallas, Tex.	New Century	Reading & Math	875	9-12	—
Dallas, Tex.	Thiokol	Occ. Skills & Motiv.	875	9-12	—
Flint, Mich.	Dealer for E.D.L. Materials	Reading	2,160	9	210,000
Gary, Ind.	Behavioral Research Laboratories	All subjects	800	K-6	640,000
Gilroy, Calif.	Westinghouse Learning	Reading & Math	103	2-4	60,000
Grand Rapids, Mich.	Westinghouse Learning	Reading & Math	400	1-6	143,700
Grand Rapids, Mich.	COMES	Reading & Math	600	6-9	164,000
Greenville, S.C.	COMES	Reading	480	6-9	100,000
Jacksonville, Fla.	Learning Research Associates	Reading, Math, Social Studies & Science	300	1	70,000

Location	Company	Subject	Number	Grades	Amount
Oakland, Calif.	Education Solutions	Reading	400	6-8	80,000
Philadelphia, Pa.	Behavioral Research Laboratories	Reading	20,000	1-2, 7-8	800,000
Providence, R.I.	New Century/Communications Patterns	Reading	1,500	2-8	145,000
Savannah, Ga.	Learning Foundations	Reading	1,000		97,000
Texarkana, U.S.A.	Educational Developmental Laboratories	Reading, Math & Dropouts	300	7-12	100,000
Virginia, State of	Learning Research Associates	Reading & Math	2,500	1-9	212,500
Norfolk	Learning Research Associates	Reading & Math	500	4-9	—
Buchanan Co.	Learning Research Associates	Reading & Math	500	1-7	—
Dickinson Co.	Learning Research Associates	Reading & Math	250	1-7	—
Lunenberg Co.	Learning Research Associates	Reading & Math	250	4-7	—
Mechlenburg Co.	Learning Research Associates	Reading & Math	250	4-6	—
Prince Edward Co.	Learning Research Associates	Reading & Math	250	4-6	—
Wise Co.	Learning Research Associates	Reading & Math	500	4-9	—

Table 13-3
Office of Economic Opportunity Programs, Fall 1970

Educational Agency	Learning System Subcontractor	Program	Students		OEO Grant[a]
			Number	Grades	
Anchorage, Alaska	Quality Education Development	Reading & Math	600	1-3,7-9	$444,632
Clarke Co., Ga.	Plan Education Centers	Reading & Math	600	1-3,7-9	301,770
Dallas, Tex.	Quality Education Development	Reading & Math	600	1-3,7-9	299,417
Duval Co., Fla.	Learning Foundations	Reading & Math	600	1-3,7-9	342,300
Fresno, Calif.	Westinghouse Learning	Reading & Math	600	1-3,7-9	299,015
Grand Rapids, Mich.	Alpha Systems	Reading & Math	600	1-3,7-9	322,464
Hammond, Ind.	Learning Foundations	Reading & Math	600	1-3,7-9	342,528
Hartford, Conn.	Alpha Systems	Reading & Math	600	1-3,7-9	320,573
Las Vegas, Nev.	Westinghouse Learning	Reading & Math	600	1-3,7-9	298,744
McComb, Miss.	Singer/Graflex	Reading & Math	600	1-3,7-9	263,085
McNairy Co., Tenn.	Plan Education Centers	Reading & Math	600	1-3,7-9	286,991
New York (Bronx), N.Y.	Learning Foundations	Reading & Math	600	1-3,7-9	341,796
Philadelphia, Pa.	Westinghouse Learning	Reading & Math	600	1-3,7-9	296,291
Portland, Me.	Singer/Graflex	Reading & Math	600	1-3,7-9	308,184
Rockland, Me.	Quality Education Development	Reading & Math	600	1-3,7-9	299,211
Seattle, Wash.	Singer/Graflex	Reading & Math	600	1-3,7-9	343,800
Taft, Tex.	Alpha Systems	Reading & Math	600	1-3,7-9	243,751
Wichita, Kans.	Plan Education Centers	Reading & Math	600	1-3,7-9	294,700
Mesa, Arizona	Association of Teachers	Reading & Math	600	1-3,7-9	33,976[b]
Stockton, Calif.	Association of Teachers	Reading & Math	600	1-3,7-9	55,154[b]

[a]The OEO grant includes the target payment to the subcontractor and $30,000 to $50,000 for the LEA management team.
[b]This payment is in addition to regular salaries.

Table 13-4
Teacher Achievement Programs, Fall 1970[a]

Educational Agency	No. of Teachers in Training Program	Target Payment
Alachua Co., Fla.	40	$24,000
Orangeburg, N.Y.	40	24,000
Port Jefferson, N.Y.	30	18,000
Royal Oak, Mich.	30	18,000
Yellow Springs, Ohio	40	24,000

[a]The contractor for all these programs is the Institute for the Development of Educational Activities (I/D/E/A). I/D/E/A is teaching individualized instructional techniques to teachers by means of in-service training sessions. Criteria for evaluating the teacher's abilities upon completion of the program are being developed jointly by I/D/E/A and the local educational agencies. These criteria will be applied by a team of I/D/E/A and LEA officials to evaluate the teacher's skill and thereby provide a basis for payments to I/D/E/A.

The second dimension in which the contracts vary is in program authority. In the majority of the programs the contractor exercises a very high degree of control over the learning program. For example, in the programs at Gilroy, Greenville, and Texarkana the contractors have, in effect, designed the classrooms, selected the equipment, materials and teachers, and operated the complete learning system. In other programs, such as those under OEO sponsorship, the contractor's authority is tempered somewhat by the requirement that the contracting agency (OEO) has final approval over all aspects of the program and over all changes to the program. However, even in these programs the contractors have almost complete authority over the day-to-day operation of the programs.

In a few programs, however, the LEA has retained almost complete operating authority. In Philadelphia the BRL contract is only for materials and some counseling and training. The Open Court program in Portland was similar. The EDL contracts in Flint and Portland call for equipment, materials, and consulting. In all of these cases the contractors are simply supplying educational materials to the districts and training the districts' teachers in the use of the materials. In each case, however, the price for the materials is contingent upon the achievement of the students in the programs.

The programs also differ in other respects. One difference is the contractors involved in these programs. They are a heterogeneous group. They range from some of the nation's largest corporations to individual English teachers though, at present, most are profit-oriented educational firms.

In most programs the contractors are directly involved in the classroom teaching and learning process. There are differences of opinion, even among the private firms, about whether this involvement will continue in the future, however. Some of the firms view their classroom activities as a rapidly passing phase. Soon they hope to be only consultants assisting school districts with "turnkeyed" systems, that is, learning systems operated by the district as part of their regular programs. Other contractors question whether the current phase will pass so rapidly.

Another difference among programs is the curricula and teaching techniques used. Most programs are based on individualized instruction approaches, but techniques vary substantially. Some LSCs use teaching machines extensively. Others use no machines or, at most, simple cassette-players. The majority fall somewhere between these two extremes. Some programs emphasize extrinsic incentives others rely exclusively on intrinsic motivation. Some stress the importance of changing the classroom environment. Some use new materials, others use only well-known materials.

What are the implications of this diversity? First, it is important to remember that performance contracting is a technique for addressing educational needs; it is not a ready-made program nor does it furnish ready-made solutions. Any LEA using this technique faces the task of designing a project specific to its needs, resources and situation.

Second, despite the inherent flexibility of performance contracting, in one sense its applications to date have been very limited. Few programs have involved subjects other than reading and mathematics, largely because of measurement problems. Even for reading and mathematics, the current state-of-the-art in achievement measuring has raised many questions about the use of performance contracting. The concentration on skill development and achievement measurement is a paramount issue in performance contracting to which we shall return.

A third implication is probably the most important. Performance contracts involve more than the responsibilities assigned to the contracting firm or teacher group. A performance contracting program involves the activities not only of the LSC but of the school district and perhaps other contractors. It is also likely to have impacts on students and schools in addition to those called out in the contract for fee-determination purposes. At first blush, the prescription for applying the performance contracting concept to education appears disarmingly simple: "Call in an LSC and let a contract specifying various levels of achievement. Then give a test at the start of a program and at the end, compute the gain, and pay off the LSC." In fact, developing, managing and evaluating a performance contracting program is a complex task.

The Scope of Performance Contracting: Present and Future

The implications of the focus of performance contracting on reading and mathematics deserve further consideration. Every LEA that has entered into a performance contract with an LSC has contracted out some portion of a reading program. It is thought to be relatively easy to set up objectives for such programs, particularly if they are remedial. Most people agree that students who are two or more grade levels behind in reading or mathematics deserve special assistance to improve their skills. Some districts, notably Gary, Dallas, and Jacksonville, have contracted for a wider curriculum. These districts apparently believe they have specified meaningful objectives for all the subjects under contract, but payments to the contractors in Gary and Jacksonville are nevertheless based on reading and math achievements.

Contractor responsibility for teaching subjects other than those that determine the fee poses a special issue. It is reasonable to believe that the more time a student spends practicing reading, the more likely he is to progress in reading. Thus, if other things were equal, we would not be surprised to find the reading programs in Gary and Jacksonville more successful than their counterparts in other districts. This time allocation may be very useful in upgrading basic skills, however some observers feel that other important educational objectives may be sacrificed in the Gary and Jacksonville programs to achieve reading and math gains. In short, while it is possible to include a wide variety of tasks in a performance contract, only a relatively few behaviors lend themselves to rigorous measurement. Broad programs, therefore, result in the contractor's fee being based on only a part of his responsibilities.

Many LEAs have been unprepared for the great amount of testing required and the possibility of "overtesting." There are, of course, the initial and final achievement tests. A set of diagnostic tests is usually necessary to structure an individual program for the student. Interim tests will be required, both for payment purposes and so the contractor can modify his program if it is not having the expected results. The district will probably have a regular testing program. Special tests for evaluative purposes may be desirable. All this can put a strain on the bewildered student, and scheduling can become a problem for the school.

Contractors and school officials are properly worried about over-testing, but for the time being there seems to be no escape. We are going through an experimental, evaluative period in the history of performance contracting, with millions of dollars being spent on such projects. It would be foolish not to generate the data required for a sound assessment of the concept and its results. Nonetheless, balancing the need for data against the burdens of testing remains a major operational issue.

Another problem is maintaining measurement integrity. Clearly, any contractor who is going to be paid on the basis of a test has an incentive to "teach to the test." There is also the obvious temptation for the contractor to go one step further and actually teach the test—instruct the students in some test questions.

If this were the only difficulty with the use of standardized tests for achievement, the controversy could be easily resolved. Rules governing how closely teaching materials may correlate with test questions could be established with serious penalties for violation. This procedure has been adopted in the Jacksonville program. The OEO and Virginia programs have adopted blind testing, whereby the contractor does not know what tests are going to be used. In short, using standardized tests for achievement measures creates contractor-motivation problems, but these can be countered. The more basic and serious issue is the statistical reliability and validity as well as the philosophical implications of measuring educational achievement by means of standardized instruments.

The discussions of this issue have centered on five statistical and conceptual questions: (1) Do standardized achievement tests measure what they purport to measure? (2) Do the tests reflect the content of the performance contracting programs to which they are being applied? (3) Do the tests yield statistically reliable measures of achievement gains? (4) Are the achievement gains measured by standardized tests relevant for the cognitive goals of the schools? (5) Are the achievement gains measured by the tests relevant to the overall goals—including affective and other noncognitive goals—of schools? (Bumstead, 1970; Cronback, 1970; Klein, 1971; Lennon, 1971; Millman, 1970).

To address these questions thoroughly would require far more detail than is appropriate for this introduction; therefore, we shall merely note the importance of the debate, and briefly explain each question. With regard to the first question, many tests have technical inadequacies. For example, some require skills different from those that are supposed to be tested; some instructions are difficult to follow; some formats are confusing; and so on. It is certainly desirable that these problems, familiar to the teaching profession but little known outside it, should be aired. These technical problems become even more important when achievement test results are no longer restricted to intraschool purposes—class assignments, counseling, program evaluations, and so forth—but are used as accountability measures and to compute contractor payments. Even so, these tests have long been used and will no doubt continue to be used for a host of educational purposes.

The second question focuses on the problem that the set of behaviors involved in a performance contracting program is not likely to match on a one-for-one basis the behaviors tested in a standardized test. Thus the school and the contractor, unable to find an appropriate test for their program, are forced either to structure the program to the available tests or they must attempt to live with the discrepancies between the course content and the testing instruments.

The reliability issue centers on the errors associated with the individual gain scores. The problem is to distinguish "true" gains from the measurement errors associated with any gain score. This task is particularly difficult for programs with short time-spans, such as four or five months, in which the measurement errors can easily exceed the amount of gain involved. Attempting to finesse this problem by using group averages raises the possibility of contractors focusing on some children and ignoring others.

The fourth question poses a broader issue. Even if one is satisfied with the measurement properties of the achievement test results, it is asked, do these results contribute to the basic cognitive goal of improved academic ability? For example, improved reading skill, as measured on an achievement test, should enhance children's enjoyment of reading and inspire them to do more reading on their own. In turn, they should show a general academic improvement in all school subjects. Whether in actual practice this chain of events will apply is subject to question, however. Thus, a recurring question about performance contracting programs is whether the increased ability is retained over some reasonably long period of time and whether the student can actually turn it to advantage in other areas.

The final question involves the measurement and testing issue, but transcends it. The question really asks if cognitive ability is the proper criterion for judging school success. In addition to cognitive skills, are not affective results important? Also, are reading and mathematics (for which achievement tests are best developed) the areas we want to emphasize to the exclusion of other skills and subject areas? This question relates to measurement but goes far beyond it to address the fundamental goals and purposes of education. This fascinating topic exceeds the scope of this paper and so we must leave the debate at this point.

In sum, the use of standardized achievement tests to define contractors' responsibilities and to compensate them poses significant statistical and conceptual problems. Alternatives to these tests, however, such as criterion-referenced tests, also pose problems (Lennon, 1971; Millman, 1970). For the near future, it appears likely that most LEAs and LSCs will regard the use of standardized achievement tests in performance contracting programs as Hobson's Choice.

Conclusions

Performance contracting is having a considerable vogue today due to the appeal of linking payments for educational services to measured, auditable results. However, this technique raises a number of hotly debated issues.

Performance contracting requires that objectives be specifiable and measurable. Skills such as reading, mathematics and some vocational abilities are easier to place under a performance contract than subjects such as history and art. Even more difficult to measure are affective and other noncognitive impacts. Thus, one of the major issues connected with performance contracting is whether it will (should?) redirect educational emphasis away from the broad range of objectives currently espoused by schools towards more stress on narrowly defined skills.

In point of fact, cognitive objectives are being defined by school districts, largely in the areas of reading and mathematics, and contractors are being paid on the basis of measured achievement based on test scores. This practice has raised a number of questions. For example, should standardized achievement tests be used to measure achievement gains? Are these tests statistically valid for accountability purposes? Can criterion referenced tests be developed as substitutes? Clearly, one of the ancillary benefits of performance contracting has been to increase professional and public attention to educational measurement.

Another set of issues raised by performance contracting concerns the role of private firms in public education. Extreme ideological positions have been taken. At one extreme the view has been expressed that the profit motive has no place in schools. At the other extreme is the view that business can revolutionize education by introducing new forces into hidebound school systems. Neither position is supported by the programs to date, or the likely future development of performance contracting. Nonetheless, performance contracting does represent a break with the past in the relationship between private firms and public schools. This has traditionally been a conventional buyer-seller arrangement involving nonrecourse sales of materials, hardware, and services. Performance contracting involves a different relationship. The LSC acquires some operational responsibilities. To a significant extent this change merely reflects LEAs desires that the "ed-bus" firms take responsibility for backing-up their claims. Even so, performance contracting blurs the formerly clear line between the educational firms who were simply developers and sellers of equipment, materials, and services and the school districts that purchased these materials, used them and were solely responsible for whatever results occurred.

The ramifications of this change in role are not easy to predict. Some observers feel that the new relationship is likely to be a passing phase. This school of thought views performance contractors as merely change-agents who get in and quickly demonstrate the cost-effectiveness of their wares and then step out and let the school-systems "turnkey" the program for in-house use. This view implies that performance contracting in any single district is likely to be temporary and that the movement in general will decline as the educational technology available in the business sector is turnkeyed into regular programs of school districts operated by the districts.

This view is supported by many contractors. They would prefer not to be operating under performance contracts but instead would like to have a consulting relationship with school districts in implementing new programs. They feel this consulting role would be more conducive to LEA-LSC interaction than the performance contracting relationship.

Other observers think the performance contracting movement will be longer lived. Some feel that we may be seeing the development of a group of firms specializing in remedial programs. Other observers feel that the accountability feature of performance contracting programs is such a useful discipline it may long continue to be used in a number of innovative programs. Still others believe that transferring technology from firms to school districts may take considerable effort and contractors will be involved in "turnkeying" systems for a considerable period.

Another question that is often asked is why schools should have to rely on profit-oriented business firms for these programs; why can't the schools' teachers do the same thing? The answer, of course, is that they can. As noted before, teacher groups have been engaging in performance contracting.

Most performance contracting programs utilize equipment, materials, and techniques that are well known to the teaching profession. The novelty of the programs comes from the contractual relationship holding the contracting group or firm accountable for measured achievement and, in the better programs at least, the use of a systems approach to learning—the attempt to combine a number of innovative features into an improved program. Teachers as well as educational firms may be given broad authority for restructuring the classroom. Realistically, however, one must admit that an outsider is often able to institute changes that an employee, working within the system, cannot.

Another question about the future of performance contracting concerns legal challenges. Critics in a number of localities have charged that performance contracts conflict with state education codes and other laws regulating public education. To date these claims have not led to many legal actions since the programs have been regarded as experimental and there has been a tendency to postpone objections in order to see what the programs can do. If performance contracting becomes a permanent part of the educational scene, however, state education departments, legislatures and the courts will likely have to adjudicate a number of questions concerning the legal status and procedures used in performance contracting programs.

Another important issue concerning the future of performance contracting is the attitudes adopted by teachers and their organizations. At the broad policy level, teacher groups have taken several positions with respect to performance contracting varying from strong opposition to cautious reservation. At the operating level, questions about the harmony of performance contracting programs and established teacher-employment policies have arisen in several cities. Again, because these programs have hitherto been regarded as experimental, objections from teachers and teacher groups have tended to be waived or left unresolved.

Finally, and perhaps most importantly, the future of performance contracting will depend to a considerable extent upon the results that are obtained in the programs during the 1970-71 years. Can LSCs provide measurable superior achievement, and what will be the overall impacts of these programs? Evidence is being collected on these questions by many LEAs, independent evaluators, governmental agencies and research organizations such as Rand.

Many of the currently debated issues will no doubt be clarified when the evaluation reports have been released. However, whatever the future of performance contracting, the programs during 1970 and 1971 have raised a number of basic issues about educational achievement and about the business-public school nexus.

Addendum

This paper was prepared in the Spring of 1971 prior to the public release of the results of the programs described. In the Spring of 1972 the authors were asked to review the manuscript before its publication. We were tempted to revise the paper to reflect the data on program outcomes, but decided to leave the paper unchanged and add this brief addendum to reflect our additional 1972 perceptions.

In the paper we cited four forces that led to the sudden popularity of educational performance contracts:

1. Compensatory education problems
2. Barriers to educational innovation
3. Desires for educational accountability
4. Searches for new forms of business-governmental relationships

Let us now examine the implications of the experiences gained from the 1970-71 programs for each of these considerations.

Performance contracting has not been a "quick-fix" for poor student achievement. During the 1970-71 school year a Rand team studied eight performance contracting programs involving seven LSCs, 15 schools and five LEAs (Carpenter and Hall, 1971). The cities involved were Norfolk, Virginia; Texarkana, Arkansas, (with Liberty-Eylau, Texas); Gary, Indiana; Gilroy, California and Grand Rapids, Michigan. (See Carpenter (1971), Carpenter, Chalfant, and Hall (1971), Hall and Rapp (1971), Rapp and Hall (1971), and Sumner (1971) for descriptions of each project.) The contractors were Alpha Systems, Behavioral Research Laboratories (BRL), Combined Motivation and Educational Systems, Inc. (CMES), Dorsett Educational Systems, Inc., Educational Development Laboratories, Inc. (EDL), Learning Research Associates (LRA), and Westinghouse Learning Corporation (WLC). The major purpose of this study was to draw implications from these programs that would be of general use for school districts that might be considering or entering into such arrangements. (These implications have been summarized in Carpenter and Hall (1971).) Although the purpose was not to evaluate or compare the specific programs studied, a number of different impacts were examined, among them the achievement gains realized. These latter results are summarized in Table 13-5. Overall, the gains realized were similar to those observed in many conventional remedial programs. There was variation from program to program but, in general, the LSCs did not achieve the large increases in test scores that they had sought. In some cases the test results were better than those realized by comparable groups of students but in some cases they were worse. The overall picture, however, does not indicate that performance contracting is quickly going to solve America's compensatory education problem.

267

Table 13-5
Mean Gains on Standardized Tests

City	LSC	Test Used[a]	Mean Gains	Remarks
Gary	BRL	MAT	1.7/1.7	Reading/math, 1st grade
	BRL	MAT	0.7/1.2	Reading/math, grades 2-6
Gilroy	WLC	SAT	0.6	Reading—for contract payment
	WLC	SAT	0.8	Math—for contract payment
	WLC	MAT (Reading)	0.6	Regular district test
Grand Rapids	Alpha	Various	NR[b]	Test identification not released by OEO. Three tests used.
	CMES	EDS	1.2/1.0[c]	Reading/math
	WLC	MAT	0.7[c]	Reading/math
	WLC	MAT	0.6[c]	Math
Norfolk	LRA	Various[d]	0.1	5th grade
	LRA	Various	0.5	7th and 9th grades
Texarkana	Dorsett	ITBS	NR	Arkansas
	Dorsett	SRA	NR	Texas
	EDL	ITBS	0.5/0.3	Arkansas and Texas, reading/math, grades 6-12

[a]Test abbreviations:
  MAT: Metropolitan Achievement Test
  SAT: Stanford Achievement Test
  EDS: Educational Development Series, Scholastic Testing Service
  ITBS: Iowa Test of Basic Skills
  SRA: Science Research Associates Achievement Tests

[b]NR: data not released.

[c]Mean gains for those students who attended at least 150 days and for whom pre- and post-test scores are available.

[d]Three tests used at each grade, chosen from SAT, MAT, ITBS, California Achievement, and Stanford Reading Achievement. Means computed only for students who took both a pre-test and a post-test.

Source: P. Carpenter and G.R. Hall, *Case Studies in Educational Performance Contracting: Conclusions and Implications*, R-900-HEW, The Rand Corporation, December 1971, p. 14.

The results of the OEO experiment reinforce this point. The OEO's summary report (Battelle Columbus Laboratories, 1972) asked and answered a straight-forward question:

"Was performance contracting more successful than traditional classroom methods in improving the reading and math skills of poor children? The answer . . . is 'No.' "

The basic OEO data are summarized in Table 13-6. Comparing the students (experimental group) who were in performance contracting programs with their

Table 13-6
OEO Performance Contracting Experiment, Aggregate Mean Gains (in Years of Achievement Gain)

Grade	Experimental Gain	Control Gain	Difference
	READING		
1	NA	NA	+.1
2	.4	.5	−.1
3	.3	.2	+.1
7	.4	.3	+.1
8	.9	1.0	−.1
9	.8	.8	−
	MATH		
1	NA	NA	−
2	.5	.5	−
3	.4	.4	−
7	.6	.6	−
8	.8	1.0	−.2
9	.8	.8	−

Source: Office of Economic Opportunity, *An Experiment in Performance Contracting: Summary of Preliminary Results*, OEO, February 1972, pp. 35-36.

respective control groups indicates no consistent pattern. More extensive statistical analysis also failed to yield any relationships that would, in the judgment of OEO, justify a belief that the performance contracts that the agency had sponsored had made any unusual contribution to remedial education.

In short, the weight of the evidence is that, despite some variations among the outcomes of the various programs, performance contracting has not proven to be a simple way to close the gap between the achievements of students from different backgrounds.

There is some evidence that the educational systems used by performance contractors may have some cost advantages over conventional approaches to compensatory education (Carpenter and Hall, 1971). The performance contractors have typically used less labor-intensive approaches than the usual remedial program.

Turning to the second issue, the impact of performance contracting on the barriers to educational innovation, the evidence is somewhat more encouraging. Many of the programs seem to have facilitated the introducion of new materials, curricula, or procedures into school systems that sponsored programs. An "outsider" motivated by the link between payments and achievement scores often appears to be better able to overcome the organizational inertia which frustrates so many efforts to effect changes in schools. Whether these innovations will prove to be lasting is another question. However, on the basis of the 1970-71 experience its potential as a change agent appears to be the most interesting aspect of performance contracting.

Performance contracting has been enlightening about the drive for educational accountability. As discussed in the paper, standardized achievement tests have many drawbacks as measures of instructional effectiveness. These drawbacks were brought home to everyone involved in performance contracting programs. Many had hoped that criterion-referenced tests would prove to be a more effective accountability-measurement technique. The evidence in the OEO Virginia and Texarkana programs, however, indicates that substantial development work will be required before this hope can be realized. The performance contracting experience to date has shown that the state-of-the-art in educational testing and measurement needs much advancement before the current educational accountability goals can be realized.

Finally, did performance contracting forge a successful new type of relationship between LEAs and LSCs? Few if any contractors made substantial profits on their projects. Four of the six OEO contractors, to illustrate this point, no longer are in the performance contracting business. Other LSCs that have had performance contracts are now reluctant to enter such an arrangement. This last fact may not be too significanct since LSCs generally have preferred some "consulting" or other arrangement that permitted them to sell goods or services without accepting the responsibility for student achievement. The pressure to engage in performance contracting arose from two related conditions. School districts were unhappy about having bought new equipment and materials and then discovering that they couldn't be or weren't implemented in the classroom. Second, firms trying to break into the educational market, which has been dominated by established textbook manufacturers, found it hard to get LEAs to accept them without some form of "guarantee."

The performance contracting programs of 1970-71 permitted a number of new firms to break into the educational market and a number of old firms to expand into new areas. The number of bankruptcies and market withdrawals implies, however, that in the future firms are likely to appraise performance contracts with a sharper pencil. We doubt that many established LSCs will have much interest in entering into performance contracting. We expect, nonetheless, that new firms will from time to time use performance contracts as a way to try to establish themselves by means of sharing some of the risks LEAs bear when they sponsor a new program.

The 1970-71 experience dashed the hopes of those who believed that performance contracting would be an easy and dramatic solution to America's compensatory education problem. It is also clear that problems of obtaining valid and reliable measures of instructional success remain. Thus, it is unlikely that performance contracting will regain its past popularity.

Performance contracting, however, might play a limited educational role. As a means to facilitate curriculum innovation and as a way for new firms to share some of the risks involved in new materials or procedures it has some attractive features. Moreover, some of the learning systems used by performance contractors may have modest cost advantages relative to conventional approaches to remedial education. If so, even if achievement gains do not increase substantially these modest cost advantages might be converted into modest improvements in instructional cost-effectiveness. Such conclusions must be stated in tentative terms since all the 1970-71 programs involved extensive start-up friction and costs as well as major development efforts and so it is difficult to extrapolate to some future "steady-state" period.

In short, performance contracting is no panacea for America's educational problems in general and its compensatory education problem in particular. It may, however, be a technique that can make a modest contribution to education.

References

Allen, J.E., Speech to the National Association of State Boards of Education, September 23, 1969.

Bumstead, R.A., "Texarkana, The First Accounting," *Educate,* Vol. 3, No. 2, March 1970, pp. 24-37.

Burkhart, R.C., *The Assessment Revolution*, Buffalo State University, Buffalo, New York, 1970.

Carpenter, P. and G.R. Hall, *Case Studies in Educational Performance Contracting: Conclusions and Implications*, R-900/1-HEW, The Rand Corporation, December 1971.

Carpenter, P., *Case Studies in Educational Performance Contracting: Norfolk, Virginia*, R-900/2-HEW, The Rand Corporation, December 1971.

Carpenter, P., A.W. Chalfant, and G.R. Hall, *Case Studies in Educational Performance Contracting: Texarkana, Arkansas and Liberty-Eylau, Texas*, R-900/3-HEW, The Rand Corporation, December 1971.

Cronback, L.J., and L. Furby, "How Should We Measure 'Change'—Or Should We?," *Psychological Bulletin*, Vol. 74, No. 1, July 1970, pp. 68-80.

Education Turnkey Systems, Inc., *Performance Contracting in Education*, Research Press, Champaign, Illinois, 1970.

"Evaluation Cites Texarkana Project," *Education Daily*, September 17, 1970, pp. 1-2.

Hall, G.R., and M.L. Rapp, *Case Studies in Educational Performance Contracting: Gary, Indiana*, R-900/4-HEW, The Rand Corporation, December 1971.

Harrison, C.H., "Who is Accountable?," *Scholastic Teacher: Supplement*, November 1970, pp. 6, 18, 26.

Lessinger, L.M., *Every Kid A Winner: Accountability in Education*, Simon and Schuster, New York, 1970.

Klein, S.P., "The Uses and Limitations of Standardized Tests in Meeting the Demands for Accountability," *U.C.L.A. Evaluation Comment*, Vol. 2, No. 4, January 1971, pp. 1-7.

Lennon, R.T., "Accountability and Performance Contracting," paper presented to the American Educational Research Association, New York, February 5, 1971.

Millman, J., "Reporting Student Progress: A Case of a Criterion-Referenced Marking System," *Phi Delta Kappan*, Vol. 52, No. 4, December 1970, pp. 226-230.

Rapp, M.L., and G.R. Hall, *Case Studies in Performance Contracting, Gilroy, California*, R-900/5-HEW, The Rand Corporation, December 1971.

Reading Crisis: The Problem and Suggested Solutions, An Education U.S.A. Special Report, National School Public Relations Association, Washington, D.C., 1970.

Sigel, Efrem, *Accountability and the Controversial Role of the Performance Contractors*, Knowledge Industry Publications, Inc., 1971.

G.C. Sumner, *Case Studies in Educational Performance Contracting: Grand Rapids, Michigan*, R-900/6-HEW, The Rand Corporation, December 1971.

Office of Economic Opportunity, *An Experiment in Performance Contracting: Summary of Preliminary Results*, OEO, February 1972.

Battelle Columbus Laboratories, *The Office of Economic Opportunity Experiment in Educational Performance Contracting*, Battelle Memorial Institute, Columbus, Ohio, January 1972.

Bibliography

Planning Guides

Adams, John W., and Karen H. Kitchak, *A Guide to Performance Contracting*, Wisconsin Department of Public Institution, Madison, Wisconsin, 1971.

Hall, G.R., P. Carpenter, S.A. Haggart, M.L. Rapp, and G.C. Sumner, *A Guide to Educational Performance Contracting*, The Rand Corporation, R-955/1-HEW, March 1972; S.A. Haggart, G.C. Sumner, and J. Richard Harsh, *Technical Appendix*, R-955/2-HEW, March 1972.

Michigan Department of Education, *An Introduction to Guaranteed Performance Contracting*, Lansing, Michigan, March 1971.

National School Boards Association, *Performance Contracting: A Guide for School Board Members and Community Leaders*, Evanston, Illinois, 1971.

Newspapers, News Services, and Magazines with Regular Coverage of Performance Contracting

American Teacher, American Federation of Teachers AFL/CIO, Washington, D.C.

Educational Marketer, Knowledge Industry Publications, Inc., White Plains, New York.

Education Daily, Capital Publications, Washington, D.C.

Educational Technology, Englewood Cliffs, New Jersey.

Education Turnkey News, Education Turnkey Systems, Washington, D.C. (ceased publication, fall 1971).

Phi Delta Kappan, Bloomington, Indiana.

Books, Articles, and Papers

Asbell, Bernard, "Should Private Enterprise Direct Your Child's Education?," *Redbook*, Vol. 138, No. 4, February 1972, pp. 56-63.

Barro, Stephen M., "An Approach to Developing Accountability Measures for the Public Schools," *Phi Delta Kappan*, Vol. 52, No. 4, December 1970, pp. 196-205.

Bhaerman, Robert D., "A Paradigm for Accountability," AFT-Quest Paper 12, American Federation of Teachers, Washington, D.C., August 1970.

———, "Accountability: The Great Day of Judgment," *Educational Technology*, Vol. 11, No. 1, January 1971, pp. 62-63.

Blaschke, Charles, "Educational Technology—A New Perspective," *Educational Technology*, Vol. 8, No. 1, January 15, 1968, pp. 17-18.

Blaschke, Charles, "Performance Contracting Costs, Management Reform and John Q. Citizen," *Phi Delta Kappan*, Vol. 53, No. 4, December 1971, pp. 245-247.

——, *Performance Incentive Remedial Education Experiment*, Final Report to the Office of Economic Opportunity, Contract No. B00-5114, Education Turnkey Systems, Inc., Washington, D.C., August 31, 1971.

Bumstead, Richard A., "Lessinger's Logic" (review of L.M. Lessinger, *Every Kid a Winner*), *Educate*, Vol. 4, No. 2, March 1971, pp. 25-30.

——, "Texarkana, the First Accounting," *Educate*, Vol. 3, No. 2, March 1970, pp. 24-37, 52.

"Briton to Expound New Learning Approach on TV," *New York Times*, September 28, 1970.

"Business-Run School Runs into Problems," *Washington Post*, May 2, 1971.

Carpenter, P., A.W. Chalfant, G.R. Hall, M.L. Rapp, G.C. Sumner, "Case Studies in Educational Performance Contracting," R-900-HEW The Rand Corporation, December, 1971.

Campbell, Robert E., "Accountability and Store Soup," *Phi Delta Kappan*, Vol. 53, No. 3, November 1971, pp. 176-178.

Carlson, Elliot, "Education and Industry: Troubled Partnership," *Saturday Review*, Vol. 53, No. 33, August 15, 1970, pp. 45-55.

Clapp, Stephen, "Performing for Profit," *P.I.C. News*, Public Information Center, Washington, D.C., Vol. 1, No. 4, September 1970, pp. 3-4.

Coleman, James S., "Toward Open Schools," *The Public Interest*, No. 9, Fall 1967.

Cronbach, Lee J., and Lita Furby, "How We Should Measure 'Change'—Or Should We?," *Psychological Bulletin*, Vol. 74, No. 1, 1970, pp. 68-80.

Donaldson, T.S., *Subjective Scaling of Student Performance*, The Rand Corporation, P-4596, March 1971.

Dyer, Henry S., "Can We Measure the Performance of Educational Systems?," *NASSP Bulletin*, May 1970, pp. 96-105.

Education Turnkey Systems, Inc., *Performance Contracting in Education*, Research Press, Champaign, Illinois, 1970.

EPIE (Educational Products Information Exchange), "Performance Contracting Game Continues," *Educational Product Report*, EPIE Report 38, Vol. 5, No. 2, November 1971, pp. 1-5.

"Free Enterprise for Schools," *Time*, August 24, 1970, pp. 58-60.

Gillis, James, "Performance Contracting for Public Schools," *Educational Technology*, Vol. 9, No. 5, May 1969, pp. 17-20.

Glennan, Thomas K., "OEO Experiments in Education," *Compact*, Vol. 5, No. 1, February 1971, pp. 3-5.

Hall, George R., and James P. Stucker, "The Rand/HEW Study of Performance Contracting," *Compact*, Vol. 5, No. 1, February 1971, pp. 6-9.

Harmes, H.M., "Specifying Objectives for Performance Contracts," *Educational Technology*, Vol. 11, No. 1, January 1971, pp. 52-56.

Harrison, C.H., "Who Is Accountable?," *Scholastic Teacher: Supplement*, November 1970, pp. 6, 18, 26.

Heddinger, Fred M., "New Leverage for Funding Agencies," *Compact*, Vol. 5, No. 1, February 1971, pp. 35-37.

"Hucksters in the Schools: The Performance-Contract Phenomenon," *American Teacher*, Vol. 54, No. 1, September 1970, pp. 9-11.

Klein, S.P., "The Uses and Limitations of Standardized Tests in Meeting the Demands for Accountability," *U.C.L.A. Evaluation Comment*, Vol. 2, No. 4, January 1971, pp. 1-7.

Kruger, W. Stanley, "Educational Performance Contracting: Another Perspective," (mimeographed) paper presented at the National School Boards Regional Conference on Performance Contracting, Chicago, Ill. (February 4-6, 1971), Denver, Colo. (February 7-9, 1971) and San Francisco, Calif. (February 11-13, 1971).

Lennon, R.T., "Accountability and Performance Contracting," paper presented to the American Educational Research Association, New York, New York, February 5, 1971.

Lessinger, Leon M., "Accountability in Public Education," *Today's Education*, Vol. 59, No. 5, May 1970, pp. 52-53.

_____, "After Texarkana, What?", *Nation's Schools*, Vol. 84, No. 6, December 1969, pp. 37-40.

_____, *Every Kid a Winner: Accountability in Education*, Simon and Schuster, New York, 1970.

_____, and Dwight H. Allen, "Performance Proposals for Educational Funding: A New Approach to Federal Resource Allocation," *Phi Delta Kappan*, Vol. 51, No. 3, November 1969, pp. 136-137.

Locke, Robert W., "Accountability Yes, Performance Contracting Maybe," *Proceedings of the Conferences on Educational Accountability*, Educational Testing Service, Princeton, New Jersey, March 1971, E1-E9.

Mayrhofer, Albert V., "Factors to Consider in Preparing Performance Contracts for Instruction," *Educational Technology*, Vol. 2, No. 1, January 1971, pp. 48-51.

McAndrew, Gordon, "Gary, Indiana Contracts for Operation of Entire School," *Compact*, Vol. 5, No. 1, February 1971, pp. 10-11.

Megel, Carl J. and Robert D. Bhaerman, "Teachers Voice Their Opposition," *Compact*, Vol. 5, No. 1, February 1971, pp. 31-34.

Millman, J., "Reporting Student Progress: A Case for a Criterion-Referenced Marking System," *Phi Delta Kappan*, Vol. 52, No. 4, December 1970, pp. 226-230.

National Education Association, "Policy Statement by the NEA Executive Committee on Performance Contracting," Washington, D.C., December 5, 1970 (mimeographed).

"New Ways of Teaching on Trial," *New York Times*, April 24, 1971.

Office of Economic Opportunity, *An Experiment in Performance Contracting:*

Summary of Preliminary Results, OEO Pamphlet 3400-3, Washington, D.C., February 1972.

"Performance Contracting: The Issue," *I/D/E/A Reporter*, Winter Quarter 1971, pp. 1-10.

Randall, Ronald, and Charles Blaschke, "Educational Technology: Economics, Management and Public Policy," *Educational Technology*, Vol. 8, No. 12, June 30, 1968, pp. 5-13.

Rapp, M.L., *Performance Contracting*, U.S. Department of Health, Education, and Welfare, 1971.

Rice, Carolyn, "Will Performance Contracts Really Produce?," *Virginia Journal of Education*, Vol. 6, No. 4, January 1971, pp. 71-73.

Saretsky, Gary, "Every Kid a Hustler," *Phi Delta Kappan*, Vol. 52, No. 10, June 1971, pp. 595-596.

Schwartz, Ronald, "Performance Contracts Catch On," *Nation's Schools*, Vol. 86, No. 2, August 1970, pp. 71-73.

Schwebel, Milton, Review of Lessinger, *Every Kid a Winner: Accountability in Education, Educational Technology*, Vol. 11, No. 10, October 1971, p. 19.

Shanker, Albert, "Possible Effects on Instructional Programs," *Proceedings of the Conferences on Educational Accountability*, Educational Testing Service, Princeton, New Jersey, March 1971, pp. F1-F11.

Sigel, Efrem, *Accountability and the Controversial Role of the Performance Contractors*, Knowledge Industry Publications, Inc., White Plains, New York, 1970.

Stake, Robert E., "Testing Hazards in Performance Contracting," *Phi Delta Kappan*, Vol. 52, No. 10, June 1971, pp. 583-589.

Stenner, Jack, "Education Performance Contracting: Varied Approaches," The Council of the Great City Schools, Washington, D.C., and Dallas Independent School District, Dallas, Texas, n.d. (mimeographed).

——, "Performance Contracting: Some Policy and Legal Considerations," The Council of the Great City Schools, Washington, D.C., and Dallas Independent School District, Dallas, Texas, n.d. (mimeograph).

Stucker, James P., *The Performance Contracting Concept, Appendix: A Critique of the Theory*, The Rand Corporation, R-699/2-HEW, May 1971.

——, and George R. Hall, *The Performance Contracting Concept in Education*, The Rand Corporation, R-699/1-HEW, May 1971.

"Teaching for Profit," *Newsweek*, August 17, 1970, p. 58.

Voegel, George H., "A Suggested Schema for Faculty Commission Pay in Performance Contracting," *Educational Technology*, Vol. 11, No. 1, January 1971, pp. 57-59.

Waldrip, Donald R., "Performance Contracting: The Dallas Experiment," unpublished paper, Dallas Independent School District, Dallas, Texas, n.d.

Wardrop, James L., "Was New Century Teaching the Gates-MacGinitie Reading Test in Connection with its Providence (R.I.) Contract?," Opinion Prepared at the Request of the American Federation of Teachers, AFL/CIO, Washington, D.C., 1971 (mimeograph).

Willingham, Edward, "Education Report/Performance Contracting in School Tests Administration's 'Accountability' Idea," *National Journal*, Vol. 2, No. 43, October 24, 1970, pp. 2324-2332.

Wilson, John O., "Statement Submitted for the Record on Performance Contracting Before the House Committee on Education and Labor," Office of Economic Opportunity, April 20, 1971 (mimeograph).

Zaharis, James K., and Fenwick W. English, "Performance Contracting: Hobson's Choice for Teachers?," paper delivered to California Teachers Association, Good Teaching Conference, Los Angeles, California, January 29, 1971, Mesa Public Schools, Mesa, Arizona.

Zazzera, Edmund, "A Contractor's Viewpoint," *Compact*, Vol. 5, No. 1, February 1971, pp. 13-16.

14

The Emerging Intersection of Economics and Psychology in Educational Research

Henry M. Levin and Richard E. Snow

A Brief Review of Psychology in Education

Psychologists have been engaged in educational research almost since the beginnings of psychology as a science about a century ago. Many of the "Great Names" of psychology, men like G. Stanley Hall, William James, E.L. Thorndike, and John Dewey, along with Francis Galton, James McKeen Cattell, Charles Spearman, and Alfred Binet, formed a strong bridge between psychology and education in the early days. Some of the names mentioned represent research on learning and instruction. Others were concerned more with the measurement and understanding of individual differences, particularly in intelligence. These two streams of psychological work in education, experimental research on learning and psychometric research on individual differences, have been quite distinct throughout history. They represent psychology's two major contributions to current educational research and development and thus to today's discussion. Since Cronbach provided a detailed historical review of these "two disciplines of scientific psychology" in his 1957 presidential address to the American Psychological Association (Cronbach, 1957), only a very brief sketch of the history of each stream is given here. Then we can concentrate on the most recent developments related to educational research.

The Psychometric Tradition began with Galton's studies of hereditary genius in the 1860s which were heavily influenced by Social Darwinism and the concepts of selection and competition. Cattell broadened the field in the 1890s through the study of individual differences in reaction times and other sensori-motor measurements. The expanded movement emerged from World War I, having clearly demonstrated the usefulness of group mental tests. Combined with the work of Binet and others on intelligence scales for school children, the way was opened for broad development of the testing movement through the decades that followed. The invention and development of factor analytic methods by Spearman, Thurstone, and others during these years, and their application to the study of many kinds of individual differences emphasized a multidimensional view of the nature of man, although the concept of general intelligence remained the centerpiece of differential psychology. World War II saw further expansion of testing of all kinds and demonstrated the importance of tests as selection devices in many personnel and training applications. Then, from 1945 to 1960, the measurement stream reached its peak. There was vast expansion in work on the prediction of academic success at all levels, in factor analytic investigation of mental ability and personality by Guilford, Cattell, and others, in developing the statistical foundations of measurement theory in technology, and in correlational psychology generally.[a] Virtually every school and college, industrial firm and government agency had its testing program, for admission, placement, guidance, and evaluation purposes. In education particularly, the general intelligence, aptitude, and scholastic achievement tests reigned supreme, both for regulating admission to more advanced work and for evaluating the outcome of this work.

Cronbach describes the social philosophy guiding this movement, from its beginnings with Galton in the 1860s up to the 1960s as follows:

Aristocracy had to be supplanted by an elite selected on the basis of individual merit. . . . An open system of *laissez-faire* competition could in theory bring to the top the individuals fittest to survive. Educational and vocational opportunity would not be open, however, if judgments of merit were impressionistic, and colored by awareness of the young person's family connections. The objective mental test, the Civil Service examination, and other formal tests came into use as liberal devices, intended to break down the barriers of caste and class so as to bring every talent to fruition. (Cronbach, 1970, p. 480)

The application of this view can be seen in operational terms in Figure 14-1. A mental test X given before instruction shows positive relation to achievement Y after instruction. By deciding what level of achievement is considered satisfactory, a cutoff point is established for the selection test X to divide future applicants into those accepted and those rejected, or, what is more common for public schools today, into fast track and slow track. In most cases the nature of the instruction intervening between X and Y was ignored by the measurement psychologist. The objective was to produce test instruments that, singly or combined in multiple prediction equations, would maximize prediction of general achievement criteria regardless of content of instruction. There was work on predicting, or factor analyzing, achievement in specific courses or subject-matters, but rarely were recommendations made on the basis of these predictive data regarding *changes* in instructional conditions. Differential aptitude and interest batteries for predicting success in different subject matters were developed for guidance and counselling purposes only. Thus, educational psychology produced a strong measurement technology for use in a static, generalized educational environment dictated by the institution.

The past decade has seen a dramatic change, however. Where earlier the "equality of opportunity to compete" provided by tests was seen as a liberalizing influence, testing has now come to be regarded as an instrument of

[a]For summaries of work in this tradition, see Cattell (1971), Cronbach (1970), Cronbach and Gleser (1965), and Guilford (1959, 1967).

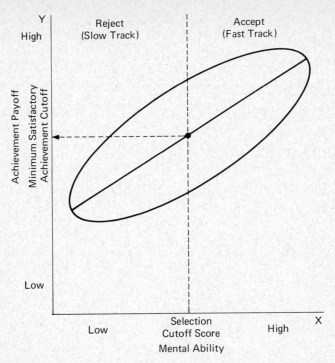

Figure 14-1. The Relationship Between Ability and Achievement Showing the Effects of Selection on Payoff. Note that Average Payoff is Improved by Rejecting Lower Ability Group.

conservative establishment, supporting a meritocracy little better than the aristocracy it replaced. Overreliance on general mental tests has produced a "single-rank-order" conception of scholastic ability in the minds of many educators and researchers. Thus, concern over racial and ethnic bias in tests or their influence as self fulfilling prophecies on pupil achievement has led to the banning of intelligence tests in some school situations, random selection for school admissions in other situations, and some new attempts to develop culture-fair tests. But attacks on the tests and on the educational measurement tradition are misguided. Tests, and research using tests, can be useful for guiding educational decisions. As suggested later in this paper, it is the "single-rank-order" conception of merit that should be attacked. First, the history of psychology's other great contribution, the experimental tradition, must be traced.

The Experimental Tradition in educational psychology was strong from psychology's beginnings well into the 1920s. James, Dewey, and particularly E. L. Thorndike led the search for improved educational practices based on experimental analysis of learning and manipulation of instructional stimuli and sequences. The philosophy guiding this stream took a generalized undifferentiated conception of man and sought to design the best educational environment for him. Aided by Fisher's contributions in experimental design, the investigator could conduct complex experimental comparisons, isolating and manipulating the key stimulus combinations that maximized average achievement. After Thorndike, however, many experimentalists took their Fisherian methods back into the learning laboratories. The scientific pursuit of learning theory required a degree of purification and control of stimuli not possible in the study of school learning, perhaps not even in the study of human learning at all. But World War II and the cold war that followed brought experimental psychologists into military training research. Then, Skinner's development of programmed instruction, Sputnik, and new Federal legislation turned research interests again toward educational improvement. With renewed effort and an attitude akin to Frederick Taylor's efficiency-expert experimentalism, the construction and comparison of instructional treatments has multiplied up to the present day.[b] Skinner best states the guiding purpose of this work: "We need to find practices which permit all teachers to teach well and under which all students learn as efficiently as their talents permit." (Skinner, 1968, p. 705)

Figure 14-2 shows the experimental approach operationally, for a simple example. Two instructional treatments, A and B, are designed to be similar except for stimulus variables that are manipulated systematically between treatments. For this example, let us say that the stimulus variable of interest is the frequency with which questions are inserted into the instructional sequence. The basic treatment might be a teacher presentation into which many or few questions to students are inserted or text material or programmed instructional sequences including many or few questions. The experimental hypothesis might be that including more questions produces a better instructional treatment, since student attention is increased and active response to the material is ensured. An actual experiment would probably contain a number of such stimulus variations. Then, using an accepted criterion measure of achievement, statistical comparison would show which treatment was best on the average. Individual differences in initial student ability are typically ignored or used only for statistical control purposes and it is assumed that the relation between ability and achievement is constant across all treatments.

In most such experiments the emphasis is on tight experimental control so that if a difference is found, it can be attributed clearly to the operation of a specific stimulus variable. Such research is *conclusion-oriented,* not *decision-oriented*—that is it aims at producing generalizable conclusions about psychological effects of, say, inserted questions. While this finding may presumably be of use to teachers or instructional designers, the organization of such findings to improve instruction in a particular setting is left to others.

Many educational experiments have constructed and compared alternative treatments in this way. When summarizing experimental findings from several

---

[b]For summaries of the history and current state of this tradition, see Boring (1957), Hilgard and Bower (1966), Gagné (1970), and Ausubel (1968).

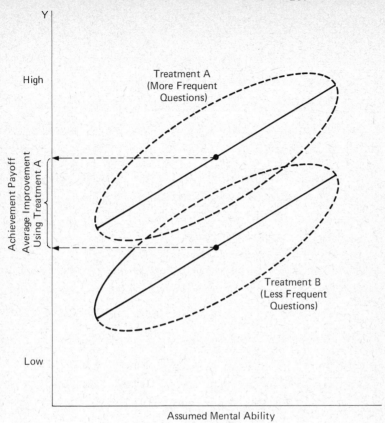

Figure 14-2. Comparison of Achievement Payoff for Two Alternative Instructional Treatments, Assuming Ability Regression Equal in Each Group.

studies or a particular stimulus variable, however, one often finds that no clear decision can be made about which treatment is best. For example, five studies may show that Method A is best, four that Method B is best, and three studies show no significant difference. Actually, a very large number of educational method comparisons have shown no difference on the average. To give just a few examples,

1. Schramm (1962) shows that comparisons of TV and live classroom instruction have shown no consistent differences. Of 393 experimental comparisons, 255 showed no difference, 83 favored televised teaching, and 55 favored conventional teaching.
2. Dubin and Taveggia (1968) report no differences in comparisons of most college teaching methods, e.g., of 88 comparisons of lecture vs. discussion, 45 favored lecture and 43 favored discussion.

3. Anderson (1952) summarized studies comparing learner-centered (democratic) classrooms and teacher-centered (authoritarian) classrooms. Eight studies favored the teacher-centered approach, 11 favored the learner-centered approach, and 13 found no difference.

Also, although some studies are able to demonstrate consistent statistically significant differences, critics have argued that rarely are such differences large enough to be of practical importance.

Thus, although the experimental tradition has developed a tremendous facility for designing and handling complex manipulations of experimental variables, particularly when considered within controlled environments like programmed or computerized instruction, its results have not led to consistent findings or theories, or to systematic educational improvement. They have instead often been regarded as practically irrelevant. Again, in my view, it is not the technology of experimental research that should be criticized here. It is the idea that instructional methods or treatments can be listed from good to bad in a single rank order conception of educational quality.

Aptitude-Treatment Interaction

The two traditions of psychology were earlier described separately because for most of psychology's history they have developed separately. Recently, however, there have been increasing attempts to unify the two approaches, particularly for educational psychological research. The two earlier questions of educational psychology were:

1. What kind of individual is most likely to succeed in a particular educational setting?
2. What kind of instructional method is best in a particular educational setting?

These questions must now be adandoned in favor of an approach which attempts to optimize the match between individual difference variables and instructional method variables. This is a search for what we have elsewhere (Cronbach & Snow, 1969) called aptitude-treatment interactions (ATI).

To put the ATI problem formally—assume that an educator is interested in a certain set of educational outcomes and has various alternative educational programs or treatments to consider. His question is: In what manner do the characteristics of learners affect the extent to which they attain the outcomes from each of the treatments that might be considered? Or, considering a particular learner: What outcome will each treatment produce?

For an example of ATI, see Figure 14-3. In this hypothetical example,

Treatment A, consisting of more frequent questions during instruction, is better for lower ability students than it is for higher ability students. Treatment B, on the other hand, is better for higher ability students, in terms of achievement payoff. The intersection of the two regression lines marks the point of the ability continuum at which students could be divided for assignment to different treatments, for this particular learning situation. Perhaps students below a certain general ability level need questions to keep them involved and actively responding, while students above that ability level are bored or bothered by instrusions that slow their pace. They do well without the inserted questions, while the low ability students do not.

Of course, this example is a simple one. There are many possible aptitude variables, from both the ability and personality domains that could be considered in such interactions. There are likewise many possible treatment

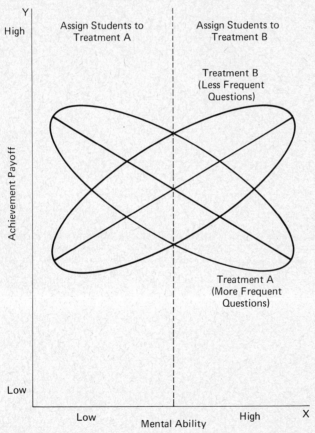

Figure 14-3. Aptitude-treatment Interaction Showing that Treatment A is Best for Students Below a Certain Level of Aptitude While Treatment B is Best for Students Above that Level.

variables, ranging from small changes in test materials, through major curriculum alternatives, to variations in teacher styles. Also, there are many criteria that could be used to examine such interactions. Today we are not interested only in achievement, but also in attitude, achievement motivation, self-concept, social development, and the growth of aptitude itself. There are likely to be complex interactions among variables from all these categories.

This kind of approach is consistent with the social philosophy and the educational needs of the 1970s. Persons can be characterized by many dimensions; so can instructional treatments. The goal of educational psychological research must be to determine the interactions among these two sets of dimensions so that instruction can be *adapted* to individuals. Adaptation to the individual has been a slogan widely held among educators. Ability grouping, individualized instruction that allows only differences in pace, various compensatory programs—these are examples of crude superficial and, often, misguided adaption. Such adaptation has never been systematic because no one yet knows the principles that govern the matching of learner and instructional environment.

This is the task for *current* educational research—from the psychological view.

History of Economic Research in Education

In contrast with the lengthy sojourn of the psychologist in the sphere of educational research, the economist has just begun his travel. While references to the economic aspects of education can be found in writings produced over the last three centuries, serious inquiry in this area is a product of the last fifteen years (Kiker, 1966). The rod that guided economists into studying education was a paradox that had developed in the econometric investigation of economic growth. Forecasting models relating changes in the labor force and changes in the stock of physical capital (plant and equipment) to changes in economic output tended to understate substantially the growth of the economy.

As a partial solution to this paradox, economists began to focus on adjusting labor force measures for changes in the quality of labor, and it was assumed that improve the explanatory power of economic growth models (Bowman, 1964). productivity (Denison, 1962). Adjustments for the quality of labor seemed to improve and explanatory power of economic growth models (Bowman, 1964). Thus a new approach to the labor input was born under a very traditional branch of economists, capital theory.

Human capital represented a counterpart to physical capital in the economic analysis of investment and productivity. For example, dollars invested in the education of the population bore fruits in terms of higher productivity and output. This return to investment in human capital could be compared with investment in physical capital in order to maximize the economic product of society. Moreover, the human capital approach was used to explain the demand for education of individuals where the rational person was expected to undertake additional schooling whenever the present (discounted) value of additional earnings was greater than the costs incurred by the individual for taking that option (Becker, 1964). This approach had important implications for explaining dropout rates, patterns of enrollment among various curricula, and so on.

Accordingly, the blossoming of the human capital approach stimulated a flurry of research activities. These included investigations of the relationship between education and earnings, education and economic growth, education and technological change, investment in on-the-job training, allocating educational investment, and so on.[c]

But none of these endeavors attempted to examine the internal economics of the educational systems themselves. Only in the last seven years or so have economists begun to examine how education is produced and how educational resources might be used more effectively. In general, this inquiry is based upon studies of the educational production function, the nexus between inputs and outputs. Stimulated particularly by the controversy over the Coleman Report on these matters, several economists have made attempts to understand the relationships of school, family, and other characteristics to educational outcomes (Coleman, et al., 1966).[d] Moreover, indices of effectiveness of various programs and resources have been combined with their relative costs in order to suggest strategies which maximize educational outcomes under budgetary constraints (Levin, 1970b).

Research Approach of Economists

In the early states of development of the economists of education, there was little overlap between the economic research and psychological research applied to education. Psychologists were not concerned with capital theory and economists were not addressing themselves to any aspect of education other than its effect on earnings and economic growth. As economists ventured into the production of education, the commonality between the two sets of researchers increased. Clearly this has been an increasing phenomenon, and its salience has been reflected by the fact that economists presented invited papers at both the 1970 and 1971 annual meetings of the Psychometric Society (Goldberger, 1970 and Levin, 1971b). This consonance of interests was also recognized by the U. S. Office of Education at a recent conference on the topic, "Do Teachers Make a Difference?" The conference participants were mainly selected from among economists and psychologists who had been researching the

[c]For an excellent review, see Bowman (1969).

[d]Criticisms of the report are found in Bowles & Levin (1968), and Cain and Watts (1970). Input-output studies are reviewed in Averch, Carroll, and Donaldson (1971).

area of school effectiveness, and the published monograph of the papers and discussions, mirrors clearly the emerging overlap between the endeavors of economists and psychologists in the field of educational research.

Traditionally, economists have taken a very different research approach than have psychologists and this has been mirrored in their contrasting styles of educational research. These differences are reflected in the research questions that have been raised by educational economists as well as the methodologies that they have used to answer them.

Economists are principally concerned with using resources in such a way as to maximize outcomes, benefits, or welfare. Accordingly, the approach of economists to the analysis of education processes addresses the questions: 1) How do differences in the amounts, types, and organization of educational resources create differences in educational results? 2) Given this knowledge, what is the least cost approach for achieving a particular set of outputs? and 3) What are the social priorities among outcomes (so that we can select that combination for any resource constraint that will maximize social welfare)?

Since economists are concerned not only with "effects" but with costs as well, they do not find much of the traditional psychological research to be useful for solving their problems. That is, the psychologist may ask whether treatment A shows significant educational gains over treatment B, but he does not ask whether the significant differences in effect are greater than the differences in relative costs of the two treatments.

Moreover, the psychologist uses prediction in a way that differs from the economist. The psychologist seeks the set of factors that will allow him to predict with the greatest degree of assurance a particular outcome, for example, reading scores or college success. He is much less concerned than the economist about the "causal" structures of the relationship. Thus, when the educational psychologist says that high school grade point average or college entrance examinations or some combination of the two represent the best predictors of college success, the economist asks the question: "But what are the determinants of the predictors?[e] That is, the economist does not see any causal link between high school grade point average (GPA) and college success (CS), and he needs this information for making inference on public policy. Thus he is concerned that there is a third set of factors that determine both GPA and CS, and it is this third set of influences that are important to the economist for suggesting educational policies that will improve resource use.

Methodology of Economists

More generally, the economist relies heavily on a deductive method of reasoning while the psychologist tends to pursue the inductive means of inquiry. The

[e]Of course the psychologist is asking different questions because his concerns are different from those of the economist. Non-causal models are useful for "statistically" predicting behaviors even though one cannot ascertain the underlying behavioral structure of the phenomenon.

economist begins with a phenomenon that he is interested in explaining, for example achievement levels of students. He then pursues the relevant literature in order to obtain theoretical insight into the relationship. Finally, he constructs causal models of the phenomenon based upon the theoretical underpinnings that he has gleaned and a set of logical constructs.

Generally, the model will take the form of an equation or system of equations with well-defined mathematical properties. Moreover, this first stage of analysis is carried out without concern for measurement or other procedures. It represents an attempt to set out the best theoretical model of the world which is being examined. Since it is the structure of that world which is the focus of the research, this is known as a structural model. Thus the model of educational achievement might be posited as follows:

$$A_{it} = g[F_{i(t)}, S_{c(t)}, P_{i(t)}, O_{i(t)}, I_{i(t)}]$$

where A_{it} = a vector or educational outcome for the ith student at time t,

$F_{i(t)}$ = a vector of individual and family background characteristics cumulative to time t,

$S_{i(t)}$ = a vector of school inputs relevant to the ith student cumulative to time t,

$P_{i(t)}$ = a vector of peer or fellow student characteristics cumulative to time t,

$O_{i(t)}$ = a vector of other external influences (community, etc.,) relevant to the ith student, cumulative to t,

$I_{i(t)}$ = a vector of initial or innate endowments of the ith student cumulative to t.

This model underlies much of the work on estimating structural relations in the educational sector (Hanushek, 1971; Levin, 1970a). Educational outcomes are assumed to be an increasing function of the cumulative effects of school, student and community environment, and family background. The operationalizing of this model requires the choice of a particular a) sample, b) structural model, c) variables, d) measures of the variables, e) analysis of possible errors in the equations and variables, f) estimation, and g) interpretation of results. These steps are discussed broadly in most tests on econometrics, and they are discussed specifically for estimation of educational relations in others.[f]

The outcome of these efforts are equations or systems of equations that

---

[f]For an introduction to econometrics, see Klein (1962); more advanced expositions are found in Johnston (1963), Christ (1966), and Goldberger (1964). Specific applications to education are found in Bowles (1970), Michelson (1970), Levin (1970a), and Kiesling (1971).

represent an attempt to approximate the causal relations between inputs and outputs of the schools. These estimates have been carried out for national samples and regional ones, samples of white students and racial minorities, and the units of observation have included individual students, schools, and school districts (Kiesling, 1971; Averch, Carroll, & Donaldson, 1971). While most of the structural models are represented by a single linear equation, nonlinear and multi-equation systems have been tested.[g] The variables and their measures that have been employed in these studies have been exceedingly diverse. Generally they have included conventional measures of student socio-economic status, indicators of school organization and resources, and characteristics of student bodies.[h] Estimation has generally been carried out with ordinary or multi-stage least squares multiple regression analysis, and errors of measurement and specification have been scrutinized (Bowles, 1970; Michelson, 1970). Moreover, the interpretations and policy usefulness of these studies has been heavily discussed and debated (Cain & Watts, 1970; Levin, 1971a). In at least one case an attempt has been made to compare effectiveness with the cost of different strategies (Levin, 1970b).

Of particular interest is the implication of aptitude-treatment-interaction—ATI—(Cronbach and Snow, 1969) to this type of research. While the educational literature is heavily documented with the rhetoric of individualized instruction, it is difficult to find examples in educational practice. Rather, a highly uniform approach to instruction is used in most schools. Teachers, facilities, instructional materials, and curriculum tend to be assigned interchangeably to students with widely differing cultural backgrounds and learning styles. Even the criteria used to group students for instructional purposes are rarely based upon instructional strategies.

Yet, what if the types of teachers, curriculum, and materials reinforce the learning characteristics of one group of students but show only a nominal effect or a deleterious one on another group of students. For example, the standard approach to teaching reading may have differential effects between white and nonwhite students (Baratz and Shuy, 1969). In particular, it appears that the standard educational approach reinforces the attributes of white students and middle class ones for more than their nonwhite and poor counterparts. Thus, the question that arises is how can we allocate our budget to obtain the proper types and combinations of resources that will maximize educational outcomes for each group of children.[i]

In order to identify the nature of these relations, Michelson estimated separate "average effects equations" for both black and white students in a large

---

[g]See Averch, Carroll, and Donaldson (1971) for a general review, and Levin (1970a) for a simultaneous-equations system.

[h]See the review in Averch, Carroll, and Donaldson (1971) and Kiesling (1971).

[i]Notice the parallel between this problem in budget allocation and public policy with the conceptual model presented by the ATI phenomenon discussed in this paper.

northern city (Michelson, 1970). He found statistically significant "effects" of various school resources on standardized test achievement between blacks and whites (Michelson, 1970: 134-140). Indeed, resources that appeared to have a positive effect on the achievement of whites (e.g., teacher experience) showed no statistical effect or an insignificant one on the achievement of black students. F tests performed on the equations showed significant differences between the two samples for verbal, reading, and mathematics scores. If this analysis could be refined, we might better be able to identify appropriate schooling experiences for children with different attributes. Clearly, such an accomplishment would have important implications for the attainment of equal educational opportunity.

This example illustrates a natural intersection of psychological and economic analysis in an important educational problem. Clearly, if there exist some treatments that work better with students of one type than with those of another type, one approach will always produce differential results, even if the same level of resources (equal dollar expenditures) are applied to each child. More specifically, schools that work well for white children might not be productive for black ones, even when such schools are equally well endowed with resources.[j] Both the economist and psychologist have become interested in the phenomenon, albeit from the vantage points of different methodologies and concerns. Given the focusing of these interests on matters of public policy, it seems reasonable that formal collaboration between the two groups would be very useful.

Prospects for the Future

The great significance of ATI for both psychological and economic research in education suggests that joint endeavors in that area might be highly productive. Yet, it is probable that even this important inter-section of interests might be nominal relative to the larger issues that might be addressed profitably by cooperative efforts between the two areas. In order to denote more generally the potential directions in which further collaboration might develop, it is useful to show economic and psychological inquiry in the context of the larger social domain.

Figure 14-4 represents a schematic diagram of economic and psychological research as they appear to relate to educational policy. The central column indicates a flow of processes as they reflect the social concern for education. More specifically, society sets out particular goals to be satisfied through educational means. These goals must be translated into concrete educational

---

[j]For a more general view see Fein (1970). Indeed, the expenditure of compensatory education funds on "white" resources may be largely responsible for the failure of such programs to alter educational outcomes for black students.

294

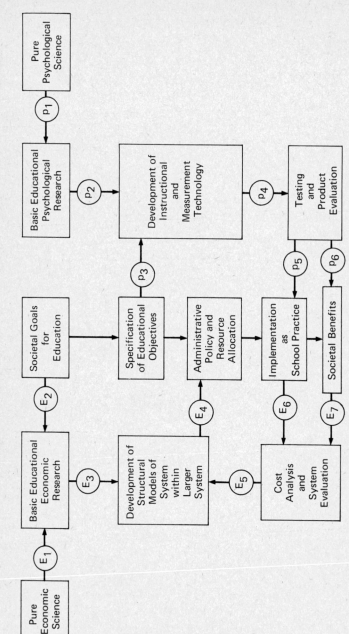

Figure 14-4. Economic and Psychological Research and Educational Policy.

objectives for policy implementation, and resources must be organized and allocated to these ends. Through the implementation of these policies, certain outcomes are derived which yield social benefits.

The contributions of economics to this process are reflected on the left side of the diagram. Basic concepts of economics are applied to educational research (E_1). The nature of the educational research is determined by an attempt to assess social goals (E_2), but this link is a two-way flow since the economist also explores whether education or some other type of social investment (e.g., health) might best fulfill the social aims set out. That is, in enhancing the welfare of the population, there are many potential strategies of which education is only one. While education may represent a relatively efficient route for achieving some ends, it may be a poorer choice for attaining others.

A major activity of economic analysis in education is reflected by (E_3), the development of structural models of the educational system as it relates to the larger social, economic, and political system. That is, not only are economists concerned with the determinants of educational outcomes, they are also interested in the relationships between educational outcomes and income, employment, occupational attainment, and other social goals (Bowman, 1969). The historical development of inquiry in the economics of education was much more concerned with the latter activities than the study of educational production. This activity is enhanced by the feedback of cost and other information resulting from ongoing and *ad hoc* evaluations. That is, data are derived primarily from operating systems through (E_5) rather than through the experimental route of the psychologists.

The results of the structural modeling represent potential inputs into administrative policy and resource allocation (E_4), and in turn the results in terms of implementation and outcomes flow back into the research and evaluation process via (E_6) and (E_7). What is important to note is that economics offers both strengths and weaknesses to the study of education.

Its strengths are (1) its direct concern for policy; (2) its methodology for linking research phonomena with social consequences by implementing causal or structural models; (3) its preoccupation with examining the costs of different strategies in relation to their effects or benefits; (4) its overall view of integrating social goals, costs, and benefits in an evaluative framework. On the other hand, economics has two very significant weaknesses: (1) its lack of tradition in experimental research, and (2) its lack of sophistication in measurement and the analysis of measurement problems.

For psychology, our historical sketch noted P_1—the early relation of pure psychological science to educational psychology. P_2 is the current recognition, growing out of earlier basic work in the educational psychological traditions, that ATI is the proper goal and approach. It remains now to determine how this approach can be implemented in research and development that will be of direct practical relevance to education.

Another contribution of the psychological tradition is represented by P_3. Although psychology has not directly confronted societal level thought about education since Dewey, the analysis of more specific educational objectives has led to a multivariate conception of educational outcomes and the specification of these outcomes in behavioral and/or content referenced terms. Both experimental and psychometric traditions have contributed to this development. It is quite important, because it makes us treat student output as multivariate just as student input and instructional treatment must be multivariate. The conceptual and methodological problems posed by this are highly complex.

P_4 indicates the strong emphasis on empirical evaluation of instructional technological development and the importance of psychological measurement technology therefore. Given proof of adequacy in evaluative research, such developments are often implemented in practice, via P_5. Through local, state and national testing programs (P_6), societal benefits can be, and sometimes are, assessed. Note, however, that psychological research and development takes place under special circumstances. Evaluative feedback is rarely received after implementation in schools. And rarely is there any direct concern with general social benefit.

Thus, the very weaknesses of economics represent the strengths of psychology and vice versa. There are several points where complementary relationships can be built.

First, a bridge is needed between the two large upper boxes in Figure 14-4. The development of structural economic models of educational systems provides powerful analytic methodology for handling and reasoning about multivariate relationships. While multiple regression techniques are not strange to psychologists, and general linear hypothesis analyses have supplanted analysis of variance in some circles, the idea of actually reasoning about causal relationships in complex networks of regression equations, including not only multiple treatment variables but also multiple outcome variables, is hardly widespread. This, apparently, is the economist's bread and butter. With the techniques of structural modeling from economics combined with the measurement techniques of psychology, it should be possible to mount large scale studies in which multiple aptitude and criterion information is gathered and related to many school variables, perhaps including *manipulated* treatment conditions within and/or between some schools and classrooms. It is noted that large scale economic or sociological research rarely involves treatment manipulation and, from the psychometrician's view, usually rests on very gross measurements often employing a single score as proxy for a host of other variables. On the other hand, psychological studies of ATI may use two or three aptitude variables to compare two, three, or four treatments, but rarely include enough of the personal situational, background and environmental variables needed for comprehensive evaluation of effects in real situations.

Another problem plagues both economic and psychological work in this regard. While psychological measurement technology for *persons* is highly developed, there is little so far in the way of measurement technology for *environemnts.* As Shulman (1970, p. 374) put it, ATI ". . . will likely remain in empty phrase as long as aptitudes are measured by micrometer and environments are measured by divining rod." But psychological studies, whether aimed at ATI or not, have rarely involved continuous changes in treatment variables across many real situations. If environments could be measured continuously, the study of such regression surfaces, using the economist's structural modeling approach, might greatly facilitate the research for practically useful ATI. Interdisciplinary pursuit of this development would benefit econometrics work since the economist's tradition in measurement is considerably less substantial than that of the psychologist's.

Psychological research and development in instructional technology has been advancing rapidly in recent years, but it has rarely had any connection with policy consideration in schools. That is, what is investigated and developed may make psychological sense, but decision alternatives or priorities are not influenced by policy or resource allocation issues in schools. In contrast, economic research is closely related to policy.

To cite one example of how research might be improved by cooperation, consider the following example: Economic analyses may show the teacher verbal ability is far more important influencing reading achievement in certain populations than is teacher experience or type of training. School policy may thus be persuaded to put more dollar resources into hiring of such teachers. Meanwhile, psychologists, having read the old literature showing that teacher characteristics are not related to achievement, may increasingly ignore the analysis of teacher verbal ability, and its correlates in classroom behavior, in favor of other research on teacher education or other variables not significant in economic thinking and not likely to capture school priorities.

As another example, consider the fact that psychological research on instruction rarely operates with regard for practical limits. It seeks the best treatment as one that is *psychologically optimal* regardless of cost. A better strategy for real educational improvement might impose economic constraints, asking the psychologist to produce the best treatment possible in a given situation for a fixed cost in time and money. This might prove to be a better exercise for training educational researchers than some of the one-shot, theory-based experiments held as ideals in the past. It also leads to a rather different fundamental attack on psychological phenomena, as advocated by some researchers (e.g., McClelland, 1965). Historically, experimental research has started at elementary levels, adding stimulus conditions systematically from experiment to experiment. As the best combination of treatment variables was slowly built up, one would know precisely why it worked. The alternative now suggested puts application before scientific understanding, requiring that a complex treatment be put together using the best current facts and hunches and tried first. If it worked, one could *then* satisfy the scientific need for understanding by analytic experimentation to find out why it worked.

The discussion of costs suggests that another bridge is needed between the two lower large boxes in Figure 14-4. Psychologists have become quite proficient at small scale evaluation (what is here called *product* evaluation). Once products are implemented in schools, however, there is rarely feedback to the technological research and development arm or evaluation as part of a system in terms of costs. Similarly in production of large scale societal level evaluation (e.g., a national assessment) there is no planned regular feedback loop to continuing research and development effort. Psychological research and development has too often been conceived as a one-way street from scientific research to social benefit. In contrast, economic research is based on continuous cycles of feedback through modeling, policy implementation, cost analysis and remodeling. Thus, connections are needed between the two lower large boxes so that cost analysis and system evaluation can augment psychological styles of evaluation, and new educational phenomena can be brought back from the firing line for systematic psychological analysis and development.

Thus, psychology's strengths in experimental research, in measurement technology, and now in its growing interactional views, combine with the multivariate structural models and the cost-benefit and policy emphases of economics. The combination provides a strong interdisciplinary attack on educational problem

References

Anderson, R. C. "Learning in discussions: A resume of the authoritarian-democratic studies." *Harvard Educational Review,* 1959, 29, 201-215.

Ausubel, D. P. *Educational Psychology: A Cognitive View.* New York: Holt, Rinehart & Winston, 1968.

Averch, H., Carroll, S., & Donaldson, T. "What do we know about educational effectivenesses?" Working note prepared for the President's Commission on School Finance, WN-7516-PCSF, Santa Monica, California.: The Rand Corp. July, 1971.

Baratz, J., & Shuy, R. *Teaching Black Children to Read.* Washington, D.C.: Center for Applied Linguistics, 1969.

Becker, G. S. *Human Capital.* New York: Columbia University Press, 1964.

Boring, E. G. *A History of Experimental Psychology.* New York: Appleton-Century-Crofts, 1957.

Bowles, S. S. "Towards an educational production function." In W. L. Hansen (ed.), *Education, Income, and Human Capital,* Studies in income and wealth, No. 35. New York: National Bureau of Economic Research, 1970.

Bowles, S. S., & Levin, H. M. "The determinants of scholastic achievement—An appraisal of some recent evidence." *The Journal of Human Resources,* 1968, 3, 3-24.

Bowman, M.J. "Schutz, Denison, and the contribution of 'Eds' to economic growth." *Journal of Political Economy,* 1964, 72, 450-464.

Bowman, M. J. "Economics of education." *Review of Educational Research,* 1969, 39(5), 641-670.

Cain, G., & Watts, H. "Problems in making inferences from the Coleman report." *American Sociological Review,* 1970, 35(2).

Cattell, R. B. *Abilities: Their Structure, Growth, and Action.* Boston: Houghton-Mifflin, 1971.

Christ, C. *Econometric Models and Methods.* New York: Wiley, 1966.

Coleman, J. S., et . al. *Equality of Educational Opportunity.* OE 38001. Washington, D. C.: U. S. Government Printing Office, 1966.

Cronbach, L.J. *Essentials of Psychological Testing* (3rd. ed.). New York: Harper, 1970 (a).

Cronbach, L. J. & Gleser, G. C. (Eds.). *Psychological Tests and Personnel Decisions* (2nd. ed.). Urbana, Ill.: University of Illinois, 1965.

Cronbach, L. J. & Snow, R. E. Individual differences in learning ability as a function of instructional variables. Final Report, OEC 4-6-061269-1217. Bethesda Maryland: ERIC Document Reproduction Service, ED-029001.

Denison, E. F. *The sources of economic growth in the United States and the alternatives before us.* Supplementary paper No. 13, New York: Committee for Economic Development, 1962.

Dubin, R. & Taveggia, T. C. *The Teaching-Learning Paradox.* Eugene, Ore.: Center for the Advanced Study of Educational Administration, 1968.

Fein, L. "Community schools and social theory: The limits of universalism." In H. M. Levin (Ed.), *Community Control of Schools.* Washington, D. C.: The Brookings Institution, 1970.

Gagné, R. M. *Conditions of Learning* (2nd. ed.). New York: Holt, Rinehart, & Winston, 1970.

Goldberger, A. *Econometric Theory.* New York: Wiley, 1964.

Goldberger, A. "Econometrics and psychometrics: A survey of communalities." Paper presented at 1970 Meetings of the Psychometric Society, Stanford, Calif.: March 21, 1970.

Guilford, J. P. *Personality.* New York: McGraw-Hill, 1959.

Hanushek, E. "Teacher characteristics and gains in student achievement." *American Economic Review,* 1971, 61(Papers and Proceedings), 280-288.

Hilgard, E. R. & Bower, G. H. (eds.). *Theories of Learning* (3rd ed.) New York: Appleton-Century-Crofts, 1966.

Johnston, J. *Econometric Methods.* New York: McGraw-Hill, 1963.

Kiesling, H. J. "Multivariate analysis of schools and educational policy." P4595, Santa Monica, Calif.: The Rand Corp., 1971.

Kiker, B.F. "The historical roots of the concept of human capital." *The Journal of Political Economy,* 1966, 74(5).

Klein, L. R. *An Introduction to Econometrics.* Englewood Cliffs, N. J.: Prentice Hall, 1962.

Levin, H. M. "A new model of school effectiveness." Chapter 3 in *Do Teachers Make a Difference?* Washington, Education, 1970 (a).

Levin, H.M. "A cost-effectiveness analysis of teacher selection." *The Journal of Human Resources,* 1970, 5, 24-33. (b)

Levin, H.M. "Concepts of economic efficiency and educational production." Paper presented at the Conference on Education and Industry, National Bureau of Economic Research, Chicago, June 1971. (Mimeo) (a).

Levin, H. M. "Frontier functions—An economic approach to evaluation." Paper presented at 1971 Meetings of the Psychometric Society, St. Louis, April 8, 1971. (b).

McClelland, D. C. "Toward a theory of motive acquisition." *American Psychologist,* 1965, 20, 321-333.

Michelson, S. "The association of teacher resourceness with children's characteristics." Chapter 6 in *Do Teachers Make a Difference?* Washington D. C.: U.S. Office of Education, 1970.

Schramm, W. "Learning from instructional television." *Review of Educational Research,* 1962, 32, 156-167.

Shulman, L. S. "Reconstruction of educational research." *Review of Educational Research,* 1970, 40, 371-396.

Skinner, B. F. "Teaching science in high school—What is wrong?" *Science,* 159, 704-740.

Index

Abt Associates, study by, 158
Academic: curriculum, 82; development, 204; freedom, 207, 209; seclusion, 207; skills, 154–155; subjects, 251
Academy for Educational Development, 213
Accountability, theory and definition, 3, 12, 39, 124, 207, 209, 229–234, 238–242, 262, 264, 267, 270
Accreditation: associations, 172–175, 188, 199, 230; loss of, 173
Achievement: levels of, 59, 282, 288; measurement of, 260–265, 284; scholastic, 58, 72, 82–83; scores, 130, 170, 173, 190, 270; student, 98, 199, 251–256, 270
Activism and activists, 12, 104–105, 109
Administrators, duties of, 3–5, 10–11, 16–17, 90, 95, 109, 113–114, 118, 157, 171, 195. *See also* Supervisors
Admission requirements, 230, 282–283
Adoption, problems of, 63–64, 74, 77
Adult education, 132, 218
Advertising and merchandising, 36–37
Advisory Commission on Intergovernmental Relations, 137
Africa, policies in, 80–81, 229
Age: segregation by, 151; teacher's, 195
Agencies, federal and state, 219, 240. *See also* specific agency
Agriculture, instruction in, 167, 215
Aid programs, 125, 131, 134–140, 159, 172
Aims of Education (Whitehead), 13
Air Force Academy, 214
Alcohol, dangers of, 174
Allegheny County, Penna., study of, 185
Allen, James E., cited, 252
Alpha Systems, 258, 267
American Association for the Advancement of Science, 179
American Association of School Administrators, 17–18, 241
American Council of Learned Societies, 179
American Federation of Labor, 119, 181
American Federation of Teachers, 103, 111–115, 118
American Educational Publications, 179
American Educational Research Association, 5–6
American Indians, problems of, 75–76, 80–81
American Institute for Biological Sciences, 179

American Mathematical Society, The, 179
American Psychological Association, 281
Americanization, curriculum issue, 164
Anderson, R. C., cited, 286
Anthropology, 110, 217
Antiintellectualism, creeping, 179
Aptitude-treatment-interaction, 286, 292–297
Aptitudes, scholastic, 71, 82–85, 170, 195, 242, 282, 288
Arithmetic, 153, 166–167, 204
Armed forces, intelligence tests, 188–189
Arts, the, 167, 177, 263
Associations, professional, 172, 174, 178–181, 187, 234, 258
Athletics, 183
Atkin, J. Myron, cited, 170, 173
Atlanta, Ga., 218
Attendance policies, 50–51
Attitudes: "do-it-now," 14, 16; parents, 148–149; toward sex, 3; on strikes, 112–118; student, 4, 12, 14; teacher, 114, 195, 265, 288; on test-taking, 76; "why change," 7
Audio-lingual approaches, 173
Audio-Visual Supply Co., 255
Authority and authoritarian concepts, 15, 20, 29, 95, 108, 118–119, 135, 166, 169, 259, 286
Automation, effects of, 31, 158
Autonomy, 186–188
Averch, H., cited, 292

"Balance of power," educational field, 4
Banfield, Edward, cited, 171
Bank Street School, 153
Baratz, J., 292
Battelle Columbus Laboratories, 268
Bauer, Raymond, 171
Beatniks, problem of, 14
Becker, G. S., 110, 289
Behavior: deviant kinds of, 106, 112–113, 152–153, 170; objectives, 39, 229, 235; science of, 217; teacher, 106, 203; traits, 66, 80
Behavioral Research Laboratories, 254–259, 267
Bender-Gestalt, Illinois Test of Psycholinguistic Abilities, Draw-A-Man, 79
Bendiner, Robert, cited, 89
Bennis, Warren, cited, 30
Bereiter, Carl, cited, 59–60, 152, 168
Bergson, Henri, creative evolution of, 35

301

About the Contributors

James E. Bruno is a consultant to The Rand Corporation and coordinator of the Rand Seminar Series on Emerging Issues in Education. He received the Ph.D. from the University of California at Los Angeles and is presently assistant professor in their Graduate School of Education. His primary research interests lie in systems analysis-operations research applied to problems in educational planning and the development of methodologies for evaluation of instruction.

C.R. Carpenter is presently research professor of psychology and anthropology at the University of Georgia and professor emeritus at Pennsylvania State University. He completed the Ph.D. at Stanford University in psychology and his research interests are in instructional media and primatology. He has served on numerous review groups for instructional technology development. He was appointed to serve on the national commission on instructional technology and elected to its executive committee.

George R. Hall is a Senior Economist in Rand's Management Sciences Department. He received the M.A. and Ph.D. degrees from Harvard. At Rand his studies have centered in the areas of government regulation of business and public policy towards education. He was the project director for Rand's study of Performance Contracting in Education sponsored by the United States Department of Health, Education and Welfare.

Willis W. Harman is presently director of the Center for the Study of Social Policy at the Stanford Research Institute and professor of engineering-economic systems at Stanford University. He received the Ph.D. in electrical engineering from Stanford and has written several texts in this field. His present research interests concern the projection of alternative futures of and analysis of major future societal problems. He was featured speaker at the 1972 White House Conference on the Industrial World Ahead.

Harold W. Horowitz is presently professor of law at the University of California at Los Angeles. He received the L.L.B. from Harvard, the L.L.M. from the University of Southern California and the S.J.D. from Harvard. His main research interests are in constitutional law; he served as co-counsel for plaintiffs in *Serrano vs Priest*, the California school finance litigation.

Arthur R. Jensen is presently professor of educational psychology and a research psychologist for the Institute of Human Learning at the University of California at Berkeley. He received the Ph.D. in psychology from Teachers College, Columbia University. His principal research interests concern individual differences in human learning and cultural, developmental, and genetic determinants of intelligence.

Michael W. Kirst is currently assistant professor of education and business administration at Stanford University. He completed the Ph.D. in political economy and government at Harvard. His research interests are in the areas of politics of education, political systems, and school finance.

Leon M. Lessinger is Dean, College of Education, University of South Carolina. He received the Ed.D. from UCLA and was Associate United States Commissioner for elementary and secondary education. His main research interests are in the area of applying systems analysis to the management of education.

Henry M. Levin is an Associate Professor in the School of Education and a member of the Affiliated Faculty in the Department of Economics at Stanford University. He received the M.A. and Ph.D. in economics at Rutgers. He is a specialist in the economics of education and human resources and has published several books and monographs and about forty articles on the economics and financing of education.

Erick L. Lindman is presently professor of education at the University of California at Los Angeles. He received the Ph.D. in education from the University of Washington. He has served as chairman of the Committee on Educational Finance of the National Education Association and as consultant to the House Committee on Education and Labor. As chief of the School Administration Branch of the U.S. Office of Education he administered Public Law 874 during its first two years of operation. His main research interests are in state school finance and administration.

Alexander M. Mood is presently director of the Public Policy Research Organization at the University of California at Irvine and teaches courses in the Graduate School of Administration there. He received the Ph.D. degree in mathematics from Princeton and served as Assistant U.S. Commissioner of Education and Director of the National Center for Educational Statistics. His areas of interest are educational evaluation and measurement.

Richard R. Rowe is presently lecturer in education at Harvard and director of the program in clinical psychology in public practice there. He completed the Ph.D. at Teachers College, Columbia University. His primary research interests are in early childhood education and clinical psychology.

Jay D. Scribner is presently associate professor of education at the University of California at Los Angeles and chairman of the Urban Educational Policy and Planning Program at that institution. He received the Ed.D. from Stanford; his major research interests lie in the areas of political systems analysis, school decentralization and urban educational problems.

Richard E. Snow is associate professor of education at Stanford University and chairman of the area of psychological studies in education. He received the Ph.D. from Purdue University in psychology. His research interests include the use of audiovisual media in instruction, the nature of aptitude in relation to learning, and teaching styles and learning.

James Stucker is an economist in the Management Sciences Department of The Rand Corporation. He received the B.S. in education from Illinois State University and the M.A. and Ph.D. in economics from Northwestern University. His work at Rand is concerned with issues of public policy in the fields of education and transportation economics.

Decker Walker is assistant professor of education at Stanford University. He obtained the Ph.D. degree from Stanford in 1971 and the B.S. and M.A. from Carnegie-Mellon University. His primary research interest is in school curricula, and he is the author of several articles on curriculum, curriculum development, and policy-making published in *School Review, The Review of Education Research, Curriculum Theory Network,* and *Studies in Art Education.*

Harmon Zeigler is presently professor of political science at the University of Oregon and program director at the Center for the Advanced Study of Educational Administration. He received the Ph.D. from the University of Illinois in political science and has written numerous books and articles in state and local politics. His research interests include the politics of education and analysis of voting behavior.

Selected List of Rand Books

Bagdikian, Ben H. *The Information Machines: Their Impact on Men and the Media*. New York: Harper and Row, 1971.

Bretz, Rudy. *A Taxonomy of Communication Media*. Englewood Cliffs, N.J.: Educational Technology Publications, 1971.

Dalkey, Norman C. (ed.) *Studies in the Quality of Life: Delphi and Decision-making*. Lexington, Mass.: D.C. Heath and Company, 1972.

Davies, Merton and Bruce Murray. *The View from Space: Photographic Exploration of the Planets*. New York: Columbia University Press, 1971.

Downs, Anthony. *Inside Bureaucracy*. Boston, Mass.: Little, Brown and Company, 1967.

Fisher, Gene H. *Cost Considerations in Systems Analysis*. New York: American Elsevier Publishing Company, 1971.

Gruenberger, Fred and George Jaffray. *Problems for Computer Solution*. New York: John Wiley & Sons, Inc., 1965.

Gruenberger, Fred J. and Daniel D. McCracken. *Introduction to Electronic Computers: Problem Solving with the IBM 1620*. New York: John Wiley & Sons, Inc., 1963.

Haggart, Sue (ed.), et al. *Program Budgeting for School District Planning*. Englewood Cliffs, N.J.: Educational Technology Publications, 1972.

Hirshleifer, Jack, James C. DeHaven, and Jerome W. Milliman. *Water Supply: Economics, Technology, and Policy*. Chicago, Ill.: The University of Chicago Press, 1960.

McKean, Roland N. *Efficiency in Government Through Systems Analysis: With Emphasis on Water Resource Development*. New York: John Wiley & Sons, Inc., 1958.

Meyer, John R., Martin Wohl, and John F. Kain. *The Urban Transportation Problem*. Cambridge, Mass.: Harvard University Press, 1965.

Novick, David (ed.) *Program Budgeting: Program Analysis and the Federal Budget*. Cambridge, Mass.: Harvard University Press, 1965.

Coleman, James S. and Nancy L. Karweit. *Information Systems and Performance Measures in Schools*. Englewood Cliffs, N.J.: Educational Technology Publications, 1972.

Pascal, Anthony. *Thinking About Cities: New Perspectives on Urban Problems*. Belmont, California: Dickenson Publishing Company, 1970.

Pascal, Anthony. *Racial Discrimination in Economic Life*. Lexington, Mass.: D.C. Heath and Company, 1972.

Quade, Edward S., and Wayne I. Boucher. *Systems Analysis and Policy Planning: Applications in Defense*. New York: American Elsevier Publishing Co., 1968.

Sharpe, William F. *The Economics of Computers*. New York: Columbia University Press, 1969.

The Rand Corporation. *A Million Random Digits with 100,000 Normal Deviates.* Glencoe, Ill.: The Free Press, 1955.

Williams, John D. *The Compleat Strategyst: Being a Primer on the Theory of Games of Strategy.* New York: McGraw-Hill Book Company, Inc., 1954.